A GOOD TAX

LEGAL AND POLICY ISSUES
FOR THE PROPERTY TAX
IN THE UNITED STATES

A GOOD TAX

LEGAL AND POLICY ISSUES
FOR THE PROPERTY TAX
IN THE UNITED STATES

JOAN YOUNGMAN

LINCOLN INSTITUTE
OF LAND POLICY

Cambridge, Massachusetts

ISBN 978-1-55844-342-6 (alk. paper)

Library of Congress Control Number: 2016931766

Designed by Milenda Lee

Composed in Minion Pro by Westchester Publishing Services in Danbury, Connecticut.
Printed and bound by Puritan Capital, in Hollis, New Hampshire.
The paper is Rolland Enviro100, an acid-free, 100 percent PCW recycled sheet.

MANUFACTURED IN THE UNITED STATES OF AMERICA

For Karl E. Case

Who has inspired generations of students to work for better tax policy

Contents

Preface

Public debate on property taxation in the United States is extremely unbalanced. An avalanche of criticism on every possible ground, often exaggerated and sometimes inaccurate, is not matched by correspondingly vigorous attention to its significant strengths or to constructive recommendations for its improvement. The property tax is a mainstay of independent local government revenue in this country. It is the largest single local tax and supplies nearly half of all general revenue from local sources. It accounts for most school district independent revenue and almost all school district tax revenue. An enormous array of legal, accounting, and administrative resources are devoted to the federal corporate income tax, but the property tax is a far more powerful revenue instrument. In the decade from 2005 to 2015, average inflation-adjusted collections from the federal corporate income tax were $297 billion, but average local property tax revenue was $472 billion.

A good property tax is stable, efficient, and fair. A tax on immovable property is an important fiscal tool in a time of globalization and international competition for mobile capital. A tax that has been capitalized into property values reduces the economic burden on purchasers; an asset tax can help balance increasing reliance on regressive consumption taxes. Asset taxes have a special role at a time when growing economic inequality has brought proposals for wealth taxation into public debate.

A highly visible tax will always attract more attention than a hidden levy, and asset taxes that are not withheld at the source or added to cash transfers are the most visible of all. But visibility carries with it accountability. Proponents of fiscal restraint should appreciate a transparent system that allows taxpayers to evaluate the cost of local services, even as those who seek to strengthen those services should appreciate a resilient source of local revenue. The property tax deals with the central administrative and political challenges facing wealth taxation: imposing a charge on nonliquid assets, taxing unrealized gains, and levying a tax on holdings of great personal significance to the taxpayer, none more significant than a home.

Extreme attacks on the property tax have deflected attention from the detail-oriented legislative and administrative reforms that could improve its operation, enlarge its base, and reduce its rates. In particular, the valuation process is central to the improvement of the property tax and a more equitable distribution of its burden. Outright exemptions may pale in comparison to the loss of revenue incurred by complex and little-understood approaches that understate values of entire classes of property. Many taxpayers would be shocked to learn how little tax is paid by various types of extremely valuable property, from farmland being prepared for development to enormously expensive condominiums and cooperative units in New York City. A well-functioning tax based on market value would obviate the need for narrow and limited "mansion taxes" to address the undertaxation of luxury residences. Other aspects of the tax similarly receive scant public attention although their fiscal impact can be enormous. For example, tax increment financing has channeled general tax revenue to specific development projects in a manner that is opaque to all but those professionally involved in these efforts.

This volume examines a number of the policy challenges to the property tax, with special attention to questions of valuation. At a time when many governments are facing fiscal difficulties and the need to address delayed or deferred financial obligations of all types, an effective property tax can be a valuable instrument for the common good.

This project has benefited greatly from the advice of the staff and fellows of the Lincoln Institute, which under the leadership of George McCarthy has made municipal fiscal health an overriding theme for its work. Daphne Kenyon, Gerald Korngold, Adam Langley, Jane Malme, Bethany Paquin, Sally Powers, and Andy Reschovsky patiently worked to help clarify and refine the ideas presented here. Maureen Clarke, Ann LeRoyer, and Emily McKeigue provided expert editorial and publications guidance that greatly improved the manuscript and brought it to reality as a book. Debbie Masi's careful production editing deserves special thanks. The analysis here has been informed by the wealth of knowledge and experience that colleagues such as Roy Bahl, Gary Cornia, Wallace Oates, Robert Schwab, and Steven Sheffrin have brought to the Institute's tax studies. Although this work deals with taxation in the United States, it has been informed by the insights of Martim Smolka at the Lincoln Institute and our international colleagues, particularly Riël Franzsen and William Mc-Cluskey. Semida Munteanu's substantive and managerial contributions are reflected in this, as in all of the tax department's work. Many of these ideas have been developed through articles in *State Tax Notes*, and the editors, readers, and publishers of that publication, particularly David Brunori, have offered valuable support, reactions, and suggestions. All errors, of course, are the responsibility of the author.

1 The Property Tax as a Good Tax

The property tax presents many seeming paradoxes. It is a familiar and long-standing levy, often traced to ancient and medieval times, with a direct lineage to the statutes of Queen Elizabeth I.[1] At the same time, it is constantly changing in response to political, economic, and administrative developments. Perhaps the central paradox is that the property tax, although it is the target of ceaseless attacks from every quarter, can actually be a good tax and an important instrument of land policy.

This assertion can seem extraordinary, or even foolhardy, but the property tax has important unappreciated strengths and serves a crucial role in the complicated fiscal system of the United States. The tax is far from perfect, but no means of raising revenue is without serious drawbacks. Many of its flaws can be addressed by legislative measures and administrative reform, and its significant benefits can be strengthened.

The unsung benefits of the property tax begin with its generally visible and transparent nature. A tax computed as a percentage of value can be clear and understandable—a dramatic contrast to the enormous complexity of the federal income tax or to the relative invisibility of a sales tax collected over thousands of transactions annually but never totaled for the taxpayer, so that its cumulative impact is unknown. The property tax imposes no filing burden, and taxpayers need not employ experts simply to determine the amount they owe.

Because property tax bills send a visible signal concerning the cost of local public services, they provide vital information to the electorate. Hidden or unclear taxes reduce the accountability of public officials and diminish taxpayer oversight. At the same time, this important benefit is in fact one reason for the unpopularity of the property tax.[2] As John Stuart Mill wrote, "[T]he very reason which makes direct taxation disagreeable makes it preferable. Under it every one knows how much he really pays."[3]

A second benefit of the property tax is its ability to provide fiscal support for independent local government. Immovable property is a tax base well suited for local identification, administration, and decision making. More than a half century ago, in her survey of tax policy in the developing world, Ursula Hicks observed, "If local bodies are to play any significant part in economic or social development, they must clearly have access to adequate finance. If they are both to act responsibly and to show initiative, some, not negligible, part of this control over resources must be independent, in the sense that the local councils are free to choose the rates (and to some extent the conditions) of their taxes or service charges."[4] Similar concerns for decentralization and accountability led the European Union to recognize "subsidiarity"—assignment of responsibility and authority to the most decentralized level of government feasible for a particular task—as a formal constitutional principle.[5]

Many taxes do not lend themselves well to local control. A uniform statewide rate for sales or income taxes does not reflect local budgets and revenue needs, but it is very difficult for small units of government to impose rates significantly higher than those in neighboring cities and towns. Few jurisdictions are able to set a truly independent sales tax rate if consumers may buy goods in a nearby locality with a lower tax rate, or with no sales tax at all. Not even states are immune to competitive pressure of this type. Analysts have long noted that "border-tax rate differentials induce consumers to shop in low-tax locales when the value of tax savings available in such areas exceeds the transportation costs associated with obtaining the tax savings."[6]

Similarly, local ability to impose independent wage or income taxes is limited if individuals or businesses can avoid the tax by relocating across a municipal border. It has been estimated that increases in Philadelphia's wage tax over more than 30 years resulted in the loss of at least 170,000 city jobs.[7] A proliferation of local income taxes can also impose heavy compliance costs on multijurisdictional businesses, sometimes nearly equaling the burden of the taxes themselves.[8]

Locally generated property taxes afford a measure of protection against fluctuating intergovernmental aid. The distribution of tax proceeds collected by the state can easily take on the character of a grant, vulnerable to changes in state revenues, priorities, and policies. Funds designated for other levels of government are often the first to be reduced or eliminated in an economic downturn, although these are exactly the times when local governments are most in need of assistance.

The property tax offers other important economic advantages as well. Any benefit or burden of ownership that affects the price of property has been capitalized, or reflected in the value of the capital asset. To the extent the tax has been capitalized, a new owner who has paid a lower price as a result does not bear that part of its economic burden. This is one case in which an old tax truly is a good tax.

The tax on land is also one of the few available means of raising public revenue that does not impede economic efficiency, because the fixed supply of land cannot be altered in response to the tax. A change in taxpayer behavior in order to avoid taxation can reduce economic welfare without any corresponding transfer of funds to the government for public benefit. A notorious example of this excess burden or deadweight loss—a pure loss to the taxpayer with no corresponding social gain—concerns the window tax that was introduced in England in 1696 on the theory that the number of windows was a gauge of property wealth. For more than a century and a half, homeowners boarded up windows or built homes with very few windows, with deleterious effects on public health, aesthetics, and enjoyment of property.[9] By contrast, a land tax can avoid this loss of economic welfare because the supply of land is essentially fixed and taxpayer actions cannot affect its supply.

Political commentators often describe the property tax as regressive, but most economists would disagree. An economic analysis of the tax burden looks beyond the legal or statutory incidence, which only identifies the person who receives the tax bill. The economic incidence may differ from the legal incidence if the nominal taxpayer has the ability to shift some portion of the tax burden, as by raising prices or rents, or reducing payments to suppliers or workers. The property tax can be analyzed as a tax on capital across the nation, with individual changes in tax rates acting as local subsidies or additional excise taxes. Because overall capital ownership rises with income levels, this introduces elements of progressivity. The property tax can also be considered to function as a payment for local public services, and to this extent concepts such as regressivity and progressivity developed in the context of taxation have limited relevance.

The property tax will always face serious challenges. Any tax can be poorly structured and badly administered, and for long periods of its history the property tax suffered from assessment practices intended to minimize political disputes rather than estimate values correctly. Assessments that accurately track rapidly rising market prices can produce unacceptable tax bills if rates are not reduced proportionately, as happened in California at the time of Proposition 13. Estimating taxable values is never easy, and special problems arise in times of market volatility. An asset tax can give rise to liquidity problems when the tax obligation is not accompanied by receipt of cash with which to make the payment. In addition to these administrative issues, there are legitimate concerns about the appropriate use of the property tax for specific functions, most notably in the financing of public schools. This important question actually does not involve the property tax itself, but rather local taxes in general, because it would arise with any local source of funding.

The visibility and transparency of the property tax are important civic benefits, but they also ensure that this tax will always be the subject of vigorous debate. Well-informed fiscal decisions require that such debate acknowledge the many strengths of the tax as well as the means for its improvement.

This book examines the operation of the property tax and alternative ways of addressing the policy challenges it faces. In particular, it considers the most important ways in which the tax deviates from a uniform levy on fair market value, including special treatment of residential property, agricultural land, and open space, as well as tax exemptions and limitations. Any tax preference should be periodically reviewed and justified, for it narrows the tax base, increases the burden on the remaining property owners, and so leads to pressure for new tax benefits. Only continual efforts toward policy improvement can allow the property tax to achieve its potential as a good tax.

Heritage of the Property Tax

Property taxes originally were intended to reach all forms of property—not only real or immovable property, such as land and buildings, but personal or movable property as well. Personal property includes both tangible items such as machinery and equipment and intangibles such as stocks, bonds, and bank accounts. This original "general" property tax on all types of assets came closer to approximating a tax on wealth than do modern counterparts that reach only one particular form of property, such as real estate.

The goal of taxing all types of property grew administratively impossible once financial instruments became a major source of value, because they could be readily concealed or moved from the taxing jurisdiction before the assessment date. Personal property so easily escaped taxation that nineteenth-century public finance reformers sought to limit the property tax to real estate and to reach financial instruments through a tax on their income. The influential economist Edwin R. A. Seligman, a Columbia University professor and an adviser to Theodore Roosevelt, wrote in 1895, "Personal property nowhere bears its just proportion of the burdens; and it is precisely in those localities where its extent and importance are the greatest that its assessment is the least. The taxation of personal property is in inverse ratio to its quantity; the more it increases, the less it pays."[10]

As a result of these changes over time, the property tax in the United States today is overwhelmingly a tax on land and buildings. Much movable and intangible property has been gradually withdrawn from the tax base, with specific exceptions.[11] Motor vehicles are movable personal property, but their taxation is administratively feasible as part of the local or state registration process. There have been continual efforts by the business community to remove items such as machinery, inventory, and equipment from the tax base, and their abatement often figures in tax incentives offered to new or expanding enterprises.

Even when personal property and intangibles are exempt from taxation, important controversies remain about whether valuation of real property that includes intangible elements actually constitutes taxation of the intangibles themselves. Enormous public utility property, for example, might have little value without regulatory permits, just as a restaurant might suffer a reduction in market value if it were to lose its liquor license and a hotel might be less valuable without the name recognition of a premium national chain. A famous California personal property tax case involving film producer Michael Todd questioned whether motion picture film negatives should be valued at the cost of their physical materials, approximately $1,000, or at the millions of dollars represented by the copyrighted film production. The complexities of such issues can be seen in the California Supreme Court decision upholding the higher assessment,[12] limitation of this approach by later legislation,[13] and other studios' use of the higher number in claiming tax credits for motion picture master files.[14]

The evolution of the property tax from a levy on nearly all assets to a tax largely limited to real estate was a practical response to the growth of intangible financial instruments and the administrative impossibility of taxing them at a local level. The exemption of most stocks, bonds, bank accounts, and other intangibles from the property tax, replaced by an income tax on their earnings, served to rationalize tax administration and restricted the property tax base to very specific, although very important, forms of wealth.

This transition from a general property tax to a real property tax also reflects the special nature of immovable property. A tax base that cannot be concealed or taken from the taxing jurisdiction offers obvious advantages, particularly for local tax administration. Moreover, in an era of increasing national and international tax competition, any tax on a mobile entity or factor of production has the potential to harm the taxing jurisdiction's competitive standing. The smaller the jurisdiction, the greater the risk of business loss from taxing mobile assets. An immovable tax base can help promote local autonomy in taxation that may not otherwise be economically feasible, even if it is legally authorized.

Characteristics of the Property Tax

Land and Buildings

In analyzing the effect of a property tax, it is important to distinguish the two components of real estate: land and buildings. Although both are technically classified as immovable, in fact buildings are fundamentally movable. Their construction requires capital and effort, and continued investment is needed to maintain their structural integrity and value. A withdrawal of capital from a city or region soon changes the physical structure of its buildings and lack of maintenance can eventually lead to demolition. Land, by contrast, is by its nature immovable. Aside from very specialized cases of land reclamation, the unimproved site is not the product of investment or effort. Of course, many nonbuilding improvements such as grading, irrigation, and utility services, as well as intangible aspects such as subdivision and zoning changes, may affect the land's potential use and value. The land itself, however, constitutes a truly immovable asset, and one whose supply is essentially fixed.

The special economic characteristics of land have many tax policy implications. Bare unimproved land draws its value from the social development that produces demand for it, not from investment and construction on it. This gives it a special place as a subject for taxation, most notably as a means of financing public improvements that lead to land value increases. The inability to alter the supply of land leaves the burden of the tax on the owner at the time of its imposition. If the pretax rent or sale price represented the maximum that the market would offer, the addition of a tax will not raise that amount, and the owner's return will diminish accordingly. Supply cannot be withdrawn from the market to increase the price. Buyers who budget for monthly insurance, tax, and mortgage payments may lower their bids when taxes rise, and the new purchaser who has paid a lower price in light of the increased tax is to that extent free of its economic burden. The great nineteenth-century social reformer Henry George drew on these and many other economic and social arguments to call for the taxation of land value in his 1879 masterwork, *Progress and Poverty*.[15]

Considerations such as these recommend treating land and buildings as two distinct objects of taxation. Two-rate taxation, with a higher rate on land than on buildings, has the potential to increase efficiency and economic welfare.[16] This approach has encountered setbacks due to administrative failures and lack of political support.[17] But even under a single rate, the ability to tax land value is one of the most important, unappreciated benefits of the property tax. The fact that an existing, centuries-old tax actually includes a land value component is an extraordinary achievement, one that deserves efforts to strengthen and improve its operation.

A Local Tax

A special constitutional history has ceded property taxes in the United States to local and state governments. Although tariffs, excises, and other property-based impositions provided a great part of federal revenues before World War I, the U.S. Constitution contains impediments to a federal property tax. Article I, sec. 9 of the Constitution prohibits any "direct" federal tax unless it is imposed in proportion to population. This provision represented a complex compromise between Northern and Southern states over representation in Congress as well as tax policy. Under the Articles of Confederation, "[a]pportionment by population was intended as a proxy for relative wealth of the states that would be simpler to calculate than the value of land and improvements."[18]

The meaning of direct taxation has never been straightforward. At the Constitutional Convention, when Rufus King of Massachusetts asked for clarification of the meaning of a "direct tax," there was no response.[19] However, a tax on real property has always been considered one clear example of a direct tax. The establishment of the federal income tax required that the Constitution be amended to allow this, for the Supreme Court had earlier held that an income tax was a direct tax to the extent it fell on income from real property.[20] "The Court's reasoning was that the tax on income was in effect a tax upon the source of the income and, therefore, was in part a 'direct tax' upon the land from which rents were derived."[21]

Property taxes were extremely important at the state level until the early decades of the twentieth century, when the introduction of state sales and income taxes left the property tax largely the province of local governments. In the nineteenth century, property taxes supplied the major portion of state revenues; today, states claim only about 3 percent of property tax collections, accounting for less than 1 percent of state revenue.[22]

The use of the property tax as a local revenue source reflects its particular suitability for that function. Some local government services have a special relationship to real property, such as fire protection, road maintenance, and public safety. Efficient local spending can enhance property values. Well-functioning public operations, such as excellent schools, can increase the desirability and market prices of housing in the jurisdiction, encouraging even voters who do not directly utilize these services to support them.

There are also advantages to the assignment of some taxes to a specific level of government. This separation of sources[23] can promote transparency and accountability, associating one tax with a specific jurisdiction. Professor John Mikesell has written:

> This policy of dividing sources can provide useful returns to the federal system. In particular, such separation can strengthen local autonomy and accountability by ensuring access to a productive base without competition from another claimant. But probably more important is the improvement in transparency, whereby citizens can easily identify what they are paying for particular government services. When multiple governments are tapping the same base, which payment flows to which government may not be easily obvious, thus weakening the accountability chain.[24]

A separation of sources also diminishes the loss of economic efficiency that accompanies multiple federal, state, and local levies, with compound rates and compliance burdens on taxpayers. For example, the sales tax base has steadily diminished over time, with rising rates needed to maintain collections. Mikesell has noted, "The state retail sales tax is disappearing, with the result that the only way that its contribution to state revenue portfolios could be maintained is through ever-higher statutory tax rates."[25]

An Asset Tax

An asset tax such as a property tax can serve a special function in a mixed fiscal system, helping to balance taxes on income flows or sales purchases.

Wealth taxes, the most comprehensive form of asset taxation, are sometimes proposed as a counterweight to increasing international reliance on consumption taxes such as sales taxes and value-added taxes, since these can fall more heavily on lower-income households that must spend all of their earnings to meet basic needs. However, wealth taxes have been in retreat on a worldwide basis, even in limited forms such as estate or inheritance taxes. The contemporary property tax is not a wealth tax, but it does reach one significant form of wealth—real property—that is strongly connected to local services and often receives significant tax benefits.

At the same time, asset taxes face special disadvantages, especially the need for a cash payment without any necessary realization of income at the time the tax is due. This problem arises in other contexts as well, such as an income tax on noncash gains or a tax on an estate composed of illiquid assets. However, in each of those cases the taxpayer has received a new asset, which is not the case with a recurrent annual tax. Sales taxes raise fewer taxpayer objections in part because they are collected in many small and largely voluntary transactions. And for many taxpayers, regular income tax withholding avoids the need to make independent cash payments and may result in a refund at the end of the year.

A number of administrative mechanisms can help mitigate the inherent difficulties of asset taxation. Adjusting the number of payment installments may reduce the burden of payment and improve compliance.[26] Some countries have initiated direct debit systems for automatic payment, sacrificing some measure of visibility in the interests of ease of payment and political acceptability. In England, for example, over 140 million property tax payments are processed in this way.[27]

Deferral programs allow qualifying senior citizens to postpone tax payments until the sale of their property, transforming the tax into a type of transaction excise. In 2012, 24 states and the District of Columbia authorized such programs.[28] These programs are often quite restricted, because they transfer the problem of liquidity from the taxpayer to the taxing jurisdictions that need cash to pay for their ongoing operations. Large-scale deferral could require local governments to borrow funds in order to maintain their own cash flow until realization of the tax proceeds. This has not become a problem with existing deferral programs, in part because such options are often underutilized, with only a small number of participating homeowners. For example, a deferral program in Washington State attracted only 249 participants, although legislative analysts had estimated that 5,500 homeowners would enroll.[29]

This is important information in light of fears that property tax burdens may force elderly residents from their homes. The specter of displacing senior citizens is often invoked in support of outright tax reductions or exemptions, because this unacceptable prospect tends to silence any dissent. It is understandable that taxpayers would prefer tax forgiveness to a lien on an asset they hope to leave to their heirs. But if they decline the option of deferring the tax, decisions on appropriate tax policy can proceed without fears that these taxpayers are being driven from their homes. The existence of a deferral option, even if—or particularly if—it is underutilized, can thus clarify and improve property tax debate.

Valuation

Valuation is always a central challenge for asset taxation, particularly when properties have not been the subject of a recent sale. Well into the twentieth century, many jurisdictions maintained outdated values on their tax rolls in order to reduce taxpayer complaints and administrative workload. Often only property that was newly constructed or purchased would be taxed at its full value, in what came to be known as "Welcome, Stranger" assessment. As the Supreme Court observed in overturning such a policy, "This approach systematically produced dramatic differences in valuation between petitioners' recently transferred property and otherwise comparable surrounding land."[30] Even under statutory systems calling for full and uniform assessment of all classes of property, single-family residences were often underassessed, business property overassessed, and public utility property assessed at the highest percentage of market value of all. This produced a system in which classes of property were taxed at different effective tax rates.

However, instead of a classification imposing an explicit and authorized set of established rates on fair market value, a failure to reassess property resulted in a nominally uniform tax rate being applied to varying and sometimes random percentages of actual market value. As long as these inaccurate figures were well below actual market values, many taxpayers were unwilling to challenge them. When such cases were brought, courts long accepted the fiction that these underassessments represented uniform fractions of market value. A uniform percentage of full value would produce accurate tax bills, although with an effective tax rate that differed from the stated rate. These systems were sometimes termed *extralegal*, because they were sanctioned by long practice and sometimes even by judicial decisions, even when state law called for uniform assessments at full market value.

The 1960s ushered in a new period of judicial willingness to overturn such systems. These decisions, together with technological advances in computer-assisted mass appraisal, put assessment at accurate market values within reach of most jurisdictions choosing that approach. However, the political considerations that led to extralegal assessment practices were not extinguished by court decisions enforcing uniform full valuation. In many states, these rulings were followed by various methods of making extralegal practices legal: statutory and constitutional enactments permitting differential treatment of various types of property; assessment and revenue limits; and special exclusions, deductions, and valuation methods for favored classes, particularly agricultural land and owner-occupied housing. These deviations from value-based taxation have been rightly criticized for nonuniformity.[31] However, applying differential tax rates to accurate valuation represented an enormous improvement in uniformity over earlier practices.

Capitalization

The capitalization of an asset tax, its effect on price, has both equity and efficiency implications. If the market value of land is reduced when a new tax is imposed, the purchaser buying at a lower price has in that respect been freed from the economic burden of the tax. That burden fell on the owner who held the land at the time the tax was imposed and who suffered a loss in asset value as a result. Jens Jensen, an early scholar of the property tax, wrote, "The taxpayer, by virtue of the process of capitalization, has bought himself free from any calculable, unequal part of the tax, and as for the general or equal or uniform part of it, he bears that in common with others."[32]

In fact, abolition of a tax that has been capitalized would constitute a windfall gain to owners who purchased at lower prices because of the tax and now can sell at a higher level. Just as an old tax can be a good tax, a new tax may require gradual phasing in to avoid placing an unfair burden on current owners. Certainly a taxpayer who recently purchased a parcel of unimproved land with carefully accumulated savings would object to being told this acquisition was appropriate for special taxation as an un-earned gift of nature. However, if the recent purchaser bought the land at a lower price because of a long-standing land tax, no such objection would apply.

Capitalization also means that a land tax is one local revenue instru-ment that does not risk a loss of economic competitiveness. Businesses seeking to locate in the taxing jurisdiction will not bear the burden of the capitalized tax, and businesses already located in the jurisdiction cannot avoid the economic burden of a capitalized tax by selling their property.

Value Capture

The property tax can also function as an instrument of *value capture*, a term used to denote a public claim to some portion of the increase in property value due to public investment, such as infrastructure improve-ments. As one scholar has written, "On the face of it, the idea of land value capture is straightforward. Land increases in value, quite possibly as a result of intervention by public powers, and an argument can be made for diverting at least part of that increase to serve the common good rather than a private interest."[33]

Public works projects are often undertaken with the expectation that they will enhance a neighborhood or region and thus increase property values there. Value capture can thus be seen as an expression of the benefit principle of tax equity, with those enjoying the positive results of public investment contributing to its support. Special assessments that distribute the cost of new streetlights or sidewalks among the benefited property owners serve as a type of value capture instrument, but these costs are generally allocated according to physical measures such as front footage rather than by value increments.

It is both technically and politically difficult to develop special taxes for properties in proximity to major public works projects. Business owners suffering disruption and loss of sales during construction are more likely to seek mitigation payments than to feel they should be subject to new taxes. By contrast, a well-functioning value-based property tax would automatically account for these effects without any need for new legislation. For example, in the case of a new subway stop, market values during construction may reflect both diminished current business opportunity and later anticipated benefits. Once benefits are realized, market values would be expected to increase. Under an accurate property tax, costs would not be allocated to owners whose properties did not rise in value.

A Good Tax

The property tax is not a perfect tax, but perfection is not a reasonable standard for public policy. The tax has important strengths, particularly its potential to serve as a visible and transparent levy in a time when such clarity in taxation is extremely rare. The property tax provides a direct link between local payments and local services at the level of government closest to most taxpayers and allows local government a measure of fiscal independence.

The land portion of the property tax is an unusual source of public revenue that does not impose an efficiency loss and in fact addresses a tax base that draws value from public growth and investment. To the extent the tax has been capitalized into the price of the real estate, that portion is not a burden to the current owner. The property tax can also serve as an instrument of value capture in situations where a special levy for this purpose might encounter significant political difficulties. Economists would contest the charge that the tax is an overall regressive imposition and would point out that such a measure would not be relevant to its function as a benefit charge.

None of this diminishes the administrative and political challenges posed by the assessment and collection of an annual tax on property value. It does, however, demonstrate the importance of addressing those challenges in order to help the property tax achieve its potential to improve local public finance and governance for the common good.

Notes

1. Seligman (1931); Quigley (1996).
2. See, e.g., Cabral and Hoxby (2012).
3. Mill (1848), 301.
4. Hicks (1961), 277.
5. Ebke (1997).
6. Walsh and Jones (1988), 261.
7. Haughwout et al. (2004).
8. Ortega (2012).
9. Oates and Schwab (2014; 2015).
10. Seligman (1931), 23.
11. Significant Features of the Property Tax. http://www.lincolninst.edu/subcenters /significant-features-property-tax/Report_Taxable_Personal_Property.aspx. Lincoln Institute of Land Policy and George Washington Institute of Public Policy. (Taxable Personal Property.)
12. *Michael Todd Co. v. County of Los Angeles*, 57 Cal.2d 684, 371 P.2d 340, 21 Cal. Rptr. 604 (1962).
13. Calif. Rev. & Tax Code, § 988(a) ("The full value of motion pictures, including the negatives and prints thereof, is the full value of only the tangible materials upon which such motion pictures are recorded.").
14. *Walt Disney Productions v. United States*, 327 F. Supp. 189 (C.D. Cal. 1971), *modified*, 480 F.2d 66 (9th Cir. 1973).
15. George (1879). See also Dye and England (2009); Netzer, ed. (1998).
16. Dye and England (2009).
17. Bourassa (2009b); Hughes (2007).
18. Johnson (1998), 19.
19. Dodge (2009), 847, n. 17.
20. *Pollock v. Farmers' Loan and Trust Co.*, 158 U.S. 601, 15 S. Ct. 912, 39 L. Ed. 1108 (1895).
21. Harvard Law School (1963), 110.
22. Significant Features of the Property Tax. http://www.lincolninst.edu/subcenters /significant-features-property-tax/census/. Lincoln Institute of Land Policy and George Washington Institute of Public Policy. Data from U.S. Census Bureau, Annual Survey of State and Local Government Finances.

23. The concept of "separation of sources" and its role in California tax reform are discussed in Sheffrin (2010b), 666.
24. Mikesell (2010), 164.
25. Mikesell (2012), 784.
26. Reschovsky and Waldhart (2012).
27. Hutchinson (2008), 10.
28. Significant Features of the Property Tax. http://www.lincolninst.edu/subcenters /significant-features-property-tax/Report_Residential_Property_Tax_Relief _Programs.aspx. Lincoln Institute of Land Policy and George Washington Institute of Public Policy. (Residential Property Tax Relief Programs.)
29. Wasson (2011).
30. *Allegheny Pittsburgh Coal Co. v. Webster County*, 488 U.S. 336 (1989).
31. Ihlanfeldt (2013).
32. Jensen (1931), 75.
33. Booth (2012), 74.

THE NATURE OF
THE PROPERTY TAX

2 Progressivity, Regressivity, and Fairness

A new approach to political debate on the property tax might begin by examining its commonplace characterization as a regressive levy. This criticism is often found in public discussion and popular writing, yet it is not accepted by many academic experts. Although it is common for non-economists to use the term *regressive* simply as a synonym for *unfair*, regressive taxes are not always judged to be unfair. In fact, politically popular revenue sources from cigarette taxes to general sales taxes to lotteries may be very regressive, while progressive taxes such as the estate tax are often unpopular and branded "unfair" by their opponents. Survey evidence suggests that public support for the elimination of the estate tax, and for replacement of the graduated income tax with a flat tax or a retail sales tax, is often based on misconceptions about the economic impact of these measures.[1]

Although popular references to regressivity are often meant only to convey unfairness, this term draws much of its power from the suggestion of scientific classification and therefore from its technical economic meaning. For this reason it is helpful for noneconomists involved in property tax policy to have an appreciation for some of the complexities economists deal with in evaluating the ultimate incidence of a tax—that is, the party actually bearing its financial burden.

A regressive tax falls more heavily on low-income taxpayers, taking a larger percentage of their income than it takes from those with higher earnings; thus "the average rate of tax falls as income rises."[2] A progressive tax, by contrast, constitutes a higher percentage of income as income rises, and a proportional tax remains a constant percentage of income across different income levels.

Thus, an unvarying tax of a specific dollar amount would be regressive, imposing a much greater burden on a low-income worker than on a highly compensated employee. A general sales tax will be regressive if low-income consumers spend a greater proportion of their incomes on taxable purchases than do wealthier households that are able to save and invest more of their earnings. Professor Ronald Fisher writes, "Because the share of income represented by personal consumption tends to be smaller for higher-income as opposed to lower-income individuals (higher-income individuals do more saving), the conclusion is drawn that general sales taxes are regressive; that is, sales tax burdens as a proportion of income decline as one moves up the income distribution. . . . The results of many empirical studies of sales tax incidence confirm these effects."[3]

It is important to note that a regressive tax or charge may be balanced by other methods of addressing income inequality, including subsidies and progressive taxes. Considering a single tax in isolation can also be misleading if in fact it functions as one part of a complex fiscal system with various roles for different taxes and for different levels of government. A comprehensive analysis of the distributional impacts of various levies would also consider the effects of the spending programs supported by those taxes. C. Eugene Steuerle has noted that it is "limiting and often misleading to define the progressivity of a tax system independently of what is done with those taxes, or as a corollary, to measure the progressivity of an expenditure system without considering how the necessary revenues are raised."[4]

Redistributing income is often a more appropriate function for the national government than for localities or even for states. The economists Richard and Peggy Musgrave pointed out that decentralized income redistribution, where jurisdiction A might implement progressive taxes and wealth transfers while jurisdiction B might not, "breaks down in an important respect. As long as there exists ready mobility between jurisdictions A and B, high-income people will tend to move from A to B, while low-income people will flock from B to A. . . . The redistribution process thus breaks down unless the scheme covers individuals across A and B, i.e., the distribution function is carried out at the national or central level."[5]

If residents are mobile, an individual jurisdiction attempting income redistribution may lose high-income earners and firms while absorbing aid recipients from other states. Ronald Fisher observed, "State-local governments are limited in their capability to redistribute resources because different jurisdictions select different amounts of redistribution and individuals and firms can easily move among the jurisdictions to frustrate any intended redistribution."[6] In reviewing studies on progressivity in subnational taxation, Andrew Reschovsky concluded that arguments against decentralized income redistribution are strongest at the local rather than the state level.[7]

It is also important to consider the effect of substituting alternate means of raising revenue, particularly in a system involving multiple levels of government. For example, adding cumulative layers of state, local, and federal taxes upon the same base can increase the excess burden of the tax, the loss in economic welfare over and above the tax payment, out of proportion to the rise in tax rates. As John Anderson has explained, "An increase in the tax rate will have a squared impact on the tax burden. . . . If we double the tax rate . . . we can expect that the excess burden of the tax will be quadrupled."[8] A "separation of sources" that assigns primary use of different taxes to different units of government can mitigate this effect.

All of these considerations suggest that it is not necessarily the case that general welfare would be enhanced by replacing any specific regressive tax with a different method of raising revenue. However, even the charge of regressivity itself can be challenged in the case of the property tax.

Whether the property tax takes a higher percentage of income from poorer households than from wealthier ones turns out to be a remarkably complex inquiry. In recent decades economists have devoted a great deal of attention to this question, "one of the more controversial—and more interesting—issues in state and local public finance."[9] This is not surprising, given how many analytic and interpretive points it raises, including the identity of the taxpayer, the measure of income, and the nature of the tax itself.

Identity of the Taxpayer

The legal or statutory incidence of a tax refers to the person or entity officially designated as the taxpayer—the name on the tax bill. This may have very little to do with the economic incidence, which is the ultimate distribution of the actual tax burden. A tenant whose rent increases when property taxes rise bears an economic burden even if only the landlord receives a tax bill. The landlord-tenant example also illustrates the difference between short-term and long-term economic incidence. If a tenant's lease allows no change in rent, the landlord will bear the full economic burden of an increased tax in the short run. Over the long run, however, tenants will generally bear some portion of the tax, even if the legal incidence is on the landlord alone. For example, if lower returns to landlords lead to a long-term decrease in the supply of rental housing, rents may rise. Harvey Rosen has observed that "the burden of the property tax doesn't depend on whether landlords or tenants pay the property tax. This is counter to the usual perception that landlords bear the burden simply because they write the check."[10]

Statutory incidence is very important for certain legal purposes, even beyond the obvious issue of liability for the tax payment. For example, in 2015 a court rejected a taxpayer argument that New York City's decision to tax rental property more heavily than owner-occupied residences constituted a form of discrimination. It wrote, "Significantly, in arguing that 30% of their rent goes to taxes, plaintiffs demonstrate that they have no standing. There is no allegation that they have a contractual obligation to pay their respective landlord's tax bill. There is no allegation that they pay the entire bill. Absent this, plaintiffs have no standing to maintain this action."[11] The court considered legal standing in this case to depend on statutory incidence, not the ultimate impact of the tax.

Legal incidence can also govern such issues as tax liability. For example, the federal government is immune from state and local taxation, but this immunity extends only to statutory incidence—the name on the tax bill. If a private company runs a federal plant under a contract that passes along all tax costs to the government, the burden of those taxes may fall upon the public. But these taxes will not violate federal immunity so long as the statutory liability for payment is on the private contractor. The Supreme Court has explained that "tax immunity is appropriate in only one circumstance: when the levy falls on the United States itself, or on an agency or instrumentality so closely connected to the Government that the two cannot realistically be viewed as separate entities, at least insofar as the activity being taxed is concerned."[12]

But statutory incidence does not establish the progressivity or regressivity of a tax. That can be determined only through an analysis of its economic incidence, which can rarely be observed directly. Usually some combination of data and theory provides a basis for estimating the final allocation of the economic burden.

The Measure of Income

Because regressivity measures the tax burden as a percentage of income, the definition of income is crucial, and controversial. Should tax-exempt income affect these calculations? Should unrealized gains? Should a graduate or professional student who anticipates greatly increased future earnings be considered as needy as a laborer with the same cash income who has already reached his peak wage level? How should a wealthy retiree with substantial savings but modest retirement earnings be classified, or a wealthy retiree with substantial income from tax-free municipal bonds? These questions are relevant to many nontax issues as well. For example, state formulas for school aid to localities may consider, among other factors, the jurisdiction's property tax base, the average income of its residents, and its school enrollment.[13] Should the low average earnings of university students increase the aid that college towns receive for their primary and secondary schools?

The definition of income raises special questions in the case of the property tax because of the long-term nature of home purchases and financing decisions. If housing expenditures reflect income or prospects for income over many years, comparing the property tax burden to income in any single year may yield a distorted measure. This choice between annual income and long-term or "permanent" income is one specific issue that has divided professional opinion about the regressivity of the property tax.

Harvey Rosen explained, "Housing expenditures turn out to be more responsive to changes in permanent income than to changes in annual income. Indeed, although the evidence is mixed, it appears reasonable to say that housing consumption is roughly proportional to permanent income. Hence, the structures part of the tax is probably neither regressive nor progressive. Unfortunately, analyses based on annual income, which suggest the tax is regressive, have tended to dominate public discussions of the tax."[14]

The Nature of the Property Tax: Three Views

The choice of measuring progressivity or regressivity by reference to annual income, income averaged over a number of years, or some other measure of long-term income presents a data challenge. A further complexity involves not only the choice of data but the economic characterization of the tax itself.

The property tax may be considered an amalgam of various components, each with a potentially distinct economic impact. For example, the tax on land can be distinguished from the tax on buildings, because for the most part the supply of land is fixed and cannot be altered. The economic burden of a tax shifts when producers and consumers respond to the tax by changing the supply and demand for a taxed commodity and the price that is paid for it. In the long run, the supply of buildings can be increased through new construction or decreased through lack of maintenance and even eventual demolition. Because there are few opportunities to alter the supply of land, the burden of the tax on land, but not on buildings, is assumed to remain with the owner. The price that yields maximum return will not change because of imposition of the tax, but the tax will reduce the amount of net profit.

The Traditional View

The first, traditional analysis of the tax on buildings distinguished between residences and business structures. Homeowners act as both suppliers and consumers of their houses, with no power to respond to a tax by changing either the amount or price of housing. Because the economic incidence of the tax on owner-occupied housing was considered to fall on the owner, the residential portion of the tax on buildings was deemed regressive because housing expenditures do not rise as rapidly as income—although, as Rosen points out, substitution of long-term income data for annual income challenged this conclusion.

Under this approach, the tax on business structures could be analyzed only in the context of specific business opportunities to shift the tax forward to purchasers (through higher prices) or backward to suppliers and employees (through lower payments and wages), making generalizations about incidence uncertain. Under an assumption that a tax on structures used in the production of goods increased the price of those goods, the burden of the tax would fall on consumers, to the extent the tax did not increase these prices it would reduce farm, business, or property income.

With the supply of land being fixed and inelastic, landowners were deemed to bear the full economic burden of land taxes. On the assumption that landholdings, like most capital, are concentrated among higher-income taxpayers, the land portion of the property tax was generally judged to be progressive.

The Capital Tax View

In the 1960s and 1970s a second or new view, now many decades old and often referred to as the capital tax view, offered a different interpretation of the property tax, analyzing it as part of a nationwide tax on wealth and capital, with generally progressive effects. In his book *Who Pays the Property Tax?* Henry Aaron wrote:

> The idea that families with low incomes must pay a larger portion of their incomes in property taxes than do families with high incomes had been generally accepted throughout the twentieth century. Although some observers dissented, the prevailing view in economic analyses and political statements alike had been that, through this tax at least, the poor do pay more. During the past decade, however, economic analysis has shown this notion to be incomplete, even with respect to that portion of the tax levied on housing; it now suggests that the property tax is

probably progressive on the average, although some low-income families may be exposed to heavy burdens.[15]

Wallace Oates summarized the capital tax view in this way: "The basic idea is that since nearly all communities are taxing local capital, the average rate of tax essentially becomes a national tax on capital. As such, it will likely be a progressive tax overall, since higher-income households own a disproportionately large share of the stock of capital."[16] Thus, just as a tax on land was assumed to be progressive because land ownership is concentrated among high-income households, a tax on capital is deemed progressive for the same reason. In recent decades the capital tax view has proved sufficiently convincing to form the new mainstream of economic opinion, "the predominant new conventional wisdom about the property tax among many economists and increasingly among policymakers as well."[17]

It is important to recognize that a "progressive tax overall" can contain elements of regressivity. The property tax presents great variations in local tax rates. If it is viewed as a nationwide tax on capital, it is a nationwide tax with some jurisdictions imposing below-average rates and some with above-average rates. The below-average rates can be analyzed as subsidies applied to the nationwide rate, while the above-average rates can be considered as adding commodity taxes or excises to increase it. These companion subsidies and taxes can have locally dramatic effects. If mobile capital can shift location in response to the tax, the return to immobile factors such as land rents and some wages will increase or decrease accordingly. Moreover, specific tax provisions, such as homestead exemptions for principal residences or "circuit breaker" income-sensitive tax relief, will affect the distribution of the tax burden. A single classification of taxes as progressive or regressive can lose sight of these multidimensional effects.

The Benefit View

If this evolution of expert opinion were not already daunting enough to the noneconomist, a third perspective, known as the benefit view, offers yet another interpretation of the tax. It considers much residential property taxation to constitute a kind of consumer activity by which households purchase a specific mix of local services through their choices of where to live. This is a particular application of the Tiebout hypothesis,[18] which deals with self-sorting by local residents who "vote with their feet" through home purchases. This benefit view accords with many policy makers' intuitive understanding of the property tax. For example, a U.S. Treasury report described the tax as "the cost paid by citizens for public services provided by state and local governments, such as public schools, roads, and police and fire protection."[19]

The benefit view alters the entire context for regressivity studies. If the property tax is considered the price for a bundle of local services, then the net burden of the tax can be determined only by comparing what is paid with what is received. As Ronald Fisher has written:

> If consumers choose residential locations based on the property tax and service package offered by the local government, and if some mechanism arises to maintain the equilibrium (such as zoning rules), consumers who desire the same fiscal package are grouped together. The property tax is the "price" for consuming local services, with all consumers paying the costs that their consumption imposes on the government. In that case, discussing the incidence of the tax separate from the provision of public services doesn't make sense, because the tax simply reflects the demand for services.[20]

The concept of regressivity itself must be reexamined when the tax is analyzed as a payment for services. For example, it could be established that food, shelter, and other basic necessities require a diminishing proportion of income as household income rises. Increased discretionary income means that a lower proportion of income is devoted to nondiscretionary necessities. But that does not imply that prices for food or shelter are best analyzed as regressive taxes, or that society would be better served by a different price system for these commodities. If the benefit view considers the property tax as the consumer's payment for local services and amenities, the focus of the inquiry has shifted from a one-way payment— the government's collection of a specific amount from each taxpayer—to a market exchange of money for goods and services.

In this respect, both the capital tax view and the benefit view suggest a complex interaction between considerations of regressivity and efficiency.

The capital tax view analyzes the property tax as a levy on capital, which is generally progressive. This also means, however, that the tax distorts market signals, leading to changes in behavior and a corresponding loss of efficiency. The benefit view, which analyzes the tax as a payment for local services, accepts that this payment may constitute a diminishing percentage of income as income rises. However, the benefit view judges the property tax to be nondistortionary, and in fact extremely efficient. "If consumers treat the local property tax as a price for public services, then this price should not distort the housing market any more than the price of eggs should distort the housing market."[21]

The fact that the proportion of income paid for an item decreases as income rises does not establish a failure in the price system. The best way to address income inequality may not be through price changes but through transfer payments that permit low-income households to spend more on whatever goods or services are most useful to them. Another efficiency benefit that both the capital tax view and the benefit view find in the property tax is an incentive for homeowners to support useful local spending and to oppose waste, because these effects are capitalized into the market value of their property.[22]

It is worth noting here that the land component of the property tax squares this particular circle of progressivity and efficiency. Unlike a tax on buildings, it is considered progressive under both the traditional view and the capital tax view. Because the supply of land cannot change in response to the tax, a land tax does not alter economic activity, and so it avoids the efficiency losses that accompany taxes on buildings and improvements. A land tax can also signal the price of local services and provide an incentive to support productive local spending.

The choice between the capital tax view and the benefit view of property taxation remains the subject of lively debate in the economics profession. Professor Oates commented:

> My own view, and I suspect it is widely shared, is that both of these competing visions of the property tax as a local tax have some validity: both contribute in important ways to our understanding of how the property tax works in the setting of local public finance. The tax is surely not a perfect benefit tax. Consider, for example, a local resident who is con-

templating an expansion to his house. Such an addition will lead to an increase in the assessed value of the house and a higher property tax payment. This will clearly tend to discourage the extent of such improvements with a consequent "excess burden" (or "deadweight loss").

At the same time, the benefits and costs of local programs, as is well documented in the empirical literature, clearly manifest themselves in local property values, providing strong incentives for efficient local budgetary choices. . . . *Both* theories imply that the benefits and costs of local programs are borne locally—and give rise to capitalization. This is what makes it so difficult to distinguish between them at an empirical level. But this has a further important implication that deserves special note: it implies that, regardless of which view of the local property tax is more nearly correct, the tax does provide at least some of the right signals to local residents for making fiscal decisions. The fact that the benefits and costs of local programs manifest themselves in local property values provides important incentives for residents to take explicitly into account both the benefits and costs of prospective programs.[23]

Fairness Beyond Regressivity and Progressivity

Because charges of regressivity so often mean simply that the property tax is considered unfair, it is important to consider alternate ways of confronting this issue. When an essentially political question is presented as a technical issue, a technical clarification does not resolve the underlying political concern. Fairness cannot be reduced to a single measure, such as the distribution of the tax according to taxpayer income. It touches on an enormously broad array of issues, including the definition of the tax base, as in the fairness of taxing unrealized gains or illiquid assets, as well as the rate of tax. It involves procedure and administration, the manner in which the tax is assessed and collected, and the availability of an impartial appeals system to address taxpayer objections. It addresses social and cultural values, such as treatment of families, long-time residents, and the elderly.

In the history of the property tax, unsanctioned and unequal assessment practices, most notably the reassessment of property only upon sale, have been notorious. Whether caused by intentional favoritism or administrative neglect, their blatant unfairness led to judicial opposition by the mid-twentieth century. On the other hand, actions that promote progressivity and accuracy in taxation, such as long-delayed revaluations, may be considered unfair when they upset settled expectations of property owners. The property tax limitation measures of the 1970s and 1980s were in part responses to accurate assessments of greatly increased housing values. This taxation of unrealized capital gains was extremely unpopular, even if it was progressive.

The breadth of these concerns, and the irreducible element of subjective judgment inherent in them, poses a significant challenge to policy analysis. Several points can help clarify the intertwined considerations of fairness and regressivity.

One concerns the complexity of opinion research on tax fairness. For many years, annual surveys of public attitudes toward government commissioned by the Advisory Commission on Intergovernmental Relations (ACIR) included the question: "Which do you think is the worst tax—that is, the least fair?"[24] The federal income tax and the local property tax always competed for this unfortunate designation. In nineteen years that this question was posed, the federal income tax received the most responses in twelve years and the property tax in seven years.[25] When in later years respondents could designate either the federal income tax or the social security tax as the worst tax, this division usually left property taxes in first (or last) place.[26] State sales taxes almost always had the fewest respondents choosing them as the worst tax, followed by state income taxes. Yet state and federal income taxes would often be judged the worst if their ratings were combined as an opinion on income taxes in general.

It is important to distinguish fairness and popularity. The ACIR surveys, for example, made no attempt to determine the basis for the respondents' judgment. The transparency of the property tax ensures it a level of scrutiny rarely faced by less visible taxes. Professional views again diverged from the results of surveys of public opinion. A 1994 survey of National Tax Association members repeated a 1934 Tax Policy League survey of senior American public finance professors. One question asked, "Should there be retention of property tax as a major source of local revenue?" In 1934, 86 percent of the respondents agreed; in 1994, 85 percent.[27]

This presents a public policy dilemma: Should less visible taxes be substituted for those whose very accountability, whatever their other benefits or drawbacks, provokes taxpayer ire?[28] On the one hand, if accountability is an element of responsible government, it should not be grounds for rejecting a tax or policy instrument of any kind. But an even more central aspect of accountability requires that elected officials themselves be responsive to constituent views. A virtue that makes a tax sufficiently unpopular is a virtue that can lead to its demise. The challenge for policy makers is to mitigate the political drawbacks of the tax while preserving as many of its benefits as possible. "Actual tax systems may look more reasonable when political realities are considered than they do from an optimal tax perspective."[29]

Patrick Doherty, past president of the Institute of Revenues Rating and Valuation, a professional organization of British property tax administrators, made an insightful observation on the popularity of the British Council Tax, the property tax on residential property. The tax is highly regressive, valuing no property above £320,000. This is an almost laughable underestimate of the value of much London property, let alone the stately homes of Britain. Even the residential portion of Buckingham Palace is valued at £320,000. Yet Doherty stressed that in addition to such criteria as efficiency, accountability, and horizontal equity, a tax must "feel fair," for whatever reasons, in order to be successful. He pointed out that the Council Tax "gives the appearance of being progressive whilst it is, in practice, regressive in nature. It is, however, accepted by taxpayers and is actually perceived as fair."[30] This echoes the analysis of Steven Sheffrin in his pioneering work *Tax Fairness and Folk Justice*,[31] where he considers how elements such as procedural fairness, vertical equity, stability in assessments, and relationship to services can help a property tax "feel fair" to local residents.

Many decades of litigation challenging the use of property taxes to fund local schools have contributed to the perception that the property tax is unfair. However, the use to which tax revenue is put is quite distinct from the fairness or unfairness of any particular means of raising that revenue. School finance litigation focuses on the property tax only insofar as it is a local tax, with greater revenue generally being available to wealthier districts. A similar challenge could be raised against local income or sales taxes if they were used for education finance. A truly state-based property tax could be used for school funding without exacerbating local fiscal disparities. The charges of unfairness that motivate school finance litigation do not bear upon the fairness or unfairness of the property tax itself.

Fairness and unfairness do not exist in a vacuum, and any consideration of property tax reductions must also take into account the effects of replacement taxes or expenditure cuts. The most politically palatable replacement for a property tax will often be a sales tax, for the same reasons that the sales tax was judged "most fair" in the ACIR surveys. When Michigan voters chose to increase the state sales tax rather than the income tax in order to support public schools, the mayor of Bloomfield Hills explained that voters prefer to "pay taxes on items purchased than be arbitrarily assessed an income tax."[32] This might surprise those who consider income taxes far less arbitrary and potentially more progressive than either property or sales taxes, but there are several reasons for this preference. In addition to their relatively low visibility, sales tax payments are contingent on a purchase, allowing the taxpayer a sense of control over tax liability. This point is somewhat controversial, for the truly needy have little discretionary spending, but this reaction is a political reality. A less provocative formulation would stress that the sales tax offers no surprises—no liability after the fact, no need to budget for a tax bill coming due, and no uncertainty about how changes in this year's market values may affect the amount of tax to be paid.

Interestingly, some economists find a connection between property taxes and sales taxes. The Mirrlees Review of the U.K. tax system by a set of international experts acknowledged "that people just find the idea of a tax linked to the value of their property unfair. This seems to reflect the fact that perceptions of fairness in tax are more closely linked to the relationship of the tax to flows of income than to stocks of wealth. But, because consumption of housing services is as legitimate a tax base as any other consumption, and because it is a good complement to current income as an indicator of lifetime income or ability to pay, this does not seem to us to be a good objection—at least not economically."[33]

Of course, the property tax is primarily a local tax, and a state sales tax will not function as an autonomous local revenue source. Most localities cannot impose significant and truly independent sales taxes without risking the loss of retail business to neighboring jurisdictions with lower tax rates. Similar problems of independence arise with local income taxes. In addition, these are typically imposed at a flat rate and thus not progressive except for the modest effect introduced by exemptions.[34]

Conclusion

Any discussion of fairness necessarily touches on highly subjective issues that resist technical analysis. When fairness concerns are couched in terms of regressivity, however, it is possible to examine them against objective criteria. The easy use of the term *regressive* to describe the property tax in popular debate is not justified on economic grounds. When commentators use the technical language of regressivity, it is essential to appreciate the implications of that term. Taxpayers and policy analysts can raise legitimate and serious objections to the property tax no matter what the consensus of professional economic opinion on its regressivity. But these objections should be presented and explained on their own terms, rather than under a rubric that suggests a quantitative judgment concerning the incidence of the tax.

More fundamentally, the economists' technical analysis does bear on larger questions of fairness and equity in taxation. Whether or not low-income households carry a disproportionate share of the burden of any given tax is an important consideration in evaluating it. Nonspecialists can easily underestimate the complexity of incidence analysis and the difficulty of estimating the actual distribution of the economic burden of a tax. The fact that economists generally reject a blanket characterization of the property tax as regressive rebuts an important fixture of anti–property tax rhetoric.

Notes

1. Slemrod (2006).
2. Pearce, ed. (1992), 371.
3. Fisher (2007), 399–400.
4. Steuerle (2002), 270.
5. Musgrave and Musgrave (1984), 514.

6. Fisher (2007), 27.
7. Reschovsky (1998).
8. Anderson (2012), 329.
9. Zodrow (2001), 70.
10. Rosen (1999), 266.
11. *Robinson v. City of New York*, slip op. 30623(U) (Sup. Ct. N.Y. County, April 20, 2015).
12. *United States v. New Mexico*, 455 U.S. 720, 735 (1982).
13. E.g., New York Office of State Aid (2011), § IA.
14. Rosen (1999), 490.
15. Aaron (1975), 2.
16. Oates (2001), 23 (footnotes omitted).
17. Fisher (2007), 358.
18. Tiebout (1956).
19. U.S. Department of the Treasury (1984), 78. See also Shobe (2015), 551 ("Local taxes benefit those within relatively homogeneous localities and are similar to a purchase of private goods, which should not be deductible.").
20. Fisher (2007), 361.
21. Hamilton (1975), 13, quoted in Rosen (1985), 488.
22. Fischel (2001a).
23. Oates (2001), 22–23 (emphasis in the original; footnotes omitted).
24. Bowman and Rugg (2011), 14.
25. Dearborn (1993).
26. Bowman and Rugg (2011), 15.
27. Slemrod (1999), 435, 438.
28. See, e.g., Galle (2009).
29. Rosen (1999), 32, referring to Buchanan (1993).
30. Doherty (1999).
31. Sheffrin (2013).
32. *New York Times* (1994), A19.
33. Mirrlees et al. (2011), 383.
34. Indiana Fiscal Policy Institute (2010), 5–6.

3 Values and Valuation

The valuation process is central to the property tax and presents its major administrative challenge. It is a crucial step in the distribution of the tax burden and the source of most taxpayer appeals. Although market price is a quantitative measure, terms such as *fair market value* and *highest and best use* suggest the equitable dimension of this calculation. This is appropriate, because the choice of a tax base does contain elements of a larger value judgment, and each alternative necessarily presents benefits, drawbacks, and changes in the distribution of the tax burden.

Market Value and Its Alternatives

An ad valorem approach to property taxation, one based on market value, is prevalent in many countries, particularly those such as the United States that trace the origins of their tax systems to British antecedents. A tax based on market value offers three crucial benefits. It can help the tax "feel fair," as discussed in the last chapter, by coordinating the asset tax with asset value. Serious disparities in tax burdens across properties of equal value, or equivalent burdens on properties with radically different values, can undermine the acceptability of the tax even to those who object to market value and its vicissitudes. Taxes based on area, or uniform taxes on each real estate parcel, inevitably raise objections when owners of extremely valuable property pay no more—and sometimes less—than those with modest holdings.

A second important benefit of a market value base is buoyancy, the ability of the tax to respond to economic developments. A tax based on area or set at a fixed amount will not reflect market changes over time. A third significant benefit of a market value base is its function as an element of value capture, recognizing that a portion of value increases can be due to public investment. A tax set at a percentage of market value recognizes a type of partnership between the owner and the jurisdiction in which the property is located.

The first great challenge to a market value tax base is to establish an accurate assessment system. The second is to adjust the tax calculation when prices fluctuate in a dramatic and unpredictable fashion. A number of factors can help mitigate this volatility, the most important being a reduction in tax rates when values rise.[1] This, of course, requires that local officials forgo the "invisible" revenue increases that can accompany tax base growth when tax rates are unchanged. The tax revolt that led to Proposition 13 in California reacted to a very accurate assessment system that tracked rapidly rising house prices, without a corresponding reduction in tax rates. The tax revolt that led to Proposition 2½ in Massachusetts developed in response to a system that had long ignored legal requirements for accurate assessments.

All market value assessments of real estate involve some degree of estimation. The unique geographic location of each parcel of property and the specific conditions of each sale prevent real estate transactions from approximating the ideal market conditions of stock or commodity exchanges. Publicly traded share prices may be set through an impartial process in which a large number of sellers offer identical items to an equally large pool of bidders. In the case of real property, however, even two neighboring houses are unlikely to be identical, and the conditions of their sale will reflect differences in timing, information, and the situation of the particular buyer and seller.

From this perspective, various market-calibrated measures of real estate values may be viewed as a continuum. At one end, many tax systems based on nonmarket measures such as area actually reflect some value influence, often in the form of coefficients to adjust for condition and location. At the other end of the spectrum, efficient systems that reassess all properties annually rely on the best value estimates for a specific date. Between these two extremes, many jurisdictions apply periodic adjustments during multiyear valuation cycles, assign properties to various ranges or bands of value, use valuation formulas, or otherwise estimate actual market values with varying degrees of precision.

International practices and individual approaches in U.S. states provide examples of a wide range of nonmarket measures. Parcel taxes, permitted in California by local vote as a supplement to property taxes restricted by Proposition 13, exhibit the least value influence. A parcel tax cannot be based on market value, and it typically does not vary according to property characteristics. Under a basic parcel tax, each distinct property in a district would be liable for the same amount.[2] This raises obvious equity concerns, and it could have efficiency implications as well if rates were sufficiently high to encourage aggregation of parcels to reduce taxes.

Area-based taxes, such as a parcel tax allocated according to lot size, offer the benefit of simplicity and problems of equity when large landholdings have less value than desirable small lots. For this reason they are often modified to reflect factors that introduce a value element, such as geographic location or quality of construction, becoming in the process more fair but also more complex. Municipalities in the Netherlands long had the option to choose between a value basis and an area basis for taxation. Over time, equitable adjustments to the area base to reflect the property's nature, location, quality, and use essentially left this measure a variant of a market value estimate, and the tax is now based entirely on market value.[3]

Another assessment alternative utilizes rental value as the basis for the tax. Traditional British property taxes, known as *rates*, were levied on rental or annual value rather than capital or market value, and were imposed on the renter or occupier rather than the owner. This situation continues in a number of countries with a British legal heritage. In Britain itself, residential taxes are now based on capital value, while business property taxes continue to be based on rental value. Annual rental value is sometimes defended as less hypothetical than a market value that might contemplate a different use of the property. However, in practice rental value has been equally subject to criticism as unrealistic and hypothetical. The renowned 1976 Layfield Commission on Local Government Finance reported "many complaints that the assessment of houses were difficult to understand and appeared to be entirely arbitrary," because the rental value basis "is unrelated to any figure or value with which the occupier is familiar."[4]

If, in a specific market, rents generally constitute a given percentage of market value, annual value and capital value may operate as equivalents, requiring only an adjustment in the tax rate to produce equal bills. The most significant difference between the two measures concerns potential future changes in value and in use, which would affect the amount a purchaser would offer but not the amount a tenant would pay for an annual lease. British annual values were based on the rental value of the property in the exact condition in which it stood (*rebus sic stantibus*). A greatly underutilized property, such as a vacant lot in the middle of a major business center, would bear a property tax reflecting its low current rental value rather than the market value it would command if offered for sale to a purchaser able to put it to its highest economic use.

To some extent the rental value approach mitigates the crucial problem of coordinating tax bills with cash income. But disregarding unrealized economic potential produces different tax burdens on properties of equivalent market value. A valuable building site could bear a small tax if it were rented for a low amount, while a modest property used to its full economic potential would bear a higher tax on that realized rental value. At the extreme, the *rebus sic stantibus* principle traditionally left vacant property essentially exempt. This incentive for property to remain unoccupied raised problems in even the most exclusive areas of London.[5] In 2013 the British government permitted local authorities to reduce or eliminate the reduction in tax for empty residences and second homes.[6]

Unvarying Assessments

A drastic response to the problem of fluctuating and unpredictable market values sets the valuation for tax purposes at a given amount that does not change in response to future variations in price levels. The once-common practice of ignoring legal revaluation requirements sometimes almost approximated a system of arbitrary fixed assessments. For example, a 1990 study found that despite a statutory requirement for market value assessment, the average interval between revaluations in New Jersey was seven to eight years, and a number of large cities had not had a complete reassessment for decades.[7]

In many jurisdictions, outdated assessments were carried on the rolls until sale of the property, which was then accompanied by revaluation at full market value. Of course, this eliminated any hypothetical neutrality and efficiency in fixed assessments. Moreover, arbitrary assessments always violated legal standards, and many such systems were overturned in court. The potential for legal challenges undermined reliance on continuation of these practices and so prevented market values from reflecting the full benefit of undertaxation. As William Fischel has written of Massachusetts, "Homebuyers did not necessarily know that there would be a statewide mandate to reassess at market value. They simply did not think such blatantly unfair and illegal assessment differentials would last for long, and they were right."[8]

Nassau County on Long Island did not update its land values for nearly 70 years, from the 1930s until the turn of the century, and used cost data rather than market value in the assessment of its buildings. This offered the political benefit of certainty and predictability, although new construction and demolitions were entered on the tax rolls. The system also produced a powerful sense of unfairness, because the 1930s values greatly understated the proportional property wealth of desirable neighborhoods and overstated the relative value share of areas that had fallen on hard times. The practical effect was to place a greater burden on poorer residents, with economic and potentially racially discriminatory impact. These were the grounds on which the U.S. Justice Department challenged the Nassau County assessment system and obtained a consent decree for revaluation.[9]

In 2009 the Pennsylvania Supreme Court found that a statute permitting assessments to reflect values as of a given "base year," as applied in Allegheny County, violated the state's constitutional requirement that all property in each county be uniformly assessed.[10] The court found Pennsylvania to be the only state that permitted indefinite use of a past year's tax value without any requirement for periodic reassessment. Allegheny County had argued that the stability and predictability of base year assessments benefited the government and taxpayers alike by avoiding the cost and uncertainties of reassessments, but the Pennsylvania court found this system to place a disproportionate burden on taxpayers in declining neighborhoods, where assessments did not reflect falling property values. The court found these variations to bear no rational relationship to a legitimate state purpose.

Acquisition Value

Proposition 13 in California does not call for unchanging assessments, but it achieves near-complete predictability through a fixed 1 percent tax rate and an assessment generally based on the purchase price of the property (or the 1975–1976 value, for property that has not changed hands since that time), with only a 2 percent maximum annual inflation adjustment. Assessments may not rise above this level but will fall if actual property values drop below it. No sudden changes in house prices will cause an owner's tax bill to rise unexpectedly. Proposition 13 thus could be seen as transforming the property tax into a kind of sales tax paid on an installment basis over the term of ownership, with the sales tax's benefits of predictability. However, that benefit comes at a significant price in terms of the equitable distribution of the total tax burden.

The original purchase price of a residence tells little about either the benefits received from public services or the owner's ability to pay, and it may in fact bear an inverse relationship to property wealth. An owner who purchased California property many decades ago has likely experienced a dramatic multiplication of real estate value. Recent purchasers of identical property who pay full current market value, possibly with an equivalently heavy mortgage, bear an annual property tax bill that may be many times that of their more fortunate neighbors. An acquisition value system can also offer a powerful but highly inefficient disincentive against selling long-held property and purchasing a different, perhaps more appropriate residence.[11] This potential loss of economic welfare is magnified by provisions that allow heirs to inherent their parents' tax assessments as long as they hold the property.

In his dissent to the U.S. Supreme Court's refusal to overturn Proposition 13 on federal constitutional grounds, Justice John Paul Stevens characterized that measure as a windfall to those who invested in California real estate in the 1970s, whom he termed "the Squires." He wrote:

> As a direct result of this windfall for the Squires, later purchasers must pay far more than their fair share of property taxes. The specific disparity that prompted petitioner to challenge the constitutionality of Proposition 13 is the fact that her annual property tax bill is almost five times as large as that of her neighbors who own comparable homes. . . . Indeed, some homeowners pay 17 times as much in taxes as their neighbors with comparable property. For vacant land, the disparities may be as great as 500 to 1. . . . These disparities are aggravated by section 2 of Proposition 13, which exempts from reappraisal a property owner's home and up to $1 million of other real property when that property is transferred to a child of the owner. This exemption can be invoked repeatedly and indefinitely, allowing the Proposition 13 windfall to be passed from generation to generation. . . . Such a law establishes a privilege of a medieval character: Two families with equal needs and equal resources are treated differently solely because of their different heritage.[12]

It is ironic that the president of the Howard Jarvis Taxpayers Association, which is "Dedicated to the Protection of Proposition 13," should criticize parcel taxes, introduced in response to Proposition 13's limitations, as unrelated to market value. He wrote, "Parcel taxes are usually flat rate taxes imposed on property irrespective of value. Therefore, the retired couple living on a fixed income in a modest bungalow pays the same amount as the owner of a multi-million dollar mansion in Beverly Hills."[13] Efforts to detach tax liabilities from market values can rarely be contained, and later adjustments and reactions can lead to new problems to be addressed through further adjustments.

Highest and Best Use

The term *highest and best use* has caused much confusion, in part because this phrase suggests a value judgment rather than an economic calculation. It does not denote the noblest or most worthy use of property but simply acknowledges that market price generally will reflect the most profitable use that is legal and feasible. A standard of highest and best use does not deal with a hypothetical future value but with current market value. As the Colorado Supreme Court explained, "[R]easonable future use is considered because it is relevant to the property's present market value. . . . [A] tract of undeveloped land with potential for development has a higher present fair market value than the same size tract of undeveloped land with no such potential, i.e., even in its undeveloped state, a willing buyer and a willing seller would agree on a higher price for it."[14] The current price takes potential future use into account.

The highest anticipated economic return does not always accompany the most intensive use of the property. In a truly rural county where farming constitutes the most economic use of land and there is little demand for office buildings or dense residential development, the highest bid for property will often contemplate continued agricultural production. In the urban fringe, development demand will generally produce higher bids for nonfarm uses to the extent that zoning and planning regulations permit this.

The current use, or *rebus sic stantibus*, approach to valuation incurs social losses through tax-induced changes in behavior, as in the English cases of owners preferring to keep property vacant rather than offer it for rent. The efficiency benefits of a land tax stem from the inability of the owner to change the bare unimproved site value of land in response to the tax. This benefit is lost if the assessed value of the land changes with the owner's development decisions.

Current use assessment assigns farmland a sometimes arbitrary but always quite reduced taxable value, as discussed in chapter 8. By excluding potential development value from the tax, this policy is intended to promote continued agricultural use and reduce pressure on farmers to sell their land. However, farmers have multiple current uses for their land, only some of which are agricultural. Farmland can also constitute a major financial asset and store of future value. A farmer owning land under development pressure in the urban fringe would rarely be a willing seller at a price reflecting only agricultural income. The expectation of future capital gains is a legitimate element of land ownership, and speculation in this sense is not the province of financiers alone.

Defining the Property to Be Valued

A critical element of the valuation process concerns the initial definition of the property to be valued, not only in terms of physical area but also with regard to the rights to be included in a hypothetical sale. Should rights the current owner may have relinquished through a lease, easement, or other legal transaction be included in the transaction? Is current zoning to be assumed a permanent restriction on development, even if other property owners have successfully petitioned for zoning changes?

Legal discussions of property rights often utilize the image of a bundle of sticks, although this metaphor has been the subject of lively debate.[15] From this perspective, the various rights that an owner might enjoy, such as the right of use, the right of occupancy, the right to exclude others, and the right to sell or bequeath the land, are considered the individual sticks that make up the bundle. Some may not be available to the owner, either because they have been previously conveyed or because public regulation prevents their exercise. For example, an owner who has rented property for a specific term no longer has the right to occupy it for that period. Similarly, an owner whose property is subject to wetlands protection or historic preservation ordinances does not have some of the rights of use and development that owners of unprotected property might enjoy.

In a sense, the requirement of tax payments is itself an element of the bundle of rights, with the government standing in the position of a landlord. The owner has indefinite rights of use and can sell or convey those rights, but only if tax obligations are met; if they are not paid, the owner stands to lose the property. The straightforward and familiar tax on property thus constitutes a continuing public claim on a portion of its value, but not public ownership of the property itself.

This analogy might consider the property tax as placing the public in the position of a limited partner, entitled to specified payments but not to a voice in management, in recognition of the public contribution to property value. In this way a property tax can function as an effective value capture instrument, and as an element of transition in nations establishing new institutions of private property but seeking a public role in establishing, enhancing, and protecting the underlying ownership rights. This is no small claim for the public interest, but it rests on a market value assessment.

Long-Term Leases

Cases involving long-term leases and possessory interests illustrate the implications of considering real property not as a physical object but as a set of intangible rights. They demonstrate that the valuation process often defines the property to be taxed, whether this step is explicitly recognized or not. The choice between the taxable values of two distinct sets of property interests is not a valuation question; it represents a fundamental determination of the nature of the tax. Courts in many states have confronted this problem, and different tribunals applying similar statutes to similar facts have reached divergent conclusions. This situation illustrates the way in which the most challenging valuation problems proceed from the complex nature of "property" itself.

In a typical case of this type, property is leased under a long-term agreement that, although negotiated in good faith, has now become burdensome to the landlord, with rents below market levels. The owner could realize a higher sale price if the property were free of the lease and available for rent at current market rates. A prospective purchaser would not offer the full unencumbered value of the property if there were a significant period remaining under the original lease.

It is understandable that in these circumstances a landlord will feel aggrieved by an assessment that does not take into account the loss in property value caused by the long-term lease. Yet it is also understandable that an assessor would seek to assign similar values to similar properties and place equivalent taxable values on identical parcels, whether they are leased or occupied by their owners.

The choice between these two positions cannot be resolved by statutory language concerning fair market value, because they present a disagreement about what property is to be valued. The owner assumes that the taxable property consists of the rights retained by the landlord: the right to receive the rent called for by the current lease during its term, and the right to occupy the property or to lease it anew at the conclusion of that term. The sale value of the landlord's interest is indisputably diminished by the below-market lease.

However, the property can also include more than the landlord's retained rights. A purchaser who sought to be free of the unfavorable lease would negotiate its early termination through a payment to the tenant. In this case, the property that was purchased would include the interest of the tenant as well as that of the landlord. The new purchaser would pay the landlord less because of the encumbrance but would also pay the tenant for early termination of the lease.

The tenant's interest, which is the right to continue to pay below-market rent for the term of the lease, could be expected to have a value equivalent to the discounted sum of these future savings. This figure is also the estimated reduction in value suffered by the landlord, in which case the value of the landlord's interest and the tenant's interest together could approximate the value of unencumbered ownership. This situation is analogous to a cloud on title, when a potential claim must be settled before a purchaser can obtain clear ownership. The amount spent to acquire the full unencumbered fee consists of the payment to clear title as well as the payment to the prior owner.

A court considering this valuation question faces two hypothetical types of "sales" that produce two different market values—a sale of the landlord's interest and a sale of the landlord's and tenant's interests together. Either transaction might be chosen by the parties to any particular sale of leased premises. Each could be a legitimate, market value sale of property, differing only in the particular interests that make up the property transferred.

It is evident that statutory language calling for assessment of all taxable property at market value does not resolve this issue. If the property is equated with the rights retained by the landlord, the taxpayer should prevail and the assessment should reflect the reduction in the value of the landlord's interest. If the property is equated with the combined rights held by the landlord and the tenant, the assessor should prevail, for the reduction in the value of the landlord's rights by reason of the unfavorable lease is offset by the positive value of the tenant's right to occupy the premises at less than market rent. The Maine Supreme Judicial Court stated that basing an assessment on the actual rent called for by the lease "imposes an unequal tax on taxpayers who own the same or similarly situated property but manage it differently. It inherently discriminates against owners who use the property to its best potential and treats the same property differently depending on the owner's business practices."[16]

This question has arisen across the country and in international settings.[17] Among the numerous state courts that have faced this issue, a majority have found that the property to be valued consists of both the landlord's and tenant's interests together, and that therefore the existence of a below-market lease should not reduce the assessment.[18] Other courts take the opposite position,[19] and some avoid a clear statement by simply requiring that the rent be "considered" in the assessment.[20]

To some courts, the predicament of an owner required to pay tax on an amount that could not be obtained were the property offered for sale is a sign of faulty valuation. It appears to be an assessment on property that the taxpayer does not own. A concurring opinion in a Michigan case compared this to imposing an income tax on current bond interest rates rather than on the lower amount paid by bonds a particular taxpayer might actually own.[21] It is true that the property owner does *not* hold the combined interests of tenant and landlord, because the lease divided those rights between two parties. The question remains as to whether the property to be taxed consists of the landlord's rights alone.

The Wisconsin Supreme Court defended the minority view that equates the landlord's interest with all rights in the property, stating that the taxpayers "did buy all the 'bundle of rights' that comprised the property. They purchased the land the buildings stood on, the physical plant, the right to the rental income through the leases, and the reversions when the leases expired."[22] However, those rights do not constitute the entire bundle, for the rights transferred to the tenant are the cause of the reduction in the value of the landlord's interest. The New York Court of Appeals wrote:

> But it must always be remembered that an underlying aim of valuation is to assure that, in providing for public needs, the share reasonably to be borne by a particular property owner is based on an equitable proportioning of the fair value of his property vis-à-vis the fair value of all

other taxable properties in the same tax jurisdiction. Otherwise, the landlord who fails to realize the fair potential of his property would, in effect, shift part of his tax burden to the shoulders of his fellow taxpayers.[23]

In response, the Wisconsin court wrote, "We reject the invitation of the New York court to require business persons to be equipped with precognition; we refuse to second-guess their business judgments, as long as such judgments were entered into at arm's length."[24]

Many instances of divided legal interests in property cause no adjustment in the tax assessment. A mortgage lender's interest may dwarf the investment of the title holder, but the owner expects to pay tax on the full value of the property nonetheless. Any attempt to tax the mortgage lender on its interest would simply result in that tax being passed on to the borrower, together with processing fees. An assessor is not required to determine the proportionate interests of co-owners, trust beneficiaries, life tenants, or business partners holding taxable property. A single assessment of the combined property interests is anticipated and accepted. The central issue is largely one of expectations: clarifying the basis of assessment so that parties to a lease can predict how the transaction will be treated for property tax purposes. If the assessment of mortgaged property were as unclear as the assessment of leased property, requiring decisions by state supreme courts to determine the appropriate tax, owners of mortgaged property might well complain that an assessment based on full value caused them financial hardship.

The minority position could give rise to interesting new problems if assessments were limited to the value of the owner's interest. For example, a Georgia decision following the majority approach noted that the owner "elected to receive cash payments totaling $216,540 during the first four years of the term and an annual rent in the amount of $2.75 per acre thereafter."[25] If the owner chose to receive the entire present value of the rent due under a long-term lease at the outset of its term, would there be a basis for valuing the property at the nominal value a prospective purchaser might offer for it?

The Pennsylvania Supreme Court faced a similar dilemma in applying the minority approach. Like most courts requiring that valuations reflect a below-market long-term lease, it had held that to value property "in hypothetical unencumbered form . . . is to ignore the economic realities of commercial real estate transactions."[26] But in 2012 a taxpayer argued that under this reasoning $30 million in tenant-financed improvements to a shopping center must be omitted from the property tax valuation, because they would offer no economic benefit to the landlord until the end of the lease term. The court realized that in this situation, valuing only the landlord's interest would mean that "a tenant under a long-term lease could build a Taj Mahal, or an Empire State Building, and such a structure would be wholly exempt from taxation merely because it was owned as a leasehold."[27] To avoid this, the court ruled that ownership by a tenant did not exempt improvements from property tax. Ironically, the court emphasized the need to value the property as a whole, and it noted that taxation is concerned with "the particular nature of the property involved, not the means by which the property is owned."[28] Both of these arguments are frequently used to support the majority approach to the long-term lease, which disregards the effect of below-market rents.

What of the landlord who is enjoying above-market returns? The New York court suggested that this situation should not increase the assessment. This is consistent with its position that the taxing jurisdiction is not a coentrepreneur sharing in "managerial banes or boons."[29] Above-market returns may reflect shrewd bargaining or good luck, but by definition they do not reflect market value. Assessments should not be increased by business arrangements that do not reflect the value of the property.

The long-term lease problem sets the groundwork for considering numerous more complex divisions of legal interests. Some of these concern a division of rights between two or more private parties, as in agreements regarding shopping malls, condominiums, homeowners' associations, and office buildings. Another set of equally provocative cases deals with divisions of rights between public and private parties. Among these are government-imposed restrictions on property income, whether involuntary, such as rent control, or voluntarily assumed for business purposes, as in the case of some subsidized housing for low-income tenants, discussed in chapter 9. Regulatory restrictions for historic preservation and environmental protection can also have dramatic effects on property value. The long-term lease cases offer a means of approaching these more difficult situations and analyzing them as part of the definition of property itself.

Possessory Interests

Possessory interests are private rights to use real estate owned by a governmental entity or tax-exempt organization. They illustrate another form of divided legal interests that may rise to the level of "property" subject to tax. They are particularly important in the case of federal property, whose constitutional immunity from taxation cannot be restricted by state legislation. The U.S. Supreme Court has made it clear that "a state may, in effect, raise revenues on the basis of property owned by the United States as long as that property is being used by a private citizen or corporation and so long as it is the possession or use by the private citizen that is being taxed."[30] A tax on a private lessee's possessory interest in federal property does not violate federal immunity—even if the lessee's interest is valued at an amount equal to the full underlying fee. In this case, the legal or statutory incidence of the tax governs its operation, no matter which party bears the economic burden.

A leasehold is the most straightforward example of a possessory interest in which the private, for-profit use of government property is generally taxable. However, many commercial uses of public or tax-exempt property do not utilize a traditional lease. An 1859 California case held that a private mining claim on federal land could be subject to taxation, even though the underlying title was protected by federal tax immunity.[31] Other early California cases confronted the problem of homesteaders who sought to avoid taxation by refusing to take title to their property, even though they could do so for a nominal sum.

The California Supreme Court found their right to possession sufficient to justify the tax, even without complete legal title, writing, "It is not the land itself, nor the title to the land, nor is it the identical estate held by the United States. It is not the pre-emption right, but it is the possession and valuable use of the land subsisting in the citizen. Why should it not contribute its proper share, according to the value of the interest, whatever it may be, of the taxes necessary to sustain the Government which recognizes and protects it?"[32]

At the end of the nineteenth century, as tunnels, rapid transit, and utility lines began to make highly profitable use of public rights of way, the New York Court of Appeals held that these rights of way were not subject to assessment.[33] "The result: a loss of 100 million dollars—turn of the century dollars—in tax revenues for New York City alone."[34] A bill to reverse this result was considered one of the most significant and controversial pieces of legislation in Theodore Roosevelt's first year as governor.[35]

The assessment of partial interests has led to surprisingly wide applications, particularly in California. At various times courts in that state have upheld property taxation of possessory interests in the form of a defense contractor's right to use a government shipyard,[36] a forest ranger's right to use government housing,[37] and a refreshment company's right to operate concessions in a public stadium.[38] Further extensions included the right to run cable lines through public rights of way,[39] the right to operate amusement machines in a public airport,[40] and the right to rent television sets to patients in a county hospital.[41]

In this way a fairly unexceptional first step has led to surprising results that challenge tax theorists to explain why the right to rent television sets should be taxed as *real* property. Many cases seem to follow Professor Edwin Seligman's advice to Theodore Roosevelt that it was immaterial whether the right to make use of public ways was classified as real or personal property: "It is both, and it is neither."[42]

These disputes reveal how important it is to distinguish the concept of property as a set of legal rights from the common usage that identifies those legal rights with a specific, often tangible, object. It is plain, for example, that the titleholder is often not the sole "owner" of the property, in the sense of claiming all rights in it. The Restatement of Property defines as an "owner" anyone "who has one or more interests" in the property, and it comments that the quantum of interests necessary for status as an owner "is not a matter upon which any precise rule can be laid down."[43]

When taxation does not require ownership, but only possession, matters become even more uncertain. Even scholars have conceded that "possession is one of the most illusive concepts in the law."[44] "[P]ossession is often said to be a social rather than a physical fact, in the sense that a person will be held to possess a thing if he has the sort and extent of control that society, considered as being represented by the ordinary reasonable man, would regard as appropriate to the kind of the thing and the circumstances of the case."[45] Or, as the California Court of Appeal put it somewhat less eloquently, "Private and government contracts and permits create such a variety of interests that the boundaries of possessory interest definitions cannot be precisely fixed; whether a particular interest is a taxable possessory one is a question for case-by-case resolution."[46]

Valuation and Property Taxation

The valuation process is the core component of property taxation. Hotly disputed political decisions about the rate of tax, which often deal with tenths of a percent, are dwarfed by the impact of alternate valuation methods. For example, in 2015 the Alaska State Assessment Review Board considered a dispute in which the owners of the Trans-Alaska pipeline contended that it had a market value of $2.6 billion, while three municipalities claimed that its value was in excess of $15.4 billion. The Board assigned it a taxable value of $9.6 billion.[47]

At the same time, many valuation decisions, whether contained in statutes or case law, actually constitute unrecognized choices concerning the definition of the property subject to taxation. These seemingly technical determinations open a window on the operational meaning of terms such as real property, ownership, and possession. They also represent value judgments, allocating the costs of public services among different types of property. Valuation decisions determine whether vacant property is to be tax free because it yields no income, whether homesteaders in possession are to be taxed before they perfect title to their land, and whether landlords receiving below-market rent are to pay reduced taxes for that reason. Enactment and enforcement of assessment standards must balance stability in taxation against disproportionate burdens on declining neighborhoods and owners of low-value property.

At the most fundamental level, the choice of fair market value as a tax base effectuates a public role in a regime of private ownership by establishing a public share in the bundle of property rights.

Notes

1. Cornia and Walters (2005).
2. McGhee and Weston (2013); Sonstelie (2015).
3. Kruimel (1999).
4. Layfield (1976), 165.
5. Pidd (2009).
6. Lewis (2013).
7. Bogart and Bradford (1990).
8. Fischel (2001b), 59.
9. McQuiston (1999).
10. *Clifton v. Allegheny County*, 600 Pa. 662, 969 A.2d 1197 (2009).
11. Haveman and Sexton (2008).
12. *Nordlinger v. Hahn*, 505 U.S. 1, 29–30, 112 U.S. 2326, 2341–2342, 120 L. Ed. 2d 1, 24–25 (1992) (Stevens, J. dissenting).
13. Coupal (2013).
14. *Board of Assessment Appeals v. Colorado Arlberg Club*, 762 P.2d 146, 152 (Colo. 1988).
15. Smith (2012).
16. *Town of Sanford v. J & N Sanford Trust*, 1997 ME 97, 694 A.2d 456, 461 (1997).
17. E.g., *Communauté Urbaine de Montréal c. Avor Realty Corp. et Crédit Foncier et Ville de Montréal*, 57 Q.A.C. 302 (Québec 1993).
18. E.g., *Caldwell v. Department of Revenue*, 122 Ariz. 519, 596 P.2d 45 (1979); *Clayton v. County of Los Angeles*, 26 Cal. App. 390, 102 Cal. Rptr. 687 (1972); *Martin v. Liberty County Board of Tax Assessors*, 152 Ga. App. 340, 262 S.E.2d 609 (1979); *Springfield Marine Bank v. Property Tax Appeal Board*, 44 Ill.2d 428, 256 N.E.2d 334 (1970); *Donovan v. City of Haverhill*, 247 Mass. 69, 141 N.E. 564 (1923); *Demoulas v. Town of Salem*, 116 N.H. 775, 367 A.2d 588 (1976); *Swan Lake Moulding Company v. Department of Revenue*, 257 Or. 622, 478 P.2d 393 (1970); *Yadco, Inc. v. Yankton County*, 89 S.D. 651, 237 N.W.2d 665 (1975).
19. E.g., *C.A.F. Investment Co. v. Township of Saginaw*, 410 Mich. 428, 302 N.W.2d 164 (1981); *Townsend v. Town of Middlebury*, 134 Vt. 438, 365 A.2d 515 (1976); *Darcel, Inc. v. City of Manitowoc Board of Review*, 137 Wis. 2d 623, 405 N.W.2d 344 (1987).
20. E.g., *Clarke Associates v. County of Arlington*, 235 Va. 624, 369 S.E.2d 414 (1988); *Nassif v. Board of Supervisors*, 231 Va. 472, 345 S.E.2d 520 (1986); *Folsom v. County of Spokane*, 111 Wash. 2d 256, 759 P.2d 1196 (1988).
21. *C.A.F. Investment Co. v. Township of Saginaw*, 410 Mich. 428, 468, 302 N.W.2d 164, at 175 (1981) (concurring).

22. *Darcel, Inc. v City of Manitowoc Board of Review,* 137 Wis.2d 623, 405 N.W.2d 344 (1987).
23. *Merrick Holding Corp. v. Board of Assessors,* 45 N.Y.2d 538, 382 N.E.2d 1341, 410 N.Y.S.2d 565 (1978).
24. *Darcel, Inc. v. Manitowoc Board of Review,* 137 Wis.2d. 623, 405 N.W.2d 344, at 351 (1987).
25. *Martin v. Liberty County Board of Tax Assessors,* 152 Ga. App. 340, 262 S.E.2d 609, at 611 (1979).
26. *In re Appeal of Marple Springfield Center, Inc.,* 530 Pa. 122, 126–127, 607 A.2d 708, 710 (1992).
27. *Tech One Associates v. Board of Property Assessment, Appeals, and Review,* 617 Pa. 439, 462–463, 53 A.3d 685, 699 (2012).
28. Ibid., 699.
29. *Merrick Holding Corp. v. Board of Assessors,* 45 N.Y.2d 538, at 545, 382 N.E.2d 1341, 410 N.Y.S.2d 565 (1978).
30. *United States v. County of Fresno,* 429 U.S. 452, 462, 97 S. Ct. 699, 704, 50 L. Ed. 2d 683, 692 (1977). One important limitation on this power requires the state to treat its own lessees in an equivalent manner—the state may not impose a tax on lessees of federal land and exempt lessees of state land. *United States v. City of Manassas,* 830 F.2d 530 (4th Cir. 1987), *aff'd,* 485 U.S. 1017, 108 S. Ct. 1568, 99 L. Ed. 2d 884 (1988).
31. *State v. Moore,* 12 Cal. 56 (1859).
32. *People v. Shearer,* 30 Cal. 645, 647 (1866). Aside from the importance of these cases in identifying a concept of taxable interests in property, they also offer an insight into historic property values. The 1859 homesteaders, for example, refused to take title to their Marin County land at $1.25 an acre because they did not want to be subject to property tax liability. Records of early tax sales in the Marin County assessor's office tell a similar tale—a 19,650-acre parcel "called Saucolito" sold for $745.27, 30 town lots in San Rafael and an interest in a ranch sold for $141.39, and all of Angel Island sold for $160.50.
33. *People ex rel. Manhattan Railway Co. v. Barker,* 146 N.Y. 304, 40 N.E. 996 (1895).
34. New York State Board of Equalization and Assessment (1983), 6.
35. Ibid., 8–9.
36. *Kaiser Co. v. Reid,* 30 Cal. 2d 610, 184 P.2d 879 (1947).
37. *United States v. County of Fresno,* 50 Cal. App. 3d 633, 123 Cal. Rptr. 548 (1975), *aff'd on other grounds,* 429 U.S. 452, 97 S. Ct. 699, 50 L.Ed. 2d 683 (1977).
38. *Stadium Concessions, Inc. v. City of Los Angeles,* 60 Cal. App. 3d 215, 131 Cal. Rptr. 442 (1976).
39. *Cox Cable San Diego, Inc. v. County of San Diego,* 185 Cal. App. 3d 368, 229 Cal. Rptr. 839 (1986).
40. *Freeman v. County of Fresno,* 126 Cal. App. 3d 459, 178 Cal. Rptr. 764 (1981).
41. *Wells National Services Corp. v. County of Santa Clara,* 54 Cal. App. 3d 579, 126 Cal. Rptr. 715 (1976).

42. New York State Board of Equalization and Assessment (1983), 6.
43. *Restatement of Property* § 10, comment c (1944).
44. Cribbet (1975), 13.
45. Lawson (1958), 33.
46. *Dressler v. County of Alpine*, 64 Cal. App. 3d 557, at 563–564, 134 Cal. Rptr. 554, at 558 (1976).
47. *In the Matter of the Trans-Alaska Pipeline System*, Alaska State Assessment Review Board OAH No. 15-3060-TAX (June 1, 2015).

SPECIAL USES OF TAX PROCEEDS

4 Property Taxes and School Finance

Some of the most significant policy discussions concerning the property tax do not deal with the tax itself but rather with the use of its revenue to support local public schools. This vigorous and long-running controversy highlights the role of the property tax, but the tax itself is of secondary importance to the substantive points at issue, such as the amount of total education spending, its distribution across school districts, and the levels of government that are to provide these funds. If income taxes constituted the primary local revenue source and property taxes were imposed at the state level, the school finance debate could continue as it stands, merely reversing the names of the state and local taxes.

School funding challenges generally begin with one basic problem: how best to expand the revenue available to schools in impoverished districts whose own resources cannot support adequate public education, even at tax rates far higher than those imposed by more affluent jurisdictions. This is not a property tax problem, but a *local* tax problem. A needy area restricted to its own income tax or sales tax revenues would find it equally difficult to support a successful school system, no matter how high its tax rates. Some transfer of external resources is essential for districts that cannot fund their vital services independently. This statement may seem self-evident, but it sometimes represents the limit of consensus in this extremely heated debate.

By itself, this consensus only establishes that no local tax can serve as the sole support for basic services when the local tax base is inadequate for that purpose. This is a far cry from demonstrating the unfairness of the property tax or any other local tax. But the traditional use of the property tax as a primary support for local schools has sometimes given rise to that implication.

Although the property tax generally functions as a local tax in this country and provides the largest share of independent local revenue, this has not always been the case. Before widespread adoption of state sales and income taxes in the twentieth century, property taxes were a major source of revenue at the state level. At the same time, many local jurisdictions also impose other taxes, such as sales or income taxes. Nevertheless, the overwhelming majority of U.S. property tax collections fund local government operations, and the property tax remains the main source of autonomous revenue for most local jurisdictions, including school districts. Therefore, debate over reliance on local resources to fund education generally questions the fairness of using property taxes as the primary means to finance local schools. It is important to clarify the extent to which the property tax itself is at issue in this debate, and the extent to which it is simply the most commonly used instrument for raising the revenue whose distribution and use is in question.

The Property Tax and Equalization of School Funding

Property taxes were most dramatically linked to the equalization of school funding in the 1971 California *Serrano* decision, which ushered in a new era of state constitutional challenges to education finance. In that case, the California Supreme Court found that divergent local property tax bases led to constitutionally unacceptable variations in school budgets: "The source of these disparities is unmistakable: in Baldwin Park the assessed valuation per child totaled only $3,706; in Pasadena, assessed valuation was $13,706; while in Beverly Hills, the corresponding figure was $50,885—a ratio of 1 to 4 to 13. Thus, the state grants are inadequate to offset the inequalities inherent in a financing system based on widely varying local tax bases."[1] Within a decade, California had pioneered a new system of centralized school finance. Instead of districts setting their budgets on the basis of local revenues, budget decisions were made for each district at the state level.[2] The initial phase of school finance reform in California focused strongly on equalization of basic funding, with the very first judicial decisions seeking to limit variations in per-pupil spending across the state to no more than $100.[3]

The same decade saw California voters lead a wave of property tax limitations with the passage of Proposition 13 in 1978. In the wake of this initiative, the state legislature changed the system for distributing property tax revenue as well. As a result of these measures, state law now governs the property tax rate, the budgets of local school districts, and the distribution of property tax collections. Approximately one-third of property tax revenue is allocated to K–12 school districts.[4] The California experience demonstrates that the property tax can be a tool for centralization and equalization of school finance as well as for decentralization and local variation.

Complexities of Centralized School Finance

Although Proposition 13 closely followed school finance reform in California, the causal connection between the two remains controversial. One perspective considers centralized, standardized school finance and administration to erode homeowners' support for the property tax.[5] "Homeowners were willing to pay higher property taxes if they were convinced this led to quality schools. The school finance litigation movement essentially breaks this tie—local property tax revenues tend now to be redistributed statewide and not directed, on the margin, to local schools."[6] At the same time, other scholars vigorously contest this hypothesis on statistical and historical grounds: "[T]he evidence does not support the claim that *Serrano* caused Proposition 13."[7]

Whatever their connection, these two elements—constitutional challenges and property tax limitations—reinforced one another in shifting authority and responsibility for school funding from localities to the state government. This process also exposed school budgets to new political pressures. At the local level, school spending is often the single most important element of the budget, but wider state needs include public health and safety, transportation, corrections, and higher education. Centralization also carries the challenge of maintaining parental contact and involvement if crucial educational decisions are perceived to be the province of state or other higher-level officials.

The California experience has demonstrated that these concerns should be taken seriously. In 1969–1970, before centralization of its school finance and the introduction of Proposition 13, California ranked 11th among all states and the District of Columbia in per-pupil K–12 spending. By 2013, it had fallen to 36th.[8] Its shortfall in spending is even greater than per-pupil figures indicate, because California teacher salaries, to be competitive, are above the national average. Eric Brunner and Jon Sonstelie observe, "California students performed considerably better in the period before the transformation from local to state finance. . . . This apparent decline in average performance would be less troubling if it were accompanied by equalization across districts and income groups. There is little evidence of equalization across school districts, however." They note that the decline in performance cannot be attributed to resources alone. "The dismal performance of California students on achievement tests is a disappointment, but that performance is due more to the inefficiency with which funds are deployed than to the paucity of those funds."[9] This situation is the result of many complex factors, but it is clear that state support for local education in California has not fulfilled the high expectations of early proponents of school finance reform.

Michigan undertook a major centralization of its school finance system in 1994, but the state's continuing economic difficulties have diminished its ability to maintain funding levels. As in California, changes in school funding were part of a set of sometimes contradictory goals, including educational improvement, enhanced equity, and tax relief. Michigan's 1994 "Proposal A" reduced property taxes dramatically and substituted a number of other sources, such as portions of state income tax collections and revenue from state sales tax increases, for school purposes.

Ten years later, two analysts who judged the results of Michigan's centralization to be "decidedly positive" nonetheless expressed concern that the state's revenue base for its school aid fund was "dangerously vulnerable to cyclical fluctuations."[10] In 2010 the Citizens Research Council of Michigan reported:

> Given the practical realities of the current financing system, state-controlled revenues (directly or indirectly) comprise nearly 85 percent of the total operating funding for local schools. As a result, state, not

local, policy makers control the purse strings of Michigan's local schools. . . . In addition to the fiscal challenges posed by Michigan's near-decade-long economic malaise, which have been exacerbated by the Great Recession, public education finances also face another serious long-term problem. Since the early 2000s, the state has failed to come to grips with the dual structural deficits affecting its major operating funds, General Fund and School Aid Fund.[11]

In a little-noticed provision of Michigan's 1994 legislation, typical of the intricacies of such enactments, the state government's former annual payments to the school retirement fund became a local responsibility.[12]

A shift to centralized school finance does not in itself address the issues of adequacy and efficiency crucial to education reform, no matter what tax is utilized as the source of education revenue. The substantive challenges of education reform are larger than the choice of a tax instrument.

Property Taxes and Local Supplementary Spending

Local taxes can also be controversial when they are used to supplement centrally set spending levels. No state is likely to fund all schools at the level the wealthiest districts might set for themselves if they made these budgetary decisions independently. This presents a choice when a state intervenes to ensure that less wealthy districts receive necessary funding. The state may direct resources to needy districts without guaranteeing them a per-pupil budget equal to that of the highest-spending jurisdictions. Alternatively, it may impose spending restrictions that limit the ability of affluent districts to supplement their budget from their own resources. Under the former approach, use of the property tax to increase the local school budget would be acceptable; under the latter, it would not. For example, Michigan does not permit local districts to seek additional tax revenue for school operations. High-spending districts that have seen their funding decline brought a new dimension to school finance litigation by considering legal action against the state.[13]

One of the attorneys who filed the original challenge to California education funding argued that it is unfair to permit parents to raise funds for local schools: "If we have a lousy education system, then the parents of the rich have to be just as concerned as the parents of the poor."[14] The opposing position considers some variations in spending a reflection of legitimate local choice, particularly if parents who cannot supplement baseline budgets may withdraw from the public school system altogether and instead send their children to private schools.

Vermont experimented with a unique approach to the issue of above-average spending after the state's Supreme Court overturned its method of school funding.[15] The legislature responded with Act 60, which from 1999 to 2004 provided a uniform statewide allowance for all elementary and secondary students. At the time, 90 percent of Vermont's school districts were already spending more than that standard amount per pupil. However, under Act 60, districts that chose to spend more had varying amounts of these additional local funds allocated to a state pool to benefit poorer areas. The wealthier a district, the greater the amount that was allocated to this "sharing pool." The state could reallocate more than two-thirds of the funds raised from the wealthiest districts to support schools in poorer districts. As reported in 2004, "Roughly 91 percent of Vermont's school districts receive more funding under the new scheme, and the residents of property-poor districts have actually experienced tax reductions. Taxes have more than doubled in the wealthiest districts, though, and per-pupil spending in those districts has decreased. These results engendered an intense response from Vermont's wealthier districts, sparking civil disobedience, local withholding from the state education fund, circumvention of the 'sharing pool' through the use of tax deductions, and an unsuccessful lawsuit challenging the constitutionality of Act 60."[16]

This controversy was a major reason for later legislative change. In Vermont, as in other states, limitations on school budgets also led to extensive private fundraising and the use of charitable foundation grants to replace tax revenues lost to local schools. In California, for example, private voluntary nontax contributions to public schools accounted for $547 million in 2011 alone.[17]

To some observers, the ability of affluent parents to purchase extra educational resources for their children's schools signals a return to the situation that gave rise to education finance court challenges in the first place. A New York teacher expressed the view that the very concept of public education "suppresses all distinctions between groups of individuals as inherently unjust."[18] On the other hand, the opportunity for local support can help foster a broad-based commitment to the public schools.

From Equalization to Adequacy

A 1986 California decision in the long line of related *Serrano* cases offered another perspective on the problems faced by spending equalization. "The adverse consequences of years of effective leveling down have been particularly severe in high spending districts with large concentrations of poor and minority students. Some of the state's most urban districts, with high concentrations of poor and minority students, are high-revenue districts."[19] As this opinion noted, "high wealth" jurisdictions with large amounts of commercial or industrial property can be home to low-income urban residents who could actually lose funding under a strict equalization approach. Many large cities with poor students need to spend more, not less, than the statewide average per student on public education.[20]

Efforts to address the needs of underserved students have shifted the focus of school finance reform from equalization to provision of sufficient funds for adequate achievement. "In 1989, the Kentucky Supreme Court declared the entire state system of public elementary and secondary education unconstitutional and held that all Kentucky schoolchildren had a constitutional right to an adequate education. The decision resulted in a dramatic overhaul of the state's entire public school system, and sparked what many scholars have called the 'adequacy movement.'"[21] Yet it is far easier to calculate differences in funding than to provide an operational definition of an adequate education. This influential decision by the Kentucky Supreme Court interpreted the state's constitutional requirement of "an efficient system of common schools" in terms of seven fairly abstract goals, including "sufficient oral and written communication skills to enable students to function in a complex and rapidly changing civilization" and "sufficient self-knowledge and knowledge of his or her mental and physical wellness."[22]

In the absence of a federal constitutional claim to equality in school finance these cases are left to state courts.[23] However, challenges to state systems cannot address the most important source of nonuniformity in education spending: differences in spending across states. These are far more significant than differences among districts in any individual state. "[R]oughly two-thirds of nationwide inequality in spending is between states and only one-third is within states, and thus school-reform litigation is able to attack only a small part of the inequality."[24]

Complexities of Per-Pupil Spending

The shift in focus from strict equalization in spending to directing adequate resources to needy districts can weaken the argument against allowing localities to choose to tax themselves to supplement state-mandated revenues. If many disadvantaged and low-performing urban districts need to spend far more than the average per-pupil budget, uniformity will not be an optimal outcome.

Nevertheless, uniform spending will always have an intuitive appeal. In California, decades of centralized school finance have effectively broken the connection between education spending and local property wealth. However, a 2011 report by the Center for Investigative Reporting's "California Watch" illustrated the ways in which per-pupil spending continued to vary widely across districts. The report quoted the president of the Alameda Education Association: "For us not to receive the same amount as other districts near us is like saying, 'We are going to value one child more than another.'" This report went on to describe California's post–*Serrano* funding system:

> In the landmark 1971 *Serrano v. Priest* ruling, the court found that using local property taxes to fund schools resulted in vast differences between a wealthy district like Beverly Hills and Baldwin Park, a low-income community east of Los Angeles.
>
> The Supreme Court ruled that differences in the basic amount spent per student—so-called "revenue limit" funding—had to be within $100 across all districts. Taking inflation into account, the permissible difference is now $350 per student. Although larger differences remain among some districts, disparities in the basic amount districts receive from the state have been substantially reduced.
>
> But that reduction has been wiped out by local, state and federal funds for close to a hundred different programs. A large part of the money is based on formulas established in the 1970s for meals, transpor-

tation and other services that often have little connection to current student needs.

The inequities the court sought to alleviate with its *Serrano* ruling persist. About two-thirds of districts now spend at least $500 above or below the state average, according to California Watch's analysis.

"What happened since the *Serrano* case is that we tried to equalize base funding for students across the state," said [Julia] Brownley, the Santa Monica assemblywoman. "But since then, we have instituted hundreds of different categorical funds that added to the base. That has taken it to another level and skewed spending again."[25]

Several aspects of this report are noteworthy. From a property tax perspective, perhaps the most significant conclusion is that continuing disparities in district budgets are not the result of differences in local property tax collections, since the allocation of property tax revenue is determined by the legislature and the governor.

Moreover, the goal of equalizing spending to within a few hundred dollars per student across a state as vast and varied as California is inappropriate. Costs of goods and services differ dramatically across regions, and between urban and rural centers. One of the major criticisms of Michigan's centralization of school finance concerned its failure to account adequately for cost differentials faced by school districts in different areas serving different populations.[26] The same criticism was applicable to California.

Many shortcomings of the post–*Serrano* funding system in California were addressed in landmark legislation signed by Governor Jerry Brown in 2013, "the most sweeping changes to the way California funds its public schools in 25 years."[27] This legislation seeks to direct more funds to needy districts, such as those serving low-income students and nonnative English speakers, rather than to equalize spending among districts.

As a numerical measure, per-pupil spending can sometimes offer a misleading suggestion of exactness. The calculations vary according to a multitude of choices about the figures to be included, such as capital expenditures, debt service, adult education, after-school programs, retirement contributions, and state administrative expenses, to say nothing of the many ways in which enrollment may be measured.[28] Appropriations may differ from budgeted amounts, and both may differ from actual spending. Thus, it is possible for the U.S. Census Bureau to calculate New York City's 2011 per-pupil spending as $19,770 and for the City's Independent Budget Office to find that figure to be under $8,000.[29] Comparisons of individual school district budgets can also be distorted if a few very small or remote districts necessarily incur very high per-pupil costs. And of course it goes without saying that the use of school funds, and not the amount of spending alone, is critical to improving instructional results.

All of these crucial issues are far removed from property tax policy, yet property taxes are still used as a convenient target in seeking blame for poor school performance. A 2013 *New York Times* editorial considering the reasons for this country's low ranking in international math and science tests took this position:

> American school districts rely far too heavily on property taxes, which means districts in wealthy areas bring in more money than those in poor ones. State tax money to make up the gap usually falls far short of the need in districts where poverty and other challenges are the greatest. . . .
>
> . . . Ontario [Canada], for example, strives to eliminate or at least minimize the funding inequality that would otherwise exist between poor and wealthy districts. In most American states, however, the wealthiest, highest-spending districts spend about twice as much per pupil as the lowest-spending districts, according to a federal advisory commission report. In some states, including California, the ratio is more than three to one.[30]

After more than four decades of extremely ambitious school finance reform, centralization, and equalization, the deficiencies of California's educational system are not the fault of the property tax. An easy resort to criticism of the tax evades the enormously challenging and far more complicated problems of improving educational outcomes.

Statewide Property Taxes

The fairness of the property tax is an issue in this debate only to the extent that local funding is deemed unfair—and then only when the property tax serves as the local tax source. Therefore, a *statewide* property tax would not be judged unfair in the same way. Some states impose a small surtax on local property taxes and use the proceeds to fund education. But statewide property taxes can encounter serious problems when they are imposed on property values computed through nonuniform local assessment practices.

This was the situation faced by New Hampshire when its school funding system, which relied primarily on the local property tax, was ruled unconstitutional by the state Supreme Court in 1997.[31] New Hampshire is the only state in the nation without either a statewide sales tax or a general income tax, leaving the property tax as an essential mainstay of public services. In response, the state imposed a tax on real property at a rate of .66 percent, based on locally assessed values equalized by the New Hampshire Department of Revenue Administration. A superior court ruled that a statewide tax could not be based on nonuniform local assessments.[32] However, a sharply divided state Supreme Court quickly reversed this decision, finding that a violation of the state's uniformity clause could only be established by "specific facts showing a 'widespread scheme of intentional discrimination.'"[33]

Other states have also made use of local property taxes to fund centralized school budgets. In Michigan, a property tax on nonhomestead property, such as vacation residences and second homes, is dedicated to the state school aid fund. This is not formally a statewide property tax, but districts that do not impose the tax do not obtain full state funding of their education grant. As in New Hampshire, a locally administered tax has become in substance a state levy.

In California, property tax assessments and collections remain a local responsibility, but the state legislature determines the use of the funds. With regard to education, the state determines funding according to a formula known as the revenue limit. As the state Department of Education explains, "A district's total revenue limit is funded through a combination of local property taxes and state General Fund aid. In effect, the State makes up the difference between property tax revenues and the total revenue limit funding for each district."[34] In 2009–2010, the average per-pupil revenue of California school districts was $8,801, and the average property tax received per pupil was $2,210, with state aid accounting for the difference. An increase in property tax revenue would cause a corresponding decrease in state aid. The property tax functions as an instrument of centralized state school finance. As noted, this has by no means eliminated objections to funding disparities between school districts. A report found that among small elementary districts the highest revenue limit funding per pupil in 2005–2006 was $31,237, and the lowest was $4,727.[35]

Impacts of Capitalization

School finance sometimes stands in a unique relationship to the property tax through the process of capitalization. The benefits of superior local public services clearly can have a positive influence on the value of real property within a jurisdiction. It is intuitively clear that if two houses are comparable in other respects, including their tax liabilities, the one in a municipality that enjoys a higher level of public services will command a higher price. At the same time, equivalent houses in different municipalities that receive similar services but bear unequal tax liabilities will command prices that reflect this difference in tax payments.

These two aspects of capitalization—the enhancement in price caused by superior services and the diminution in price caused by increased taxes—affect the school finance debate.[36] Excellent school systems can be expected to increase local property values, providing an incentive even for homeowners without children in local schools to support effective education spending. This also offers a reason to oppose wasteful or ineffective spending that may reduce the value of local property. There is no similar financial incentive for homeowners to support state-funded school spending, because their state tax payments do not affect their local property values. This is one potential advantage to local participation in school funding and operation decisions, and one reason for the hypothesis that centralized school finance helped gain support for Proposition 13 in California.

Clarifying the Debate

School finance reform is an immense challenge involving questions ranging from fundamental definitions of adequacy to legal interpretations of state mandates and measurement of costs. Public officials must balance sometimes competing concerns for equalization, adequacy of funding, centralization, and local autonomy. Moreover, school finance reform is only one part of the much larger challenge of improving educational outcomes. In many cases, the role of the property tax is only incidental to these overriding issues. The operation of the tax and the use of its revenues can be structured to support any of a number of desired financing outcomes, and a focus on the property tax as the cause of educational deficiencies can be a distraction from the essential and daunting task of improving school quality. Efforts to reduce schools' reliance on property tax revenue may draw as much or more support from anti-tax activists as from those motivated by a belief that these steps can foster greater equity or educational effectiveness. Debate on the property tax should proceed on its own merits and clearly distinguish between issues concerning its operation and the use of its proceeds.

Notes

1. *Serrano v. Priest*, 5 Cal. 3d 584, 594; 487 P.2d 1241, 1248; 96 Cal. Rptr. 601, 608 (1971) (citation omitted).
2. Brunner and Sonstelie (2006).
3. Fischel (1989), 465.
4. California Legislative Analyst's Office (2012), 19.
5. E.g., Fischel (1996).
6. Brunori (1999), 1722.
7. Stark and Zasloff (2003), 853. See also Martin (2006).
8. U.S. Census Bureau, Education Finance Branch (2015), 28, table 20.
9. Brunner and Sonstelie (2006), 73, 88.
10. Arsen and Plank (2004), 905.
11. Citizens Research Council of Michigan (2010), vii, 50.
12. Thiel (2012).
13. Coffman (2012).
14. Seligman (1988).
15. *Brigham v. State*, 166 Vt. 246, 692 A.2d 384 (1997).
16. Obhof (2004), 593 (citations omitted).
17. Weston (2015), 3.
18. Becker (1997).
19. *Serrano v. Priest*, 200 Cal. App. 3d 897, 226 Cal. Rptr. 584, 619 (1986).
20. Minorini and Sugarman (1999b), 38.

21. Minorini and Sugarman (1999a), 175.
22. *Rose v. Council for Better Education*, 790 S.W.2d 186, 212 (Ky. 1989).
23. *San Antonio Independent School District v. Rodriguez*, 411 U.S. 1, 93 S. Ct. 1278, 36 L.Ed.2d 16 (1973).
24. Murray, Evans, and Schwab (1998), 808. See also Corcoran and Evans (2015), 358 ("[I]n most years, 60–70 percent of the variation in spending can be attributed to between-state differences in per-pupil expenditure.").
25. Freedberg and Doig (2011).
26. Arsen and Plank (2004).
27. York (2013).
28. California Department of Education (2013).
29. U.S. Census Bureau (2013); New York City Independent Budget Office (2014).
30. *New York Times* (2013).
31. *Claremont School District. v. Governor*, 142 N.H. 462, 703 A.2d 1353 (1997).
32. *Sirrell v. New Hampshire* (Rockingham Superior Court, January 17, 2001).
33. *Sirrell v. New Hampshire*, 146 N.H. 364, 373, 780 A.2d 494, 501 (2001).
34. California Department of Education (2008).
35. Weston (2010), 2.
36. Oates (1969; 2006).

5 Tax Increment Financing

Tax increment financing (TIF) was pioneered in California in 1952 and subsequently has been utilized in nearly every state,[1] becoming "the most widely used local government program for financing economic development in the United States."[2] For that reason, California governor Jerry Brown's 2011 decision to end TIF initiatives in that state signaled a dramatic change in the fiscal landscape. Despite intense opposition by redevelopment agencies, the California Supreme Court held that their dissolution was constitutional.[3] Although Governor Brown signed legislation authorizing more limited community revitalization and investment authorities in 2015,[4] the suggestion that TIFs were no longer sustainable in California marked a turning point worth careful consideration, and one that sheds light on larger issues of debt finance now facing many state and local governments.

In theory, TIF creates a perfect closed system of self-sustaining finance, a textbook example of using value increments to fund the public improvements that create them. There are important differences among state approaches, but a set of common elements forms the basic pattern. Generally, a municipality identifies a specific geographic area for redevelopment. The redevelopment initiatives may be directed by the municipality or by an economic development agency, which typically is under municipal control. They may be funded on a cash basis or, more commonly, by the issuance of bonds. Their crucial feature is the earmarking of taxes on future increases in property values in the TIF district to pay for redevelopment costs. Because future tax base growth is set aside for TIF purposes, local governments, school districts, and other jurisdictions relying on property tax revenue from the TIF district will find this tax base frozen for the duration of the TIF.

TIFs can be invisible to taxpayers, for the assessor continues to value property as before, and the taxpayer continues to pay taxes in the same way. But tax collections are now divided between the portion attributable to values in place when the TIF district was established and the portion that represents value increases since that time. For the life of the TIF district, which may be 20 to 30 years, or even longer,[5] taxes on value increases are earmarked for TIF spending or repayment of TIF debt.

Ideally, a TIF project requires no new taxes and pays for itself by increasing the tax base. Because a finding of "blight" in the redevelopment area is often required for establishment of a TIF district, the government investment is considered to target a region that would not otherwise attract private capital. From this perspective, TIF is, as Professor George Lefcoe has written, a "win-win-win for the city, the private developer and the taxpayers."[6] It is no wonder that Sacramento mayor Kevin Johnson, in opposing Governor Brown's plan to end TIFs, called these projects "magical things."[7]

In appropriate situations TIF can produce exactly these beneficial results. A formerly blighted area may blossom, tax valuations may increase as a result, and a strengthened tax base may permit expanded public services. In less successful cases, however, the investment may fail to improve local conditions, while the freeze in future tax base growth could restrict services during the period for repayment, further diminishing the jurisdiction's economic prospects.

The promise and popularity of TIF have placed it in a position of enormous fiscal importance. Yet California's rejection of that approach signals the need to consider its risks and potential drawbacks as well.

Risks and Incentives

The risk of poor performance is inherent in any situation calling for financial judgment. An absence of private investment, which is the justification for government intervention, may signal that the market has not identified current development opportunities in a particular location. In this case, a certain number of unsuccessful investments might be the price for undertaking any ambitious redevelopment initiative. A more fundamental concern involves legislative and institutional factors that could actually encourage unproductive investments. This constitutes what economists term "moral hazard"—an incentive for misallocation of resources.

When introduced in 1952, TIF was seen as a means of raising matching funds for federal urban development grants. Several decades later, resourceful local governments facing an era of tax limitations were able to utilize this tool to support expanded spending despite such constraints. At the same time, several structural elements of TIF have proven to be especially problematic, including the interpretation of *blight*, the assumption that future increases in property value are caused by the TIF project, and above all the ability of a TIF district to appropriate the future tax base growth of other, overlapping jurisdictions, most notably school districts.

Identifying Blight

Many states require a finding of "blight" for establishment of a TIF district.[8] Yet, as Professor Lefcoe has noted, truly blighted neighborhoods offer the fewest possibilities for easy increases in property value. Citing an Iowa study that found TIFs to be most successful in "booming suburbs and metropolitan areas," he commented, "After all, that is where costly new developments have the best chance of being financed, built, and adding greatly to the property tax rolls. . . . TIF funded redevelopment built in distressed areas would seldom boost property values enough for the project to pay its own way."[9]

An instrument dependent on future value increases would not be able to support interventions in truly blighted areas that only resulted in reduced rates of decline, or even stabilized values—however heroic such an accomplishment might be in fact. Over time, the definition of blight has been stretched beyond recognition in many cases, with cities, courts, and consultants ready to accede to almost comical expansions of that term. A 2011 audit by the California state controller's office reported: "Even though redevelopment agencies must spend their money on improving 'blight,' Palm Desert dedicated almost $17 million in redevelopment dollars to improve a luxury golf resort."[10] In Coronado, near San Diego, the redevelopment area covered "every privately owned parcel in the city, including multimillion dollar beachfront homes."[11] Use of TIF as a general funding device and not as a means of assisting blighted neighborhoods is the first step in unmooring this instrument from its theoretical justification.

Cause and Effect

Nineteen states require a finding that new development would not take place in the TIF district "but for" the government intervention.[12] This has been treated as even more of a formality than a finding of blight. Blight, however subjective, at least refers to an observable physical attribute. The counterfactual prediction of what would happen but for establishment of a TIF district is so open to conjecture as to invite manipulation. Because this finding is often left to the municipality establishing the TIF district, there is no incentive for an independent review. As Professor Richard Briffault has written, "The conceptual heart of TIF is that the TIF expenditure is the but-for cause of subsequent economic growth in the TIF district. . . . But for the most part, as TIF has spread the but-for requirement has fallen away."[13]

Tax Base Growth

The inability to predict what would happen in the absence of TIF undermines its theoretical status as a self-financing device that does not raise taxes. The assumption that tax base growth is caused by the TIF justifies earmarking the tax base increment to pay for that development, and it lies behind the claim that TIF allows new spending with no tax increase. But it is extremely difficult to prove a specific cause for any change in property value. A municipality may have an incentive to draw the boundaries of the TIF district as widely as possible, including development that may be unrelated to the TIF investment. And value increases due only to general growth or inflation cannot be attributed to the TIF. If tax base growth that reflects inflation is allocated to the TIF district, the jurisdictions that depend on the property tax for basic funding may have to raise their tax rates or face budget shortfalls. Many local government budget items, such as health insurance for public employees, can rise at rates well above inflation.

The assignment of future valuation increases to the TIF district can encourage municipalities to target undeveloped land or other property with low assessed values, particularly agricultural parcels eligible for preferential farmland programs. These areas may not be blighted or underserved by private developers, but they can offer dramatic increases in assessed value simply by being reclassified as commercial or industrial. For example, one study found that almost half of Wisconsin TIFs supported construction on open space and farmland, including a Wal-Mart Supercenter on a former apple orchard.[14]

Calculations of the tax base increment can also be distorted when jurisdictions reassess property on a multiyear basis. For example, Cook County employs a three-year cycle, reassessing the northern suburbs one year, the southern suburbs the next, and the city of Chicago in the third year. In this situation, designation of a TIF district just before reassessment can ensure an increment that has nothing to do with the TIF investment.

A plethora of economic studies have reached no consensus concerning the effect of TIF on economic growth. This is not surprising, given the enormous variety of circumstances, regions, and types of projects at issue. Some studies have even found negative effects for TIF designation. For example, Professors Richard Dye and David Merriman undertook a major analysis of 235 Chicago-area municipalities and concluded that "property values in TIF-adopting municipalities grew at the same rate as or even less rapidly than in nonadopting municipalities."[15] A second study three years later did not find "the earlier provocative result of a significantly negative impact of TIF adoption on growth," but still failed to identify a positive impact, with growth in TIF districts offset by declines elsewhere.[16] Analysts who have reviewed the voluminous literature on this point generally agree that "research on the effects of TIF has raised more questions than it has answered."[17] "There is little clear evidence that TIF has done much to help the municipalities that use it, while it is a source of intergovernmental tension and a site of conflict over the scope of public aid to the private sector."[18]

Overlapping Jurisdictions

By far the greatest moral hazard posed by TIFs concerns the ability to freeze the assessment base of overlapping jurisdictions, such as school districts. The municipality establishing the TIF district may be able to appropriate value increases, including those due only to inflation, from independent districts with no power to block this transfer. Just as tax credits and deductions can make it rational to construct an otherwise uneconomic building, the ability to draw on the tax base of separate jurisdictions can encourage expenditures that would not be approved if the municipality itself needed to provide this funding. In fact, a municipality may have an incentive to set up a TIF even if it reduces growth. As Richard Dye and Jeffrey Sundberg explain:

> With a positive pre-TIF rate of growth, the district is able to "capture" that portion of the growth in property value for use in TIF financing.
> This points out what we consider to be one of the gravest flaws in TIF. If property values would grow at a high rate in the absence of TIF, even a project that results in a permanent reduction in the growth rate would be easy to finance. Policy makers unused to the concept of opportunity cost might be susceptible to making a poor decision if financial viability is confused with efficiency.[19]

The importance of tax base capture is so great that, as Professor Lefcoe points out, "In states where local governments have no opportunity to pledge tax increments from other taxing entities such as counties and school districts, there is very little TIF. . . . Why have so few states granted schools, counties and other taxing entities the right to opt out of sharing their tax increments? The short answer probably lies in an analysis of the lobbying effectiveness of redevelopment agencies, schools and counties."[20]

The effect on school districts provided a major impetus for the end of new TIF projects in California. As noted in chapter 4, the state had for decades supplemented school budgets with state resources following the landmark judicial decisions rejecting disparities in local school funding due to varying property tax wealth across districts. Tracy Gordon of the Urban Institute wrote, "The catch is that the money has to come from somewhere. In California, the state is on the hook for property taxes that would have otherwise gone to schools."[21] By 2001, California TIF districts were estimated to receive 10 percent of all property tax revenues in the state, or $2.1 billion annually, and to have accumulated $51 billion in bonded indebtedness.[22]

The ability to "capture" revenue that would otherwise go to another jurisdiction provides an incentive for undertaking TIF projects that would not be justified on their own merits.

Larger Questions

It is common for legislative enactments to rest on faulty theoretical justifications, and it is unrealistic to look for a perfect match between the conceptual basis and practical implementation of fiscal measures. Institutional structures are a principal defense against excesses and abuses, and the failure of these systemic protections is of greater concern than flawed legislative rationales for new enactments. At the most general level, transparency and clarity are essential to citizen oversight, but many TIF programs are largely hidden from taxpayer notice. At a more specific level, debt limits and the requirement of voter approval can offer a check on municipal borrowing, but legislatures, courts, and local officials have generally circumvented these measures by agreeing that bonds secured by tax increment financing do not constitute debt for these purposes.

Transparency

Professor Lefcoe writes, "Redevelopment and economic development agencies often keep the public in the dark about their transactions."[23] The rationale of self-financing can lend legitimacy to politically expedient nondisclosure. If in theory taxpayers are not required to make any new payments for these projects, lack of public participation or even awareness seems less problematic. In this way, the assumption that all future tax base growth is due to TIF investment helps justify the exclusion of overlapping jurisdictions from the decision to earmark that growth for TIF development. This theory presents the TIF process as a closed circuit: "The incremental revenues pay for the public expenditures, which induce the private investment, which generates the incremental revenues, which pay for the public expenditures."[24] Yet a frozen tax base is likely to require higher tax rates, new fees, or other mechanisms to fund ongoing government operations.

Judicial Oversight

Although courts can also provide institutional protection against abuse, judicial oversight has played little role in TIF developments. This may reflect the goodwill naturally extended to an apparently self-financing program to assist blighted areas. In addition, lack of public awareness reduces the likelihood of legal challenges to TIF programs. When even public officials do not understand TIF provisions, it is extremely difficult for taxpayers to evaluate their impact. The professionals most familiar with these complex structures often have a vested interest in avoiding conflict over them. For example, with regard to blight determinations, "The attorneys most capable of filing such challenges are jeopardizing their future dealings with the city officials they sue and with officials in other cities who get wind of their whistle-blower-like behavior."[25]

Once TIFs became the primary instrument for municipal redevelopment and even new development, the sheer magnitude of these investments, and the rise of entire businesses and professions assisting in their implementation, placed an extremely heavy burden on efforts to change their method of operation. A 2007 Florida Supreme Court decision characterizing TIF financing as debt would have required voter approval of TIF bonds. The court ruled three weeks later that its decision was not retroactive, and it reversed itself entirely the following year.[26]

Defining Debt

The Florida decision dealt with the underlying challenge of characterizing debt for legal purposes. Nearly every state imposes statutory or constitutional limitations on the amount of debt municipalities may incur, and most require a voter referendum for such "general obligation" borrowing.[27] Revenue bonds secured by a new and segregated source of funds, such as tolls for a highway or bridge to be built with bond proceeds, have long been exempt from these provisions, which are designed to protect general tax revenues. TIF debt has similarly been free of these requirements, most crucially the need for a public vote on bond issues. This practice can be justified on the theory that the TIF debt, too, is secured by a segregated account. But the TIF account consists of future growth in the basic property tax revenue that supports such general government functions as education, public safety, and transportation.

Criticism of the referendum requirement generally focuses on its costs and the barriers it places in the path of worthy projects. "In response to these criticisms, state courts have developed judicial doctrines that evade constitutional debt limitations. . . . In the last twenty years, judicial complicity with state and local officials has freed local governments to increase the number of TIF applications and push it from a 'fringe' development finance tool to a mainstream public finance method."[28] Yet the public has not been averse to supporting the issuance of debt for specific purposes. For example, H. Spencer Banzhaf, Wallace Oates, and James Sanchirico studied over 1,500 local referenda held between 1998 and 2006 dealing with open space conservation, and they found that more than three-quarters of them were approved by voters.[29]

The legal classification of borrowing secured by taxes on value increments as something other than general obligation debt reflects the larger problem of characterizing and accounting for future liabilities. Legislative and judicial interpretation may have excluded TIF claims on future tax receipts from the legal category of debt, but this does not change their effect on local governments that must deal with reduced future revenues.

Chicago's TIF Experience

Chicago's long history of TIF projects presents important lessons on their potential benefits and pitfalls. The city has made use of TIF on an extremely large scale, with former mayor Richard M. Daley repeatedly calling it "the only game in town."[30] At the same time, the city's academic community has undertaken major studies of the impact of TIF development, and investigative journalists have examined the political process of TIF approval and operation in great detail.

The Central Loop TIF, perhaps the nation's largest, was established in 1984 under Mayor Harold Washington to finance investment in the notoriously hard-to-develop "Block 37," a parcel bounded by Washington, State, Randolph, and Dearborn Streets. Mayor Washington predicted that the TIF could be closed by 1995. In fact, it was expanded in 1997 to include the area bounded by Wacker Drive, Michigan Avenue, Congress Parkway, and Franklin Street. By the time it was terminated in 2008, the TIF had brought in more than $1 billion in revenue, including $365.5 million in its final year alone. Meanwhile, the development of Block 37 remained unfinished.

This experience is not unique. As Tracy Gordon has noted, "Once redevelopment areas are born, they rarely die. For example, Los Angeles officials created the Hoover Redevelopment Project in 1966 to improve the area surrounding the city's Memorial Coliseum. In 2004, 35 years before the project was due to end in 2039, state lawmakers extended it to 2051. . . . As a Senate staff analysis noted at the time, '[T]he committee may wish to consider why it should [take] Los Angeles officials a century to redevelop the Hoover neighborhood.' "[31]

In 1997, Chicago had 41 TIF districts; during the following four years, it created 86 more.[32] At the beginning of 2009, the city had over $1 billion in TIF funds on hand, compared to an official city budget of $6 billion.[33] A single new TIF—LaSalle Central, established in 2006 in the financial district just west of the Central Loop—was projected to accumulate more than $2 billion in revenue before it expires in 2029.[34]

The large number of taxing entities within Cook County gives the city of Chicago a special incentive to appropriate these jurisdictions' future tax base growth through TIF designation. There can be as many as 15 overlapping jurisdictions in the city, including the Board of Education, the Chicago Transit Authority, the Chicago Park District, the Community College District, the Health and Hospital Commission, and Cook County itself.[35] Moreover, Illinois legislation allows a municipality special freedom in TIF operation. For example, although gerrymandering of TIF districts is not uncommon, Illinois is remarkably lenient in allowing revenue from one TIF district to be spent in another.[36]

Limited Oversight

Mayor Daley's support for TIFs as the "only game in town" confronted no significant opposition during his long tenure from 1989 to 2011. The institutional factors that diminish oversight, such as lack of transparency and the absence of legal challenges, combined with public approval for new development and successful downtown revitalization, were especially strong in Chicago. Cook County Commissioner Mike Quigley undertook a review of TIF procedures, culminating in a major public report in 2007.[37] None of his recommended reforms were adopted. His proposal to include TIF information on property tax bills failed at a County Board meeting presided over by Finance Chair John Daley, the mayor's brother.[38] After Quigley was elected to Congress, no other local official took on the challenge of reforming TIFs in Chicago.

Illinois law requires creation of a Joint Review Board (JRB) composed of representatives of affected jurisdictions and special districts to vote on TIF proposals. But as Commissioner Quigley wrote, "In practice, however, the JRB barely scrutinizes the TIF proposals that come before it, and has never voted one down. With the exception of Cook County, all JRB members are in effect representatives of the mayor of Chicago."[39]

Similarly, all 15 members of the Community Development Commission (CDC) charged with oversight of TIF projects are appointed by the mayor, providing almost unanimous approval of city proposals. Of the 812 votes cast by the CDC between November 2005 and April 2007, 808 were affirmative, and no item failed to carry a majority.[40] Quigley's report states: "We have to conclude that the CDC functions as a rubber stamp, exercising little actual oversight. . . . Four commissioners have been present for fewer than half of the votes taken since November 2005. One commissioner whose name has been read during 95 roll calls has been present for just three of them."[41]

Chicago offers an extreme example of the lack of transparency common to TIF programs. "Of the 11 aldermen who spoke with us about their TIF meetings, none was allowed to see the entire TIF budget—they were shown the revenues and expenditures planned for their wards alone and asked to sign off."[42] Quigley's report states, "The near total lack of public information readily available on Chicago's TIFs is, in a word, inexcusable. . . . Why this should be so is perplexing, but the process one must go through just to get a minimally clear picture of TIF in Chicago requires time and fortitude average citizens simply don't have."[43]

This situation is not unique to Chicago. The Maryland *Daily Record* undertook a detailed examination of "The New East Baltimore" development project, headed by East Baltimore Development Inc. (EBDI). "The Daily Record's investigation found that The New East Baltimore's public funding is so complex and poorly scrutinized that local elected officials, some of whom serve on EBDI's board, said they had little grasp of the $108.5 million in city funds committed to the project."[44]

Given this lack of oversight or opposition, it can be hard for municipalities to resist the use of TIF revenue for short-term needs. In Chicago, TIF funds were used for job training and street cleaning because, as one alderman said, "Streets and San [Sanitation] is being shortened every day."[45] This is particularly ironic, because by 2005 the TIF budget for Chicago was greater than that of the entire Streets and Sanitation and Transportation Department.[46] By 2005, 10 percent of all property taxes in Chicago were earmarked for TIF purposes, and TIF districts covered more than one-quarter of the city's area, causing overlapping entities to lose hundreds of millions of dollars in revenue.[47]

TIF's effect on property tax revenues also caused public confusion. Quigley's report estimated that TIF caused a 4 percent rise in Chicago property taxes, but a flyer distributed by the city's Department of Planning and Development titled "Tax Increment Financing: Myth/Reality" stated, "Myth: TIF will increase my taxes. Reality: TIF produces more tax revenue by encouraging growth in the neighborhood and expanding the tax base, but it does not change the way your taxes are assessed or change the way you pay taxes."[48]

Mayor Daley's successor, Rahm Emanuel, came to office in 2011 with a commitment to TIF reform. He appointed an expert panel whose report, *Findings and Recommendations for Reforming the Use of Tax Increment Financing in Chicago*, called for greater transparency, accountability, and public involvement. Journalists and analysts anticipating dramatic changes were highly critical of a 2013 proposal for a $55 million TIF development that would benefit DePaul University, charging that "Rahm's New TIF Program Looks a Lot Like the Old TIF Program," and "Mayor Ignores Own Reform Panel."[49] In 2015 Emanuel announced that the city would phase out seven downtown TIF districts and that no new projects would be undertaken that had not already been approved by City Hall. The *Chicago Tribune* wrote, "While his administration has been more transparent on TIF spending than Daley's, TIF districts, their surpluses and how the money gets transferred and spent has made the program a constant target of suspicion. Emanuel's proposals are a big step in the right direction."[50]

Long-Term Borrowing

Debt finance has an important place in funding long-term capital projects. However, the TIF experience shows that the ability to spend against future revenues for unspecified purposes with little oversight encourages excessive borrowing in other ways. Once again, Chicago offers a cautionary tale in this regard.

In 2004 Mayor Daley decided to lease the Chicago Skyway, a 7.8-mile toll road connecting the western Indiana suburbs with the Dan Ryan Expressway to downtown Chicago. In 2005 a private consortium paid $1.83 billion for a 99-year concession to operate the Skyway and collect its tolls. Political opposition was diminished in part because, although the Skyway had been operated as a Chicago municipal department, most of its users were commuters from eastern Illinois suburbs and western Indiana, not Chicago voters. The proceeds were allocated primarily to repayment of municipal debt and establishment of an $875 million reserve fund, with $100 million to be spent on current outlays.[51]

Four years later, the city sold the rights to collect its parking meter revenue for the next 75 years for $1.15 billion, with the avowed intent of putting the proceeds into a long-term reserve fund whose interest would help replace the $20 million in lost annual parking meter revenue. In fact, nearly all that amount was spent within one year. Mayor Daley had "no qualms about raiding reserves he once called untouchable, in part, to dole out $200 grants to hard-pressed homeowners."[52] This led one alderman to cast his first "no" vote on a Daley budget in 16 years. "[T]he parking meter money was billed as a 'perpetual replacement fund' when the 75-year lease was rammed through the council a year ago. 'We have breached our fiduciary duty to taxpayers. You can't break a contract in 12 months that's supposed to last for 75 years. It's unconscionable. It's irresponsible. It's disingenuous. The decision to raid this fundamental asset is mind-boggling.'"[53] The budget approved at the end of 2009 left only $773 million of the combined $3 billion realized from the lease of the Skyway and the sale of parking meter rights.

David Brunori wrote in *State Tax Notes*, "In 2007, I mentioned that the city of Chicago was considering leasing its parking meters. In 2008 it leased the 36,000 parking meters for 75 years for $1 billion. Morgan Stanley later then sold the lease to Abu Dhabi. The emirate has complete control over the city's parking meters and has ended free parking on holidays."[54]

Chicago's problematic use of debt is reflected and magnified at the state level. In February 2011, the State of Illinois sold $3.7 billion in bonds to "hedge funds, mutual funds, and non-U.S. buyers" in order to make a legally required payment to its public employee pension plan.[55] The Illinois bond rating was one of the lowest of the 50 states, and these bonds carried an interest rate approximately two percentage points greater than would be required from a private company with a similar bond rating. That same month, Governor Pat Quinn announced plans to issue more than $8 billion in bonds to pay past-due bills, such as amounts owed to state vendors. The governor said, "This is not, not new borrowing. Billions of dollars of existing bills will not go away by magic."[56] The past-due bills were already in existence, but the declaration that an $8 billion bond offering is "not, not new borrowing" had a through-the-looking-glass quality. Within two years, failure to address unfunded pension liabilities led the state's credit rating to fall to the lowest level in its history, and the lowest of all 50 states.[57]

Defining Debt

From the mayor of Sacramento to the governor of Illinois, magic seems to figure heavily in considerations of debt. More than 70 years ago, the philosophy of legal realism sought to demystify judicial decision making by removing it from the realm of scholasticism, first principles, and natural law. In his enormously influential article, "Transcendental Nonsense and the Functional Approach," Felix Cohen mocked the idea of "magic 'solving words'" such as "property rights," "fair value," and "due process." "Legal arguments couched in these terms are necessarily circular, since these terms are themselves creations of law, and such arguments add precisely as much to our knowledge as Molière's physician's discovery that opium puts men to sleep because it contains a dormitive principle."[58] The magic solving words of debt and borrowing have been much in evidence in creative finance, including TIF, in recent years.

From another perspective, perhaps Governor Quinn could be interpreted as acknowledging that functional, rather than technical, borrowing does not occur when the state undertakes a specific bond offering, but at an earlier time when it assumes an obligation for which it lacks funding. A report on the state budget by University of Illinois researchers termed this "implicit borrowing." They wrote, "Past choices to implicitly borrow by not putting aside sufficient funds to cover future pension liabilities have made Illinois pension underfunding the worst in the nation."[59] In this view, debt might include all varieties of payment obligations, whether or not they are technically subject to legislative and constitutional restrictions and referendum requirements.

After the first generation of tax limitation measures across the country, much spending was supported by borrowing that avoided the magic solving word of "debt." Transactions such as leasing parking meters, selling an expressway, and TIF borrowing secured by taxes on future value increments can avoid classification as debt for specific legal purposes. Unfortunately, the name given to these diverse fiscal instruments does not change the experience of repayment. Motorists facing increased tolls, drivers whose parking fees have quadrupled, taxpayers called upon to honor unfunded pension obligations, or property owners confronted with higher tax rates because of a frozen tax base do not bear less of a financial burden because what they are repaying is not termed debt. If the cycle of tax limitations was followed by a cycle of borrowing, then the next cycle, that of repayment, will require political, legal, and economic expertise to help local governments through this transition without the aid of magic.

Notes

1. Byrne (2006), 317; Kenyon, Langley, and Paquin (2012), 34.
2. Briffault (2010), 65.
3. *California Redevelopment Association v. Matosantos*, 53 Cal. 4th 231, 267 P.3d 580; 135 Cal. Rptr. 3d 683 (2011).
4. Jones (2015).
5. For example, in 2010 Wisconsin extended the potential life of TIF districts to 40 years. Buhl (2010).
6. Lefcoe (2011), 437.
7. Grimes (2011).
8. Kenyon, Langley, and Paquin (2012) found that 37 states and the District of Columbia required a finding of blight in order to establish a TIF district.
9. Lefcoe (2011), 444. Much political controversy over eminent domain takings of property for economic development after *Kelo v. City of New London*, 545 U.S. 469, 125 S. Ct. 2655, 162 L.Ed.2d 439 (2005), has focused on the definition of blight. See Lefcoe (2008).
10. Seipel (2011).
11. Lin (2011).
12. Kenyon, Langley, and Paquin (2012).
13. Briffault (2010), 77.
14. LeRoy (2008), 11.
15. Dye and Merriman (2006), 5, citing Dye and Merriman (2000).
16. Ibid., 6, citing Dye and Merriman (2003).
17. Weber and Goddeeris (2007), 54.
18. Briffault (2010), 83–84.
19. Dye and Sundberg (1998) (footnote omitted).
20. Lefcoe (2011), 457, 465.
21. Gordon (2011).
22. Merriman (2010), 309 n. 3.
23. Lefcoe (2011), 473.
24. Briffault (2010), 68.
25. Lefcoe (2011), 446.
26. *Strand v. Escambia County*, 992 So. 2d 150 (Fla. 2008); *Bay County v. Town of Cedar Grove*, 992 So. 2d 164, 168–170 (Fla. 2008). See also Carr and Griffith (2007), and Follick (2008).
27. For a discussion of the nineteenth-century background to debt ceilings and referenda requirements, including borrowing for railroads and canals, and New York City debt during the Boss Tweed era, see Geheb (2009) and Gelfand (1979). In Berman (2011), Professor John Wallis traces current state debt provisions to the defaults of 1841, which raised interest rates for state borrowing for the rest of the 19th century. "To this day, Mississippi hasn't paid back some of those bonds, even after a 100-year English bid to collect."

28. Geheb (2009), 736 (citations omitted).
29. Banzhaf, Oates, and Sanchirico (2010).
30. Briffault (2010), 66.
31. Gordon (2011).
32. Thompson, Liechty, and Quigley (2007), 1.
33. Joravsky and Dumke (2009).
34. Thompson, Liechty, and Quigley (2007), iii.
35. Weber and Goddeeris (2007), 12.
36. Thompson, Liechty, and Quigley (2007), 38–40.
37. Thompson, Liechty, and Quigley (2007).
38. Joravsky (2009).
39. Thompson, Liechty, and Quigley (2007), 15.
40. Ibid., ii.
41. Ibid., 46–47.
42. Joravsky and Dumke (2009).
43. Thompson, Liechty, and Quigley (2007), 41, 44.
44. Simmons and Jacobson (2011).
45. Joravsky and Dumke (2009).
46. Thompson, Liechty, and Quigley (2007), ii.
47. Ibid., 6, 9.
48. Ibid., i, 48.
49. Joravsky (2013).
50. *Chicago Tribune* (2015).
51. Gómez-Ibáñez (2010), 412–413, 422.
52. Spielman (2009).
53. Ibid.
54. Brunori (2011).
55. Corkery and Neumann (2011).
56. Setze (2011a).
57. *Chicago Tribune* (2013); Long and Garcia (2013).
58. Cohen (1935), 820.
59. Dye, Hudspeth, and Merriman (2011), 29.

SPECIAL TREATMENT OF SPECIFIC PROPERTIES

6 Classification and Differential Taxation

Property tax systems that impose different tax rates on different types of property pose a special challenge for policy analysis. They increase complexity, diminish equality of treatment, and can provide incentives for inefficient property use. The introduction of one favored category immediately creates pressure for special treatment of other properties, from historic structures to energy-efficient buildings. Minnesota began with four property classes in 1913; by 2012, depending on how various tiers and subclasses were counted, it had as many as 55.[1] Cook County, Illinois, which includes Chicago, has 15.[2]

These varied provisions can increase the tax burden on less wealthy groups that are not well connected politically. It is common for residential preferences to be limited to owner-occupied property, with renters bearing heavier rates. Business property is generally subject to higher taxes than residences, although a struggling business may have less ability to pay than an affluent homeowner. Burdensome taxes often lead local governments to offer tax reductions to specific firms considering moving to or from the jurisdiction, showing once again the importance of having broad, uniform taxes with lower rates for all.

At the same time, states that have for decades or even centuries imposed lower taxes on residential property than on business property can find it politically untenable to reverse course. When twentieth-century courts showed new willingness to enforce legal requirements of uniformity, states often responded by amending those laws and permitting legal classification. Ironically, that in itself was a major step toward tax reform, as unacknowledged tax benefits to some owners were replaced by openly acknowledged classification based on market value.

Basic Classification

There are several methods for varying the tax burdens on different types of property. The effective tax rate, which measures the tax as a percentage of market value, will obviously vary when different rates are applied to different properties. Less obviously, it will also vary when a nominally uniform tax rate is applied to assessments based on different measures of taxable value.

The political rationale for differential taxation, or classification, is straightforward, particularly in its most common form of a reduced tax burden on owner-occupied residences. Homeowners are generally voters who are well aware of their property tax bills, while residential tenants are often unaware of their building's property taxes, less politically involved, and less likely to vote than homeowners. Tenants will bear a portion of the property tax burden if their rent is increased because of the tax, but they usually have no way of calculating this impact. The visibility of the property tax, which is at once a civic benefit for accountability and taxpayer awareness and a major cause of its unpopularity, is greatly reduced in the case of rental property.

Professor Wallace Oates observed, "Occupants of rental dwellings do not pay the tax directly; the legal tax liability rests with landlords. While there is some reason to believe that property taxes on rental units are shifted forward in the form of higher rents, it is nevertheless the case that renters never see a tax bill. Moreover, there is some indirect, but pervasive, evidence suggesting that renters don't think that they pay local property taxes. . . . As is well known and documented, renters tend to be less active in local public life than homeowners. In particular, they vote with lower frequency on local issues (including budgetary measures) than do owner-occupants." Investigating the question, "How much smaller would local public budgets be if all residents were homeowners?" Oates found a typical "renter effect" on the order of 10 percent.[3] The political rationale for benefiting homeowners who tend to be politically involved while burdening renters who are unaware of their tax is self-evident. But this approach can place a heavier burden on the community's less affluent residents.

Business owners are a small fraction of the voting residents in most jurisdictions, and the real but largely invisible impact of the business property tax on renters, consumers, suppliers, and employees is rarely a political issue. To the extent these parties live outside the local jurisdiction, business property taxes are an effective means of exporting taxes or shifting the economic burden of tax payments to nonresidents. Similarly, taxes on public utility properties may be heavier if they are an allowable expense in calculating a regulated rate of return. In each case, the uncertain and nonevident economic impact of the tax on these sectors provides a political incentive to increase their relative shares.

States face few federal restrictions in imposing classified property taxes, with only a handful of specific exceptions. For example, the 1976 Railroad Revitalization and Regulatory Reform Act,[4] which has been expanded to apply to motor carriers and air carriers, sought to end the traditional practice of imposing heavier property taxes on railroads than on other businesses. In general, however, the decision to impose a classified property tax is a matter of state law. Under the federal constitution, states are permitted wide latitude to draw distinctions and create categories in matters of taxation. There is no federal impediment to heavier taxation of business property as such. "Where taxation is concerned and no specific federal right, apart from equal protection, is imperiled, the States have large leeway in making classifications and drawing lines which in their judgment produce reasonable systems of taxation."[5] At the same time, courts have long recognized a state interest in neighborhood continuity and stability that can provide legal justification for preferential treatment of owner-occupied housing.

Arguments for and Against Classification

Political and legal considerations do not address concerns of equity and efficiency to justify why one class of property should pay a higher effective tax rate than another. They do not answer, for example, the Chambers of Commerce who "see no rationale for business to be paying so much of the property tax given the level of services received,"[6] or academics who find nothing in "principles of tax policy concerning aggregate tax shares by class. . . . The economic principles of equity and efficiency (not to mention administrative simplicity) suggest that property should be assessed uniformly with respect to its market value."[7] Commentators note that "the assessment levels of certain types of properties are sometimes directly related to the legislative influence of the owners of these properties,"[8] and tax administrators "have observed in respect to the classified property tax system that it cannot work equitably; that it has no effective brake on it; and that it leads to changes in the property tax law which are inspired by politics rather than economics."[9]

In 1977 one of a series of District of Columbia tax reform commissions attempted to clarify the policy arguments for and against classification. It identified two general positions in favor of classification: (1) it could legitimize de facto classification resulting from faulty assessment practices; and (2) it could improve progressivity by favoring residential owners at the expense of "business property owners who are perceived to be in a better position to absorb or pass on property taxes." It acknowledged tax exporting as a separate issue, perhaps viewing it as a political question rather than one of equity and efficiency. "Because of the District's unique situation of not lying within any state's boundaries, a significant portion of the property tax is shifted to non-residents (tourists, commuters and national organizations)."[10]

Each of these arguments is pragmatic rather than principled. Legitimizing unauthorized fractional assessment systems does not necessarily promote good tax policy. The commission's report made clear that it was not speaking to the actual incidence of the tax when it noted that business owners were "perceived to be in a better position to absorb or pass on property taxes." The perception that business owners have greater ability to pay could be mistaken, particularly when suppliers or consumers may bear some of the economic burden of these taxes. Some enterprises may be on the verge of insolvency while some wealthy homeowners may enjoy ample income with which to pay the tax. Appeals to fairness and ability to pay are particularly inapt if owner-occupied housing is subject to a lower rate than rental property or multifamily housing, because homeowners are generally more affluent than renters. To the extent that a portion of the property tax falls on tenants, a higher effective rate is being imposed on a generally less wealthy portion of the population.

The argument for tax exporting is always politically popular within the exporting jurisdiction but can be problematic from a larger interjurisdictional perspective. A case can be made for tax exporting if it can be established that nonresidents enjoy the benefits of services for which local residents pay a tax, but the fact that a tax can be exported does not in itself justify a higher rate. The Institute on Taxation and Economic Policy considers "exportability" to be one of the five building blocks of a sound tax system, together with equity, adequacy, simplicity, and neutrality. The Institute supports this view on the grounds that "public services provided by state and local tax revenues are enjoyed by individuals from other states," but it does not detail how this connection would be established or quantified.[11] Commentator David Brunori offers a somewhat more jaded assessment of tax exporting: "Exporting tax burdens is a long-revered political tactic. The goal is to get people from outside your state to pay taxes that benefit your constituents. Your residents and businesses get the goodies—roads, police, healthcare—while others pay the freight. Whoever invented this concept is a political genius. . . . But no matter the tax, getting other people to pay it is a terribly cynical way to fund government."[12]

The 1977 D.C. commission exhibited more conviction in its four arguments against classification: (1) the lack of any pervasive economic rationale for taxing different types of income-producing property at different rates; (2) the risk that a perceived antibusiness strategy could impede economic growth; (3) the increased cost and difficulty of administering a classified system; and (4) the tendency for the number of classes to multiply and become more complex over time. Nearly admitting the lack of a principled argument for classification, the commission wrote, "Since there is no theoretical basis for singling out various classes of property for heavier taxes, there is no objective point at which further classification should stop, thereby opening up the potential of political bargaining by well organized special interest groups." The commission was "persuaded that the arguments against classification are the more convincing, and concludes that the overall effects of any such commercial/residential classification scheme would be harmful to District residents."[13]

Nevertheless, this expert recommendation did not prevail against political considerations, and by 1998 the District had a classified tax system and another tax reform commission was faced with attempting to reduce the number of rates. The 1998 commission noted that the five rates then in effect ranged from 0.96 percent for owner-occupied property to 5 percent for vacant land, and to 1.54 percent for rental property.[14] That commission's equitable argument for treating rental property in the same manner as owner-occupied residences was successful, and by the time yet another tax reform commission was appointed in 2012 the District had four property classes, with a single rate for all residential property, including multifamily housing.

A major argument against classification stems from the inefficiencies introduced when taxes alter relative prices and affect economic choices, which can leave individuals worse off without increasing government revenue. These effects will depend on many factors, including the responsiveness of supply and demand to changes in price. In the case of the property tax, it will also depend on the extent to which zoning regulations and existing improvements limit an owner's ability to change land use. When larger effects beyond the taxing jurisdiction itself are taken into consideration, predicting the effect of such distortions becomes even more complex. For example, many elements of the federal tax code intentionally favor home ownership. A property tax benefit limited to owner-occupied housing could increase the effect of this deliberate nonneutrality, and a uniform property tax might counteract it to some extent.

In 2015 the classification system in the District of Columbia imposed a tax of 0.85 percent on residential property, 1.65 percent and 1.85 percent on commercial property, 5 percent on vacant real property, and 10 percent on blighted real property. The tax on vacant land does not offer the neutrality and consequent absence of excess burden that is one of the central benefits of land value taxation, because it will be affected by the owner's actions. The long history of tax increment financing has demonstrated that terms such as blight can be difficult to define with precision, as discussed in chapter 5, so it is especially important that a classification of this type, which involves near-punitive rates of tax, be as objective as possible.

Special taxes on vacant property have taken a variety of forms. For many centuries the British taxed the occupant upon annual rental value, rather than the owner upon capital value, effectively exempting vacant parcels altogether and providing an incentive to keep property unoccupied. Hawaii allows its counties the option of differential taxation of land and buildings, but at present only Kauai distinguishes between the two. Amazingly, Kauai taxes land used for apartment houses at a lower rate than the apartment buildings themselves, but it taxes land used for single-family residences at a higher rate than the residences. Unlike nearly all other jurisdictions, Kauai taxes agricultural land more heavily than structures, but it taxes commercial, industrial, hotel, and resort lands less heavily than their buildings.[15]

In his study of Hawaii's experience, Steven Bourassa comments, "In the United States, land value taxation has been introduced largely as a way to encourage, or at least not discourage, economic development. But in one notable case in the United States, too much development led to the abolition of the tax. This is another example of misplaced blame. The overdevelopment of Waikiki, for example, was arguably due to poor planning and land use control rather than any flaw in Hawaii's land value tax system."[16]

Manhattan Borough President Scott Stringer wrote in 2007 with regard to New York City, "Today, property taxes impose no burden on landowners who fail to develop empty lots or to rehabilitate deteriorating buildings. The result is a free pass on speculative timing of the real estate market—an enormously costly state of affairs in a City desperate for affordable housing."[17] Interestingly, this report referred to the tax treatment of certain vacant land above 110th Street as an "exemption" when it actually was taxed in the favored class of one-, two-, and three-family residences. In New York City, it is understandable that those preferences might be mistaken for an exemption. The classification of empty lots again became an issue in the 2013 mayoral race.[18] The treatment of vacant residential land actually reflects the more basic problem of the city's extreme residential preferences. The very detailed exceptions introduced in response to controversies over vacant land increase the complexity and lack of transparency in its property tax.

Historical Background: De Facto Classification

Classification systems often reflect historic practice as much as legislative policy. The political incentives that encourage favorable and unfavorable treatment of specific property types have long operated in the absence of legislative sanction. Even when state law required uniform full-value assessment, local officials frequently listed property at a fraction of its market value, and these fractions themselves varied by property type.

The 1977 D.C. tax commission's first argument in favor of classification stated, "By explicitly treating specific property classes differentially, the legislative body would legalize the de facto classification which results from imperfect assessment practices."[19] This has often been the single most important motivation for establishing legal classification. Rather than a new policy adopted on its own merits, it has been a means of addressing decades and sometimes even centuries of established if unsanctioned assessment practices.

Many de facto classification systems developed as a means of favoring homeowners at the expense of businesses when state law did not permit classified taxation. This was not a consequence of imperfect assessment practices, but a deliberate attempt to avoid uniform taxation. Fifty years ago, the Advisory Commission on Intergovernmental Relations stated, "The laws of nearly two-thirds of the States appear to contemplate assessment at full value and the language of many of them is very specific on this point. . . . The assessment practice in most of the States bears little resemblance to the legal requirements."[20]

The Fiction of Uniform Underassessment

Unauthorized classification was encouraged by years of judicial decisions permitting assessments at a fraction of market value despite constitutional or statutory requirements of full valuation. In a representative 1964 case, the California Court of Appeal held that the state constitutional provision for assessment at "full cash value" did not prohibit uniform fractional assessment. The court found the constitutional arguments "hardly persuasive now when, for almost a century," administrative, legislative, and judicial authorities had sanctioned fractional assessment.[21]

If fractional assessments were actually uniform, they would simply add a step to the assessment process without changing the amount of tax to be paid. A tax of 1 percent of full market value is the exact equivalent of a tax of 2 percent on 50 percent of market value. Although the law might call for assessments at full market value, the resulting accurate tax bills would impose no financial harm. The absence of demonstrated injury often weakened early cases by taxpayers protesting illegal fractional assessment. As the California court wrote, "It should be noted that while he criticizes at length the practice of assessing all property at a fraction of its fair market value, plaintiff has neither pleaded nor offered to prove that he has suffered or might suffer any detriment or discrimination as a result."[22]

The Supreme Court of Minnesota wrote in 1897, "But why should the defendants have a right to complain when their property is taxed at only one-third its cash value? . . . The defendants cannot complain unless they are in some way injured. A disregard of the constitutional and statutory method of assessment by the assessing officers in fixing the assessment at one-third the cash valuation of the property was doubtless a public wrong, but not a private one against the defendants for which they have a right to any relief in this proceeding."[23] A vigorous dissent in the California dispute protested, "The majority in this particular case in effect hold that the long continued, systematic and intentional violation of the law somehow constitutes or has developed into a right in the assessor to violate the specific provisions of the law. . . . No amount of juggling, subterfuge, circumventions, evasions, deception, maneuvering, legalistic legerdemain or sorcery can change the plain and specific provisions of the Constitution."[24]

These and many other cases upheld fractional assessment on an assumption that all property was assessed at a uniform fraction of full market value. However, the major incentives for unauthorized fractional assessment—reducing taxpayer complaints by providing an unrealistically low valuation figure on the tax bill, favoring certain classes of property, and avoiding the administrative and political stress of revaluation—did not seek uniformity in assessment. Uniform fractional assessment would need to be based on accurate values, carrying the same administrative burden and taxpayer disruption as full-value assessments; "60 per centum value cannot be ascertained without first fixing the 100 percentum value."[25] The most powerful political rationale for fractional assessment, favoring owner-occupied residences, requires nonuniform assessment.

A 1974 Virginia tax reform study reviewed long-standing fractional assessment practices in that state, recognizing that while the state constitution required all assessments at fair market value, in fact "[i]t has not been the general practice in Virginia to assess at the full market value or any level approaching that." The report compared the level of assessment to the uniformity of assessment by comparing assessment-sales ratios with the coefficient of dispersion—the degree to which individual assessments differ from the average. It found that the city of Richmond, which had the highest assessment ratio in the state at nearly 90 percent, also had the most uniform assessments, with an extraordinarily low coefficient of dispersion of 5.9 percent. Buchanan County had one of the lowest assessment ratios in the state, 9.4 percent, and also had the least uniform assessments, with a coefficient of dispersion of 73.2 percent.[26]

In the course of remedying long-standing, flagrantly inequitable valuations in Nassau County, New York State actually provided an unintentional example of the ways in which fractional assessment can provide a misleading veneer of uniformity. As noted in chapter 3, Nassau County, protected by the state legislature from complying with court-ordered full-value assessment, for decades based its building assessments on depreciated 1938 construction costs and its land assessments on 1964 market values.[27] This practice had the effect of lowering the effective tax rate on areas increasing in value since those times and increasing the tax rate on areas in decline, with a disproportionate burden on minority taxpayers. In the settlement of a legal action challenging this discrimination,[28] Nassau County agreed to a revaluation of all its taxable property. However, the massive tax shifts caused by a change to accurate market values would clearly conflict with the state legislation limiting increases in the assessment of one-, two-, and three-family homes in New York City and Nassau County to no more than 6 percent a year and 20 percent over five years.[29]

The county sought to harmonize these conflicting mandates by adjusting its already shockingly low assessment ratio, which was set at 2.11 percent in 2002, to 1 percent for 2003. In this way, even properties whose tax bills more than doubled could be said not to have experienced an increase of more than 6 percent in their assessed values. Residential taxpayers protested this result through every level of the state judiciary, to no avail. The desire to uphold the settlement and to close the protracted and expensive revaluation led the state's highest court to emphasize legally irrelevant issues such as the fact that the settlement was "widely reported," that the revaluation could not comply with the assessment limit unless this approach was upheld, and that the revaluation had required extraordinary technical effort and the expenditure of tens of millions of dollars. The court ultimately found that the assessment limit was satisfied by this approach.[30]

Dissenting justices at both the Appellate Division and the Court of Appeals decried this "gimmick." "Can anyone doubt that what the Legislature intended was a meaningful year-to-year comparison, and not a meaningless one? . . . To hold otherwise is to license blatant evasion. It is as though the statute provided that Nassau County's budget could not increase by more than six percent from year to year, and Nassau County had sought to comply by stating the first year's budget in dollars and the second year's in British pounds."[31] It is ironic that the court that had sought to enforce the long-disregarded legal requirement of full-value assessment itself interpreted the law that followed that decision in a manner that came close to disregard.

State-Mandated Fractional Assessment

In response to court decisions enforcing uniformity, some states have enacted legislation or passed constitutional amendments explicitly permitting classification. This is an understandable reaction, given the political calculus favoring differential effective tax rates. However, it can seem puzzling for states to authorize fractional assessments rather than full-value assessments, whether or not the ultimate effective rates vary by property type. In New York City, for example, the taxable value of residential property of up to three units is 6 percent of market value, which makes nominal tax rates of 17 or 18 percent more reasonable than they first appear. New Mexico assesses all property at 33.3 percent of market value.[32] Arkansas assesses property at no more than 20 percent of market value,[33] and Ohio at no more than 35 percent.[34] South Dakota assesses property at full value for general tax purposes, but at 85 percent of value for school district funding.[35]

The cynical explanation for such complexity sees it as a means of confusing the taxpayer. As James Bonbright wrote, "Gullible taxpayers associate a larger valuation with a larger tax, or at any rate are less contentious about a relatively excessive assessment if it does not exceed their estimate of true value."[36] Some tax systems are sufficiently convoluted to achieve full confusion, whether or not that was the legislative intent. For example, Chicago homeowners seeking to calculate their 2009 tax bills had first to multiply their estimated property value by a 16 percent assessment level, then multiply that assessed valuation by 3.3701 to account for the state equalization factor, and then subtract the homeowner's exemption.[37] These figures change from year to year.[38]

Fractional assessment systems definitely have the potential to undermine uniformity, even when they are intended to be applied in a uniform manner. The State Assessor of Maine wrote:

> At its simplest, fractional valuation requires an unnecessary step in the assessment process, whereby the full value which must first be found is factored back to produce the fractional assessment to be used. This step is so unnecessary that even many assessors recognize the fact, and consequently eliminate it by never bothering to find full value in the first instance. They have noted the absurdity, but have compounded the error by eliminating the wrong unnecessary step. The result is that the assessment is then based upon speculation, not fact. . . . I do not believe there is any question but that fractional valuations constitute a very real hindrance to true equalization of assessments.[39]

In overturning the practice of fractional assessment, the New York Court of Appeals wrote in 1975, "In sum, for nearly 200 years our statutes have required assessments to be made at full value and for nearly 200 years assessments have been made on a percentage basis throughout the State.

The practice has time on its side and nothing else."[40] Uniform fractional assessment might indeed have time on its side and nothing else, but such a practice would be unlikely to persist for 200 years. Nonuniform fractional assessment, on the other hand, serves many purposes, from favoring specific property types to avoiding the need for reassessments to update valuations.

Remedies for Relative Overassessment

Unequal fractional assessment can produce relative overassessment, in which a property is assessed for less than its actual market value but at a greater percentage of full value than comparable property. Relative overassessment produces actual overtaxation when a uniform nominal tax rate is applied to the two unequal assessments. Initially, many state courts refused relief even to taxpayers who could prove relative overassessment so long as their tax valuation fell below the legal market value standard. These courts reasoned that to direct the assessor to further lower a valuation that was already less than the statutory or constitutional requirement would mandate an illegal act.

In 1890 the Massachusetts Supreme Judicial Court wrote, "[T]he question is, whether the property has been valued at more than its fair cash value, and not whether it has been valued relatively more or less than similar property of other persons."[41] The Supreme Court of Nebraska agreed: "[W]hen property is assessed at its true value, and other property in the district is assessed below its true value, the proper remedy is to have the property assessed below its true value raised, rather than to have property assessed at its true value reduced."[42] Bonbright observed that this approach provided the taxpayer with "the theoretically satisfactory privilege of suing out a writ of mandamus to compel the assessors to revalue every other piece of property in the jurisdiction."[43]

The U.S. Supreme Court reversed the Nebraska decision in 1923, holding that it would "deny the injured taxpayer any remedy at all because it is utterly impossible for him by any judicial proceeding to secure an increase in the assessment of the great mass of under-assessed property in the taxing district. . . . [T]he right of the taxpayer whose property alone is taxed at 100 per cent. of its true value is to have his assessment reduced to the percentage of that value at which others are taxed even though this is a departure from the requirement of statute. . . . [W]here it is impossible to secure both the standard of the true value, and the uniformity and equality required by law, the latter requirement is to be preferred as the just and ultimate purpose of the law."[44]

This case presented a new challenge: If an individual can "have his assessment reduced to the percentage of that value at which others are taxed," how is that percentage to be established? Given that unauthorized fractional assessments usually represent greatly varying percentages of full value, with some classes of property enjoying an advantage with regard to others, how is a taxpayer to prove the overall standard of assessment? Bizarrely, this requires the taxpayer to establish what the tax system is before protesting an assessment.

New York State for many years directed each side in an assessment dispute to choose parcels for comparison, "selecting a number of parcels from the assessment roll and proving their full value at trial. Once full value was determined, the total of the assessed values of the properties selected would be divided by the total of their full value to obtain the actual over-all ratio of assessed value to true market value in the taxing district."[45]

Such a proceeding could be extremely costly. A New York court wrote that the cases relying on parcel selection and actual sales "not only create discouraging and enormous expense for the taxpayer, but promote the search by both sides for samples which are at the extreme ends of the spectrum."[46] These shortcomings led the New York legislature to permit taxpayers to make use of state equalization ratios—administrative estimates of the ratio of total assessed value to full value in a jurisdiction—to prove relative overassessment. This process utilized a ratio developed for one purpose, generally an estimate of total property values for purposes of distributing state aid, in the entirely different context of individual tax appeals. The court's willingness to take this step demonstrated that its excessive deference to local administration in the earlier cases had been replaced by a willingness to assist taxpayers in challenging those practices.

Two decades of Massachusetts history illustrate the dramatic changes in judicial attitudes taking place across the nation. In 1959 the Massachusetts Supreme Judicial Court ruled that a challenge to illegal fractional assessments was moot as to taxes for 1958, because they had already been collected, and could not be entertained for 1959, because those assessments had not yet been issued.[47] Only two years later the same court rejected a long-standing system of fractional assessment in the city of Springfield, where the assessors openly acknowledged applying different assessment ratios to single-family dwellings, two-family units, three-family units, residences of four or more units, commercial and industrial property, farms, vacant land, and personal property. The court found this to be deliberate and intentional discrimination and overturned the assessment roll in its entirety.[48] By 1979 the court's recognition that "[t]o require the taxpayer to revalue even a substantial fraction of the property of a large city may be tantamount to a denial of relief" led it to reduce relative overassessments not to the municipal average, but to the fraction of full value found in the most favored class, single-family residential property.[49]

Classification and Uniformity

It is not surprising that many states confronted with judicial willingness to enforce uniformity in assessment changed their laws or even their state constitutional provisions in order to permit classification. Whether or not uniformity might be politically feasible on its own terms, it can become unacceptable if it produces a dramatic change in assessments and a significant shift in the tax burden from commercial and industrial property to single-family residences. Like many states, Massachusetts and New York amended their laws to permit classification. However, unlike New York, Massachusetts did not sanction existing arbitrary class shares of the tax burden borne by each property type. Instead, it permitted a limited variation in tax rates only after institution of full-value assessment.

In one respect, this approach relinquished uniformity by allowing a system of tax rates to be classified by property type. The challenge of justifying differential burdens remains unanswered. But states such as Massachusetts that adopted legal fractional assessment based on a full-value standard[50] actually took a great step toward uniformity even when they permitted tax rates to vary by property class. Legal classification imposed according to state guidelines on a full-value assessment base is a great improvement over ad hoc and even random fractional assessments representing inaccurate valuations, failures to reassess property, and sometimes reassessment only upon sale. Those systems could produce nearly as many effective tax rates as taxable parcels.

This compromise result is not inappropriate for the intensely practical property tax. It falls short of theoretical purity, as do all taxes as actually applied and administered, but it takes a major step toward accuracy and uniformity in assessment. By rationalizing the distribution of the tax burden and enhancing the fairness of the taxation process it offers a model for balancing the policy and politics that together must support any successful tax.

Notes

1. Minnesota Property Tax Working Group (2012), 16.
2. Cook County, Illinois, Code of Ordinances § 74–63 (2015).
3. Oates (2005), 420, 426 (citations omitted).
4. 49 U.S.C.S. § 11501.
5. *Lehnhausen v. Lake Shore Auto Parts Co.*, 410 U.S. 356, 359, 93 S. Ct. 1001, 1003, 35 L.Ed.2d 351, 354–355 (1973).
6. Massachusetts Department of Revenue (2004), 13.
7. Dye, McMillen, and Merriman (2006), 712.
8. Beebe and Sinnott (1979a), 296.
9. Ibid., 287.
10. District of Columbia Tax Revision Commission (1977), 70, 73.
11. Institute on Taxation and Economic Policy (2012), 2.
12. Brunori (2015), 49.
13. District of Columbia Tax Revision Commission (1977), 70, 72.
14. District of Columbia Tax Revision Commission (1998), 59.
15. Kauai County (2013).
16. Bourassa (2009a), 204.
17. Stringer (2007), 2. Specific amendments to classification of vacant land followed this report. New York City Office of Tax Policy (2009), 4; New York Laws of 2008, ch. 332.
18. Anuta (2013).
19. District of Columbia Tax Revision Commission (1977), 69.

20. Advisory Commission on Intergovernmental Relations (1963), 43.

21. *Michels v. Watson*, 229 Cal. App. 2d 404, 406, 40 Cal. Rptr. 464, 465 (1964).

22. Ibid.

23. *State v. Thayer*, 69 Minn. 170, at 175, 71 N.W. 931, at 933 (1897).

24. *Michels*, 229 Cal. App. 2d 404, 418–419, 40 Cal. Rptr. 464, 473 (1964) (Fourt, J., dissenting).

25. *State v. Birmingham Southern Railway*, 182 Ala. 475, 494, 62 So. 77, 83 (1913) (Sayre, J., dissenting).

26. Governor's Property Tax Reform Study (1974), 89.

27. *O'Shea v. Board of Assessors*, 8 N.Y.3d 249, at 256, 864 N.E.2d 1261, 1264, 832 N.Y.S.2d 862, 865 (2007).

28. *Coleman v. County of Nassau*, Index No. 97-30380 (Sup. Ct. Nassau County, March 29, 2000).

29. N. Y. Real Prop. Tax Law § 1805 (1).

30. *O'Shea v. Board of Assessors*, 8 N.Y.3d 249, 256–258, 864 N.E.2d 1261, 1264–1266, 832 N.Y.S.2d 862, 865–867 (2007).

31. *O'Shea v. Board of Assessors*, 8 N.Y.3d 249, 261–262, 864 N.E.2d 1261, 1268–1269, 832 N.Y.S.2d 862, 869–870 (2007) (Smith, J., dissenting).

32. N. M. Stat. Ann. § 7-37-3 (2012).

33. Ark. Code Ann. § 26-26-303 (2012).

34. Ohio Rev. Code § 5715.01 (B) (2012).

35. S. D. Codified Laws § 10-12-42 (2012).

36. Bonbright (1937), 498.

37. Gainer (2010).

38. See, e.g., Cook County, Illinois, Assessor's Virtual Office, http://www.cook countyassessor.com.

39. Beebe and Sinnott (1979a), 482–483.

40. *Hellerstein v. Assessor of Islip*, 37 N.Y.2d 1, 13, 371 N.Y.S.2d 388, 398, 332 N.E.2d 279, 286 (1975).

41. *City of Lowell v. County Commissioners*, 152 Mass. 372, 375, 25 N.E. 469, 470 (1890).

42. *Sioux City Bridge Co. v. Dakota County*, 105 Neb. 843, 848, 182 N.W. 485, 487 (1921), *rev'd*, 260 U.S. 441 (1923).

43. Bonbright (1937), 501 (footnote omitted).

44. *Sioux City Bridge Co. v. Dakota County*, 260 U.S. 441, 446 (1923).

45. *Slewett & Farber v. Board of Assessors*, 80 A.D.2d 186, 189, 438 N.Y.S.2d 544, 550 (1981).

46. *Ed Guth Realty, Inc. v. Gingold*, 34 N.Y.2d 440, 449, 358 N.Y.S.2d 367, 372, 315 N.E.2d 441, 445 (1974).

47. *Carr v. Assessors of Springfield*, 339 Mass. 89, 92, 157 N.E.2d 880, 883 (1959).

48. *Bettigole v. Assessors of Springfield*, 343 Mass. 223, 225–226, 237–238, 178 N.E.2d 10, 12, 19 (1961).

49. *Tregor v. Board of Assessors*, 377 Mass. 602, 609, 387 N.E.2d 538, 543 (1979); *Assessors of Weymouth v. Curtis*, 375 Mass. 493, 375 N.E.2d 493 (1978). This

approach was later reversed by legislation. *Keniston v. Board of Assessors*, 380 Mass. 888, 407 N.E.2d 1275 (1980).

50. E.g., Neb. Rev. Stat. § 77-201 (2012); Wash. Rev. Code § 84.40.030 (2012). Earlier fractional assessment systems are described in Advisory Commission on Intergovernmental Relations (1963), 43.

7 Open Space and Conservation Easements

One of the most dramatic recent developments in the usually measured evolution of property law in this country has been the explosive growth of conservation easements. All but unknown before the 1960s, conservation easements today number in the tens of thousands and restrict millions of acres from development. Estimates of the amount of land in the United States subject to conservation easements have risen from 1.9 million acres in 1990 to 6.2 million acres in 2000 to over 20 million acres in 2014.[1] Many conservation initiatives now routinely seek to protect one million acres of land in a given state. The implications of conservation easements for land use planning, environmental management, and land markets are still not fully understood, and it is not surprising that many aspects of their property tax treatment remain unsettled as well.

A conservation easement limits development on a parcel of land. An owner who conveys an easement to an exempt organization, such as a local land trust, usually expects future property tax assessments to reflect this reduction in development potential. However, state law may be unclear on this point, and the drafters of the Uniform Conservation Easement Act, which provides a model to assist states in drawing up their own legislation, deliberately avoided any legislative statement on local tax consequences. The commentary to the act states, "The relationship between the Act and local real property assessment and taxation practices is not dealt with; for example, the effect of an easement upon the valuation of burdened real property presents issues which are left to the state and local taxation system."[2]

It is often difficult to estimate the effect of an easement on property value. The terms of each easement are unique, with wide variation in permitted uses, provision for public access, if any, and authorized construction. An easement that prohibits any building on land that is under development pressure could deprive the property of the greater part of its market value. On the other hand, an easement that blocks subdivision of land whose highest and best use is as a single-family estate may not have a dramatic effect on its market price. A number of highly publicized cases of abusive overvaluation for federal tax purposes have brought new attention to the speculative nature of some of these calculations and the need for greater clarity in the tax treatment of conservation easements, including the property tax assessment of land they restrict.

Traditional Easements and Conservation Easements

An easement is an interest in land that does not rise to the level of possession. Perhaps the most familiar example is a right-of-way that permits its holder to cross land belonging to another. This right does not confer possession, ownership, or the ability to exclude others, but only the right to traverse the property. Yet that right may be extremely valuable if it allows passage to an otherwise inaccessible road or a body of water. This is an example of an affirmative easement, one which permits a specified use of property. Less commonly, negative easements convey the right to prohibit some use of the affected parcel. For example, an easement protecting a view or access to sunlight might block construction on neighboring property, or on a specific portion of it.

A right-of-way illustrates another important distinction among easements, because it would generally be held by the owner of neighboring land. After a sale of the otherwise landlocked parcel, the right-of-way would normally pass to the new owner rather than follow the prior owner to a new location. Property law historically favored easements held by neighboring owners for the benefit of their land ("appurtenant" easements), over easements that not did accompany ownership of adjacent land (easements "in gross"). In part, this practice reflected the value placed on flexibility in responding to changing economic conditions. Adjoining landowners have a vested interest in appropriate neighborhood development and less reason to block adjustments to new circumstances. They also may be more easily identified and located, particularly after the passage of time, than individuals or organizations outside the community.

The traditional easement had no special conservation function, but its terminology was pressed into service when environmental concerns required development of a new property right. The most familiar means of open space preservation—outright purchase of land by a governmental or conservation organization—is not feasible or appropriate in all cases. Expense alone limits the amount of environmentally significant property that can be protected in this way. Ownership also entails maintenance, insurance, and a host of other responsibilities and liabilities that local land trusts, nonprofit organizations, and governmental agencies may be ill-equipped to assume. Most importantly, families with the greatest appreciation for the natural beauty and environmental value of their land often are the least disposed to relinquish title to it. These owners might make a personal or contractual commitment to preserve their land, but they could not ensure that future heirs or purchasers would be bound by this promise.

All these considerations indicated the need for a new conservation tool to ensure long-term preservation of land that remained in private ownership. This seemingly straightforward approach to protecting open space actually presented a significant challenge. A traditional appurtenant easement would meet this need only if held by owners of neighboring property. An easement in gross held by a conservation organization or a land trust might not "run with the land" to constrain future owners. In fact, this conservation purpose required exactly the type of easement most disfavored by the common law: negative (to block future development rather than to permit action on the affected land); in gross (held by a conservation organization, land trust, or government agency, rather than by a neighboring landowner); and, most unconventionally of all, of indefinite or even perpetual duration, in order to preserve open space for the foreseeable future.

States across the country responded to this situation with legislation permitting just such a new device, usually called a conservation easement.

The Uniform Conservation Easement Act was drawn up to assist in this process, and a number of states adopted it in whole or in part. Since the new instrument did not fit any traditional legal pattern, the term *easement* was itself somewhat arbitrary. In Louisiana, it is called a "conservation servitude" and in Massachusetts, a "conservation restriction."[3] The drafters of the Uniform Act utilized easement terminology in part because they considered lawyers and courts to be more familiar with easements than with such alternatives as restrictive covenants and equitable servitudes. The term *restrictive covenant*, which might be the most accurate existing nomenclature, had a long and unfortunate historical association with exclusionary measures.

Federal Tax Issues

Any review of tax issues raised by conservation easements must begin with federal taxes, because the Internal Revenue Code has played a critical role in shaping their development. Although an early IRS ruling indicated that a gift of a conservation easement might qualify as a charitable donation,[4] the 1969 Tax Reform Act placed that conclusion in doubt. To curtail abusive deductions by taxpayers who retained beneficial control of assets they claimed to have donated to charity, that legislation generally required that deductible gifts convey all interests in property. In 1976, environmental groups achieved passage of an explicit exception to this rule in the case of qualified conservation easements.[5] Initially, these easements were required to last at least 30 years; this was later changed to allow deductions only for easements in perpetuity.[6]

Requirements of Perpetuity and Public Access

The perpetuity requirement was perhaps the most dramatic example of the influence that federal tax legislation exerted over the terms of conservation easements, for it ensured that most would be permanent. This in itself was a startling development, since flexibility and responsiveness to changed conditions are significant land policy considerations. A private landowner who conveys a perpetual easement has legally restricted development forever, a step that arguably merits public participation. The drafters of the Uniform Act argued that "public agency approval adds a layer of complexity which may discourage private actions. Organizations and property owners may be reluctant to become involved in the bureaucratic, and sometimes political, process which public agency participation entails."[7]

Another controversial issue concerns public access to conservation land. Environmental advocates successfully argued against any such requirement as a condition for federal deductibility. Where an easement protects animal habitat or fragile plant life, public access might undermine its conservation purpose. On the other hand, lack of public access may serve primarily to protect the privacy of landowners who have received a public subsidy for the easement on their property.

Valuation for Federal Tax Purposes

In the absence of an established market for conservation easements, federal regulations permit their value to be estimated by comparing the market price of the restricted property before and after the easement is imposed.[8] This approach is logical but frequently problematic. The easement is a useful tool largely because it does not require a change in ownership. However, this means that often there will be no recent sales data for the property, either before or after it is imposed. In that case, before and after value estimates may be hypothetical and may vary widely with appraisal assumptions.

In many transactions, review by two parties with opposing financial interests—a buyer and seller, a mortgage bank and a loan applicant, or an assessor and a taxpayer—provides some check on any pressure for an appraiser to adopt assumptions favorable to the client. This type of oversight can be absent if an appraisal is prepared for an easement donor whose deduction will be enhanced by magnifying the unencumbered value of the property and minimizing its value after imposition of the easement. The conservation organization receiving the easement must acknowledge the tax value placed on it but need not assent to the valuation or review the assumptions behind it.

Less-than-scrupulous appraisers and donors may hypothesize a development potential unsupported by market evidence or even by the physical features of the parcel. They may assume that the easement has deprived the property of nearly all value, even if it imposes minimal restrictions on the most valuable use. Unless the tax return claiming the deduction is audited and successfully challenged, unrealistic assumptions will maximize the easement's tax benefit. In the past, taxpayers claiming deductions based on inflated valuations faced little audit risk.[9]

Federal regulations require a written appraisal for any easement valued at more than $5,000. Although recommendations have suggested that appraisals be made public in order to discourage abusive overvaluations, these are private documents. A tax assessor asked to reduce the property tax valuation of land subject to a conservation easement could request a copy of the appraisal prepared for federal tax purposes but would have no legal right to it. It might contain an estimate of a "before" value far above the pre-easement property tax valuation and an "after" value far below it. The federal tax deduction is maximized by the greatest possible difference between the before and after values, whatever their amounts; the post-easement property tax is minimized by the lowest possible after value. "Even if nothing else were changed in the laws affecting easement appraisals, subjecting them to public scrutiny would have a significant effect in curtailing abuses, since appraisers would know that their work would be subject to public and peer review."[10]

The incentives for non-arm's-length valuations were highlighted in a 2003 *Washington Post* series on the Nature Conservancy. Part of that report described transactions in which the Conservancy purchased unrestricted property, imposed a conservation easement on it, and then resold it to a related party for a much lower amount. Although the reduced purchase price would seem evidence that the easement decreased the land value, these purchasers had agreed to make simultaneous donations to the Nature Conservancy in an amount sufficient to recover its initial investment. In effect, the ultimate purchasers were paying the full unrestricted price for the property and then placing an easement on it. By using the Nature Conservancy as an intermediary, they could claim a charitable deduction for the cash donation without documenting any reduction in property value. A typical purchaser received "substantial tax write-offs. . . . The easement restricting development also reduced the land's assessed value, slashing his property tax bill."[11]

Property Taxation of Land Subject to Conservation Easements

Changes in state property law to permit perpetual conservation easements have rarely faced significant political opposition, in part because they usually avoid potentially controversial questions. As noted, the drafters of the Uniform Conservation Easement Act explicitly deemed local tax issues outside their mandate. This means that local assessors often encountered this new encumbrance without definitive guidance about its effect on tax valuations. For example, in 1997 the Louisiana Attorney General was asked "whether Louisiana provides any particular income or property tax incentives or benefits to the grantor of a conservation easement." The answer was, "[W]e are not aware of any special provisions relative to conservation easements."[12]

Assessment Concerns

The most basic question for the assessor is whether the easement should be taken into account in valuation at all. Some states have explicitly provided that it should, although one state, Idaho, requires that it be ignored: "The granting of a conservation easement across a piece of property shall not have an effect on the market value of property for ad valorem tax purposes and when the property is assessed for ad valorem tax purposes, the market value shall be computed as if the conservation easement did not exist."[13] In states that have not addressed the question, courts must determine whether existing tax law mandates that an assessment reflect the effect of a conservation easement, under general market value principles, or ignore the easement, on the theory that assessments need not take divided legal interests into account.

On one hand, landowners who have made a federally recognized charitable gift of development rights understandably assume that such rights now belong to an exempt organization and should not be taxed. While this is a cogent argument, the opposite conclusion also has support. Most cases in which an owner voluntarily divides legal interests in real estate do not affect property tax assessments. The taxing jurisdiction is not responsible for prorating a bill between a landlord and a tenant, and many states will not exempt a leasehold granted to a charity by a nonexempt owner. An assessor need not allocate the tax between joint tenants, or between a life tenant and the holder of a remainder interest, or between a mortgagor and a bank extending a loan. In each such case the parties must agree among themselves how to pay the single property tax imposed on the undivided estate.

Interestingly, traditional appurtenant easements, those held by owners of neighboring land, have long been an exception to this general rule. The obscure historical development and circuitous legal reasoning behind this special treatment has led some commentators to question whether there exists a rationale for this exception at all. The scholar James Bonbright wrote in 1937, "Why the easement should have received exceptional treatment we are unable to say."[14] However, it clearly relates to the appurtenant easement's effect on two parcels of land. The owner of the benefited parcel now has new rights, such as a right-of-way over neighboring property. The owner of the burdened estate has reduced rights, in this case no longer being able to exclude the neighbors, for the easement permits its holder access that in its absence might constitute trespass.

While assessors might disregard the division of interests between a landlord and tenant, or between a mortgagor and a bank, a transfer of rights between two distinct taxable parcels is not so easily ignored. If the property suffering a loss in rights were assessed at full market value, as if no easement existed, consistency would require that the easement also be ignored in assessing the benefited estate, so that the property with expanded rights would be valued at less than its market price.

Conversely, if the tax on land carrying a right-of-way, or a right to an unobstructed view, or a right to enter a private park, reflected its full market value in light of those benefits, the correspondingly encumbered land should not be taxed as if it were available for development. Note that this analysis deals only with appurtenant easements held by neighboring property owners, and not with easements in gross held by land trusts, environmental organizations, or government agencies. Nevertheless, the historical tax treatment of appurtenant easements provided the initial context for considering the new conservation instrument. Traditional doctrine thus provided two contradictory guides: a general disregard of divided legal interests in assessment, and an exception to this rule for appurtenant easements.

If fine points of legal doctrine do not assist the assessor facing a novel claim for a reduced valuation by reason of a conservation easement, appeals to common sense and established practice can be equally unsuccessful. On one hand, relinquishment of future development rights in order to promote conservation may seem the very model of a charitable gift; from this point of view, common sense would dictate that only the rights retained by the owner be subject to tax. Most jurisdictions have in fact concluded that legislative authorization for conservation easements implies that they should be taken into account for property tax purposes. At least 18 states have enacted statutes directing assessors to consider the effect of conservation easements in the valuation process.[15] On the other hand, an official who sees no change in the use of or public access to property may question what effect a voluntary and possibly tax-motivated transaction should have on its assessment.

Voluntary Nature of the Restriction

Conservation easements are voluntary actions taken by landowners who may have many possible motives for protecting their land or restricting its use. An assessor may be puzzled if an estate with great scenic beauty or important conservation values has been subject to a voluntary transaction that has provided the landowner with a federal tax deduction but produced no physical change in the property. The absence of any right of public access may suggest that this is a private matter, with no more implications for property taxation than a lease or a family trust.

Such skepticism is not limited to the unsophisticated or to those who lack environmental awareness. The U.S. Treasury regulations on conservation easements find the owners' plans actually to develop the property a factor in determining the amount of their charitable deduction.[16] This approach reflects a commonsense concern that taxpayers not be rewarded for refraining from something they would not have done in any event. It is efficient to limit tax incentives to situations in which they make a difference. But this does not mean that the donor's own plans affect the value of development rights.

It is the market for development that is relevant on this point. Building rights on rural land with little development potential may have a low value, and if so, the transfer of these rights should not support a significant deduction. But the assessor's perhaps well-founded suspicion that the owner of a scenic estate would never develop it, however great the profit, does not bear on whether its market value has been diminished by extinction of the development rights. A donor who transfers shares of stock to a charity may never have intended to sell them, and perhaps never would have sold them, but something of value has been relinquished nonetheless. Wealthy landowners who cherish their estates might never plan to sell or develop them, but shifting financial and family situations could lead them to change their minds, and in any event their heirs might have a different view. Even if the donors would never have taken this step, they have given up the right to do so.

Effects on Neighboring Parcels

If easements are taken into account in the assessment process, assessors must calculate their effect on both the restricted property and nearby parcels. The neighboring properties are in many respects more easily analyzed. Their legal rights are unchanged, and any scenic landscape they enjoy is a familiar amenity. Direct observation of prices in the surrounding area can provide a basis for estimating the easement's impact, if any, on neighboring property values. In most cases some increase would be expected, rising with proximity to the conservation land. A legally protected scenic view generally commands a premium price, as evidenced by advertisements for homes "adjoining protected land" or "adjacent to conservation property." Moreover, in some areas, large amounts of conservation land may increase the price of developable parcels by decreasing their supply. Federal tax law anticipates a potential benefit to neighboring lots and requires that any resulting increase in the value of other land held by the easement donor or related parties reduce the charitable deduction for the gift.[17]

Although easements may enhance the value of surrounding property, they will not necessarily do so. A building restriction on rural land may not even be noticed by neighbors or by the market. Similarly, restrictions on development in an area that has become largely industrial or commercial might have no impact on the value of nearby shops and factories. It is even theoretically possible for an easement to diminish the value of neighboring land. For example, in the case of a potentially profitable large-scale development requiring assemblage of a number of component lots, building limitations on one parcel might negate this possibility for the others. Public access can also have either positive or negative effects on surrounding property. A nearby scenic recreational area might increase residential values, but proximity to an ill-maintained or poorly patrolled public park could well reduce them. These effects might be subtle, but they are not conceptually problematic; they illustrate standard market influences often seen in assessment practice.

Effects on the Restricted Parcel

The effect of an easement on the restricted property itself is more complex and open to dispute. The Treasury regulations take a neutral position on the matter, which is in fact quite controversial. They state, "Further, there may be instances where the grant of a conservation restriction may have no material effect on the value of the property or may in fact serve to enhance, rather than reduce, the value of property. In such instances no deduction would be allowable."[18]

Clearly, an easement may lower the value of the subject property. Land in the urban fringe could lose the greater part of its value under a building restriction. An easement could also have a very minor effect, as in the case ·of remote land with no ready market potential. The first question is whether an easement can actually have no effect on value, or whether a perpetual restriction must reduce value, even if slightly, below that of an identical parcel still available for development. This can seem a fairly theoretical inquiry, because the difference between an "extremely minimal effect" and "no effect" will not often have important tax consequences. But it is characteristic of the surprising ways in which conservation easements have evolved that this seemingly abstruse point has given rise to a huge controversy.

The debate opened with a 1985 U.S. Tax Court case in which a taxpayer claimed a charitable donation for a "facade easement" on a building in the French Quarter of New Orleans.[19] This easement prohibited changes in the exterior of the structure, just as a conservation easement restricts development of land. However, the already stringent historic preservation ordinances governing the French Quarter effectively prevented changes to the building exterior even before the easement was imposed. The IRS took the position that only a $24,500 reduction in value was warranted, as against the taxpayers' figure of $108,400. The Tax Court permitted a deduction of $55,278, or 10 percent of the property value. The 10 percent reduction for an easement with little practical application was widely noted. By the time a 1988 opinion allowed a similar 10 percent reduction ("for lack of evidence to the contrary") for another New Orleans facade easement, the Tax Court felt it necessary to state, "[B]y this decision we do not mean to imply that a general '10-percent rule' has been established with respect to facade donations."[20] However, that was exactly the effect of these decisions. In 2004 a *Washington Post* investigation of facade easements found "hundreds of affluent Washingtonians who have taken part in the once obscure but rapidly growing program. . . . In almost every instance, easement donors in Washington write off about 11 percent of the value of their homes."

> Such tax deductions are increasingly common although the District already bars unapproved and historically inaccurate changes in the facades of homes in the city's many historic districts. As a result, easement donors largely are agreeing not to change something that they cannot change anyway.
>
> Homeowners typically claim tax deductions of 10 to 15 percent of their home's value, according to preservationists. Until earlier this year, an IRS guide suggested that easement valuations "should" fall in that range.

In Washington, easement promoter Tim Maywalt said, "I have never seen an appraisal come in at anything but 11 percent—and I have seen 350 appraisals." The chief assessor of Washington said his office "searched in vain for evidence of lost value, to determine whether property taxes should be reduced for the donors. 'We don't see any difference in value here between the homes that have the facade easements and the ones that don't.' "[21]

Needless to say, this series sparked widespread criticism, calls for legislative reform, and defense of legitimate and beneficial facade easements.[22] This controversy had its roots in the apparently arcane question of whether an easement taking away rights already blocked by local ordinance could have a significant effect on market value.

Percentage Reductions in Value

It is sometimes suggested that assessors might reduce the taxable value of property subject to conservation easements by a set uniform percentage, or one percentage for lands with public access and another for those without. This would provide certainty and encourage easement donations but it would also ignore the effect of easements on market value. Even if all conservation easements had uniform provisions, their impact on land prices would vary greatly. Land ripe for development could experience a large reduction in value, while the price of land unsuited to development or far from the urban fringe might show little or no change. And easement provisions are far from uniform. In fact, there can be almost as many variations in easement terms as there are easements themselves.

Easements reflect the agreement of the parties and need not follow any standard form. They may prohibit all development, or only development of a specific kind, or only development in a specific location. Future building locations may be specified, or they may be "floating" lots to be set down anywhere on the easement parcel. Landowners may relinquish or retain multiple rights of use. Public access may be prohibited; if permitted, it may be limited to specific times, places, and purposes. There can be no general rule about the percentage by which a conservation easement reduces the market value of land, because there exists no general conservation easement, only specific documents with individual provisions, whose effects can be determined only for a given real estate market at a particular time.

Increases in Property Value

If an easement clearly can have a negative effect on market value, and may well have a nominal or unobservable effect, what of the third possibility contemplated by the Treasury regulations—that an easement can *increase* the value of the property it restricts? The theoretical grounds for rejecting this possibility are clear: buyers cannot be expected to bid more for a smaller set of rights. The market value of land without development potential cannot exceed the value of identical land that still carries development rights. If the New Orleans cases considered that even an extremely small diminution in property rights must reduce market value to some extent, there seem no grounds on which to argue that it could increase that value.

Powerful as this logic is, the Treasury regulations demonstrate that it is not the only possible conclusion.

One interesting source of some assessors' skepticism about changes in value is their observation that many wealthy buyers pay high prices for homes subject to restrictive conditions, whether imposed by historic districts, neighborhood associations, gated communities, or cooperative apartments. This has led some to conclude that restrictions actually add value, and that owners who voluntarily place conservation easements on their land may also anticipate an increase in property value as a result. This hypothesis has been influential and deserves a response.

Property owners benefit from restrictive agreements that prevent their neighbors from indulging in a variety of undesirable actions and inactions—whether loud parties, houses painted a garish color, or failure to remove holiday lights by the appointed time. There is clearly a value in knowing that one's investment is not at risk from this type of wayward behavior, but that does not imply that similar restrictions on oneself carry a value as well.

An instructive thought experiment might consider a homeowners' association imposing such restrictions on property owners. Suppose a prospective purchaser were offered a specific house in that development under two alternate sets of terms: either the purchaser would be subject to the same restrictions as all other community residents, or the purchaser would be the only member of the community not subject to the restrictions. Is it reasonable to expect the prospective purchaser to offer *more* for restricted property than for the right to be the only unrestricted member of the association? If this is not plausible, the observed high sales prices in such places may reflect the value of knowing that one's neighbors are subject to these restrictions, rather than any value that purchasers attach to being restricted themselves. In the context of conservation easements, where only the easement donor's property is restricted, this reasoning suggests that an easement cannot raise the value of the very property it restricts.

This example does not completely settle the question, however. Another, more limited argument for the possibility of easements increasing property value begins with the case of land not subject to current development pressure—a parcel whose highest and best use is equally available before and after imposition of the easement. For example, a large scenic lot might have its highest price as an individual residence if its value as a single estate exceeds the sum of the values of smaller parcels under a hypothetical subdivision plan. In this case, loss of future development rights might have no observable effect on market value. If in addition the easement itself provides the owner with an amenity, whether through public recognition of the property's significance or simply social cachet, it is not inconceivable that some increase in property value might follow.

In a standard real estate market, this chain of events might seem highly unlikely or even ludicrous. However, in the market for luxury properties and estates, standard conditions do not always obtain. When the *New York Times* observes that among celebrities, "Membership in the Nature Conservancy is a social calling card, and the creation of a conservation easement on personal property is a status symbol,"[23] the possibility that a conservation easement might enhance market price cannot be dismissed out of hand. When houses in exclusive neighborhoods display plaques announcing that they are protected by easements, the parallel to security systems suggests that both measures might increase property values.

Such occasionally odd behavior in the most expensive portion of the real estate market has a disproportionate impact on the conservation easement debate. Land appropriate for conservation will often be of higher than average market value, and land deserving special protection is by definition not average. Where easements are designed to protect against immediate development pressure, market values will reflect that demand. It is to be expected that in many easement cases assessors will be asked to reduce taxes on estates held by affluent residents whose claims to having voluntarily reduced their property value may be met with initial skepticism.

Public Costs and Benefits

It is entirely appropriate for a legislature addressing the tax consequences of easements to consider their public costs and benefits. The role of such policy considerations in judicial decisions is less clear, and in theory they should not enter the assessment process at all. However, subjective and imprecise interpretations of public benefit have in fact influenced every level of the property tax process as officials have struggled to clarify the effect of conservation easements.

Evolving Public and Judicial Attitudes

Judicial opinions give evidence of shifting public attitudes toward the preservation of open space and the ways in which these cultural changes have influenced tax policy. For example, the 1961 case of *Englewood Cliffs v. Estate of Allison*[24] considered an early prototype of a conservation easement, one providing the maximum possible public benefit. By his will, William Allison bequeathed more than 7,000 acres of land overlooking the New Jersey Palisades as a park open to the public without charge. Because title to the property was held by a private trust responsible for maintenance and upkeep, the community enjoyed all the benefits of the park but did not bear its costs. For many years the park's property tax was based on a nominal $500 valuation. When this figure rose to over $20,000 in 1958 and $50,000 in 1959, the trustees brought this case in protest.

From today's vantage point, a magnificent public park plainly serves a charitable purpose, and it is disconcerting to learn that New Jersey did not consider open space an exempt use of property. As the court wrote, "[T]he statute which confers tax benefits upon non-profit organizations applies by its terms to buildings. . . . There is no provision in that section for parks, playgrounds and the like where the land itself is of primary importance and any buildings are of minor importance."[25] No argument was made that the land should be free of tax, but the court did note that both the state and local governments would certainly intervene to bar any sale of the park for private purposes—and that the taxing jurisdiction had made no effort to contribute to the park's maintenance. Drawing an analogy to an appurtenant easement, the court made an admittedly imprecise estimate that 90 percent of the land value had been transferred to the public, and so reduced the assessment to 10 percent of the unencumbered amount, an interesting parallel to the Tax Court's allowance of a 10 percent deduction for the facade easements in the New Orleans French Quarter.

Allison dealt with statutes that considered "empty" land not to merit a charitable exemption and found activity and construction the only use of real estate worthy of such support. Today, New Jersey is a state committed to environmental values, where "open space" carries a positive connotation and building restrictions are often considered a social good. New Jersey also supplemented its conservation easement statute with specific legislation requiring that assessments account for the effect of easements on value.

Even before this provision, a change in judicial perspective was evident. In a 1984 case, *Village of Ridgewood v. The Bolger Foundation*, the New Jersey Tax Court refused to reduce the assessment on land subject to an easement that allowed no public access, and in fact *raised* the property assessment by $12,500.[26] On review, the Appellate Division found the Tax Court to be correct, but the state Supreme Court took a completely different approach. It emphasized the public benefit offered by preservation of open space and declared that an easement blocking development deprived the property of nearly all its market value:

By giving up in perpetuity the right to do anything with the property other than keep it in its natural state, defendant has, as the County Tax Board found, seriously compromised its value as a marketable commodity. *Allison* leaves no doubt that the adverse impact of such an encumbrance on market value must be taken into account in arriving at an assessed valuation.[27]

The New Jersey Supreme Court approved an assessment of less than 5 percent of the land's unencumbered value. This was a defensible but not a logically necessary result: the two lower court decisions to the contrary show that reasonable jurists could differ on this issue, and not every building restriction impedes highest and best use. The *Allison* and *Ridgewood* cases, 20 years apart, reflect evolving attitudes toward conservation as much as technical interpretations of property tax law.

Similar changes have influenced tax cases across the country. In 1965 the Maine Supreme Judicial Court found that a preserve for animals provided "no benefit to the community or the public,"[28] but in 2014 it found preservation of wildlife habitat to be a charitable purpose justifying a property tax exemption.[29] The court noted that decisions in states across the country, from Florida to Ohio to New Mexico and California, had similarly found land conservation to be a charitable purpose. It cited a 2014 Massachusetts case determining that the preservation of open space can serve the traditional charitable purpose of relieving the burdens of government through safeguarding natural resources and environmental quality.[30]

Sometimes assessors are encouraged or required to consider the public benefit of open space preservation. For example, one commentator recommended that they "take into account both the substantial community benefits of conservation easements and the minimal effect that granting lower assessments is likely to have on the tax base."[31] These are issues better considered by legislators setting the legal basis of the property tax rather than by local officials administering it. But statutes themselves may leave assessors with this policy determination. In Maine, for example, open space classification requires the assessor's finding of public benefit, considering such factors as size, uniqueness, scenic values, recreational use, and wildlife habitat.[32]

It is problematic to ask assessors to judge public benefit. It can take many forms, some of them contradictory, and any judgment as to net benefit will necessarily be somewhat subjective. Building restrictions may preserve scenic beauty, encourage tourism, protect wildlife, and promote agriculture. They may also encourage leapfrog sprawl, drive up land prices, block construction of affordable housing, and prevent flexible land use responses to changed conditions. One of the most powerful conservation incentives is preservation of family lands through reduction in the taxable value of real estate. Where one party might see this as an unmitigated good, allowing cherished property to remain in the hands of those who have cared for it for generations, others could see it as a benefit for one specific family and a problem for others seeking to acquire land of their own.

Moreover, the public benefit afforded by development restrictions may have no relation to the consequent loss in market value of the affected property, which is the issue within the assessor's expertise. A public park on land unsuited to development may provide enormous benefits without a correspondingly large reduction in value, while a "backyard easement" may block valuable development with no significant public benefit.[33] Assessors, already suffering from public perception that they are responsible for tax bills, are eager to dispel the notion that they set tax policy, or even tax rates. But front-line officials are sometimes left to make policy choices by default, simply because they cannot avoid a decision for which no guidance has been issued.

Fiscal Impact Analysis

An influential and sometimes controversial measure of public benefit analyzes the fiscal impact of open space conservation, estimating its effect on local revenues and expenditures. This approach has been very successful in increasing support for land conservation even among voters whose primary concern is to avoid future tax increases. Open space will almost always produce less tax revenue than residential or commercial property, but fiscal impact analysis takes this computation further and considers the increased spending needs that accompany growth, particularly the costs of public education. Schools are often the largest element in local budgets, and these calculations can show that new construction, particularly of modestly priced housing or multifamily dwellings, will fail to "pay its way" and require additional taxes from existing properties.

Costs of Development

From the perspective of conservation proponents, the discussion of costs is an entirely reasonable contribution to public debate. They see fiscal impact analysis as correcting a one-sided emphasis on forgone taxes by calling attention to larger budgetary choices involving both revenue and expenditure. However, this approach is controversial for two reasons. The first is technical, questioning specific assumptions—for example, the characteristics of anticipated residents and buildings—and therefore the accuracy of the analysis itself.[34] The second is political and philosophical. Is it in society's interest for jurisdictions to discourage growth in their school-age populations? How should regions and states respond when individual communities attempt to limit development? These issues are by no means confined to conservation. Fiscal considerations have led some communities to block construction of housing for families with children, whether by encouraging age-restricted residences or by limiting the number of bedrooms permitted in multifamily dwellings. One jurisdiction allowed an 80-unit housing development under an agreement permitting eight school-age children to live there; for every school-age child above that limit the developer incurred a $15,000 fine.[35]

Larger Regional Issues

Communities often face difficult issues concerning whether and how they should take into account the larger social impacts of local decisions. To what extent should a town be responsible for a "fair share" of the affordable housing required throughout the state? Should a locality with no currently needy residents be permitted to disclaim this allocation? These questions arise when any community rejects growth, whether through zoning, regulation, or conservation restrictions on available building lots.

One commentator suggested the mixed effect of such measures in reflecting on a New Jersey conservation vote:

> One impact of dedicating land use to green space in perpetuity is to increase the price of nearby land that is not restricted. In densely populated states such as New Jersey, removing substantial amounts of land from potential development is a massive wealth transfer from future residents to existing owners of unrestricted land. Given New Jersey's well-documented history of using land use regulation to "zone out" the poor from well-to-do communities, which led to the landmark decision of the state supreme court in *Southern Burlington County NAACP v. Township of Mt. Laurel,* a bit of skepticism about New Jersey voters embracing a means of increasing land prices might be justified.[36]

Boston magazine, like most such regional publications, issues annual comparisons on "The Best Places to Live." Its 2006 "big three" criteria examined distance from the city center, educational performance, and percentage of land area protected as open space.[37] The desirability of open space in exclusive locations is evident. In the California State House, where every county presents a display, Marin County's poster states, "Nearly half of Marin County is preserved as open space." As the following examples in Table 1 show, many affluent Boston suburbs have substantial amounts of protected open space, potentially enough to influence land markets there.

TABLE 1

Town	Median Home Price	Percentage Protected Open Space
Cohasset	$751,250	25.49
Concord	$712,000	31.08
Dover	$1,057,500	25.41
Hingham	$655,000	28.94
Lincoln	$1,141,500	35.49
Needham	$649,000	26.65
Sudbury	$681,000	26.05
Wayland	$590,000	36.94

SOURCE: Blanding (2006), 128.

At the same time, restrictions on land use have been considered a major factor in the Boston area's lack of affordable housing.[38] In response to such criticism, the Lincoln town planner noted that zoning restrictions, such as two-acre minimum lot requirements, reflect the fact that residents "value open space and spread-out country-style living."[39] The popularity of open-space preservation continues to grow, and in 2009 "permanently protected acreage in Massachusetts surpassed developed acreage for the first time in modern memory."[40] In 2014 the state increased its refundable conservation land tax credit by 50 percent.[41]

Individual communities cannot be asked to solve collective problems on their own. If existing legal and fiscal structures provide a disincentive to growth, it is not realistic to expect towns to embrace development and higher school taxes as an expression of regional solidarity. But localities' understandable wish to insulate themselves from these larger problems must be balanced by regional approaches to planning, development, and housing. Conservation easements have become enormously popular in part because they can allow private parties to enact land use controls without governmental intervention. However, perpetual development restrictions affect social and economic issues on which a public voice may be appropriate.

Conclusion

The development of a new property instrument is an unusual and noteworthy phenomenon whose ramifications can be fully appreciated only over time. In the case of conservation easements, even their property tax treatment has given rise to a surprisingly wide range of questions involving both practice and principles. Nearly three decades of experience suggest some initial conclusions on these points.

Early efforts to determine the effect of a conservation easement on property tax assessment sometimes relied on theories that have not stood the test of time. Absent an explicit statutory statement to the contrary, attempts to ignore their effect altogether have generally not been found to comport with legislative intent. It is reasonable, in the face of statutory silence, to assume that these newly created devices are to be taken into account in the assessment process. On the other hand, assumptions that easements necessarily deprive the burdened property of most of its market value will frequently be erroneous. The great variety of easements, and the lack of any standardization in the restrictions they impose, make generalization about their effects on market value treacherous. It is impossible to specify the percentage reduction in value that will follow imposition of an easement without knowing details of its legal provisions, the local real estate market, and the development potential of the property. Restricted estates may retain most of their value if their highest and best use does not require rights that have been relinquished, while land under intense development pressure could lose nearly all its value if construction is prohibited and there is no market for protected open space.

These controversies touch on fundamental distinctions between legislative and administrative competencies. Assessors cannot exempt property from tax simply because they deem it worthy of support, or because it constitutes a minor portion of the tax base, or because the costs imposed by alternative uses might outweigh the revenue lost through the exemption. Appeals to public interest as the basis for a tax reduction are properly directed to lawmakers, and exceptions to general statutory standards for valuation, abatement, or exemption should require legislative justification. Many easements make enormous scenic, environmental, or recreational contributions to public welfare, but the examples of "backyard" easements and golf course easements show that this is not uniformly the case. Even easements with significant public benefits will often impose costs, whether through higher land prices, patchwork development patterns, or loss of land use flexibility when future conditions change. Policy choices between competing values of these types are difficult and contentious, but subsidized land planning measures that cover enormous amounts of property in perpetuity merit an explicit decision on the appropriate public role in their imposition, taxation, and oversight.

Many of the challenges currently posed by conservation easements are actually a tribute to their spectacular success. Although property tax controversies form only a small part of the policy issues raised by conservation easements, their widespread, recurrent, and highly visible nature has allowed them to make a significant contribution toward understanding and clarifying this new instrument.

Notes

1. Davis (2003); Kell (2006); U.S. Endowment for Forestry and Communities (2014).
2. National Conference of Commissioners on Uniform State Laws (1981), 3.
3. La. Rev. Stat. Ann. § 9:1271; Mass. Gen. Laws, ch. 184, § 31.
4. Rev. Rul. 64-205, 1964-2 C.B. 62.
5. I.R.C. § 170(f)(3)(B)(iii).
6. Madden (1983), 125–137.
7. National Conference of Commissioners on Uniform State Laws (1981), 2.
8. Treas. Reg. § 1.170A-14(h)(3)(i).
9. Stephens and Ottaway (2003a).
10. Pidot (2005), 30–31.
11. Stephens and Ottaway (2003b).
12. La. Atty. Gen. Op. No. 1997-336.
13. Idaho Code § 55-2109.
14. Bonbright (1937), 497.
15. Eitel (2004), 78, n. 158
16. Treas. Reg. § 1.170A-14(h)(3)(ii).
17. Treas. Reg. § 1.170A-14(h)(3)(i).
18. Treas. Reg. § 1.170A-14(h)(3)(ii)
19. *Hilborn v. Commissioner*, 85 T.C. 677 (1985).
20. *Nicoladis v. Commissioner*, 55 T.C.M. 624 (1988).
21. Stephens (2004).
22. E.g., Jeane (2013); Rikoski (2006).
23. Bahney (2003).
24. *Englewood Cliffs v. Estate of Allison*, 69 N.J. Super. 514, 174 A.2d 631 (App. Div. 1961).
25. Ibid., 60 N.J. Super. 519, 174 A.2d 633.
26. *Village of Ridgewood v. The Bolger Foundation*, 6 N.J. Tax 391, 400 (1984).
27. *Village of Ridgewood v. The Bolger Foundation*, 104 N.J. 337, 342; 517 A.2d 135, 138 (1986).
28. *Holbrook Island Sanctuary v. Inhabitants of the Town of Brooksville*, 161 Me. 476, 484, 214 A.2d 660, 664 (1965).
29. *Francis Small Heritage Trust, Inc. v. Town of Limington*, 2014 Me. 102, 98 A.3d 1012 (2014).
30. *New England Forestry Foundation, Inc. v. Board of Assessors of Hawley*, 468 Mass. 138, 152–153, 9 N.E.3d 310, 321–322 (2014).
31. Stockford (1990), 846.
32. Me. Rev. Stat. title 36, §§ 1102 (6); 1109 (3).

33. Pidot (2005), 31.
34. E.g., Flint (2003).
35. Whoriskey (2003b).
36. Morriss (2004), 647–648. The *Mt. Laurel* decision found a one-acre minimum lot size not justified as substantially related to public welfare. *Southern Burlington County NAACP v. Township of Mt. Laurel*, 67 N.J. 151, 336 A.2d 713 (1975).
37. Blanding (2006), 128.
38. E.g., Glaeser and Ward (2009).
39. Greenberger (2006).
40. *Boston Globe* (2014).
41. Mass. H.4375, Chapter 286 (2014).

8 Farmland Assessment and Current Use Valuation

T he appropriate taxation of farmland touches on many complex issues: equitable distribution of the tax burden; assistance to family farmers in difficult financial straits; land use planning to avoid sprawl and protect open space; and promotion of agriculture as a source of production, a landscape amenity, and a way of life. These goals sometimes conflict, and policies addressing them often contain contradictory elements. Much uncertainty exists about whether measures such as preferential property taxation can actually help achieve long-term preservation of farmland. More than a half century of experience with agricultural taxes based on use value rather than market value provides a vantage point from which to consider these controversies.

Current Use Taxation for Farmland

The concept of "use-value" or "current use" assessment can appear deceptively simple, but its application has evolved in unexpected ways. It began as a means of reducing development pressure by taxing farmland in its current state as agricultural land rather than on a fair market value that might reflect potential nonfarm uses. Some states have extended this method of taxation to forests, open space, and other forms of property as well.

Maryland established the nation's first use-value program for agricultural land in 1956. It is not hard to see why this was a popular step, and one that led to some form of preferential tax treatment for farmland in every state, usually through use-value assessment.[1] It could be seen as a way of protecting family farms, preserving open space, and preventing urban sprawl—all by basing assessments on actual conditions rather than on values that could be realized only through sale for development. It had so much support that when Maryland's highest court found it to violate the state constitution's requirement of uniformity in taxation, the constitution was amended in the same year.[2]

The speed of that enactment is reflected in the decidedly ad hoc character of the resulting constitutional language. Article 43 of the Maryland Declaration of Rights now reads in its entirety: "That the Legislature ought to encourage the diffusion of knowledge and virtue, the extension of a judicious system of general education, the promotion of literature, the arts, sciences, agriculture, commerce and manufactures, and the general melioration of the condition of the People. The Legislature may provide that land actively devoted to farm or agricultural use shall be assessed on the basis of such use and shall not be assessed as if sub-divided."[3]

This odd phrasing accurately reflects the results-oriented nature of many farmland assessment programs. In seeking simply to reduce taxes on agricultural property, they often assign extremely low taxable values to land that can be developed at any time and is not owned by the ostensible beneficiaries of this legislation, family farmers. The popularity of use-value assessment is readily understandable, but it rests on assumptions that may be challenged. The questions it raises include (1) how value in use is to be measured; (2) whether the benefits of use-value assessment accrue primarily to hard-pressed family farmers; (3) whether this approach achieves long-term farmland preservation; and (4) whether it helps combat urban sprawl.

Use Value and Market Value

The term *use value* suggests a distinction between two elements of ownership: the right of current use and occupancy, measured by rental values, and the right of sale, which includes speculative potential for gain due to future price appreciation or demand for a different use of the property. This implies that use value might be measured by current rent, as was the case with the traditional British "rates," which based property taxes on annual rental values and required payment from the occupier rather than the owner. However, in the United States agricultural use tax provisions rarely attempt to measure rental values directly. Many states use formulas based on soil types, productivity ratings, or per-acre values that can result in extremely low assessments.

Value in Use and Value to the Owner

"Value in use" has sometimes been contrasted with "value in exchange" when property has special utility for its current owner. This concept of value in use is a variant of value to the owner and almost always *higher* than market value. It sometimes serves as an exception to the literal interpretation of market value when customized facilities with costly special features designed for a specific owner have little utility for other potential purchasers. In this situation, courts are understandably reluctant to permit a major investment fulfilling its intended purpose to escape taxation. For example, the New York Stock Exchange argued in 1927 that its building was so specialized that it would be of no use to another purchaser, even another financial exchange, and so had no market value. In fact, the owners reasoned that the value of the land should be reduced by the demolition costs of the building.[4] In rejecting this argument, the New York court held that in very limited situations unique property that is useful to its owner and that would be replaced if destroyed can be valued by reference to its depreciated cost. This particular application continues to arise in unique circumstances. For example, in 2015 the Alaska Supreme Court upheld assessment of the Trans-Alaska Pipeline System for the years 2007–2009 on a "use-value standard" producing values between $8 billion and $10 billion. The court found no error in valuing the pipeline as "special purpose property that was 'specifically designed, constructed, and adapted for its particular use.'"[5]

The subjectivity involved in identifying value to the owner, and the difficulty of quantifying its value, make it an extremely problematic basis for general assessment. Courts have consequently taken a very restrictive approach to its application. As the New Jersey Superior Court stated, "The focus must be on the value of the property in the market place, without regard to the particular or peculiar circumstances of the owner. Were this not so, adjacent parcels of land improved with identical structures might be valued differently to the extent that their respective owners' personal situations differed, even though in the open market each parcel would sell for the same price."[6]

Similarly, the Pennsylvania Supreme Court wrote, "[U]se value or value-in-use represents the value to a specific user and, hence, does not represent fair market value. . . . Because value-in-use is based on the use of the property and the value of that use to the current user, it may result in a higher value than the value in the marketplace. Value-in-use, therefore, is not a reflection of fair market value and is not relevant in tax assessment cases because only the fair market value (or value-in-exchange) is relevant in tax assessment cases."[7]

All of these considerations have generally led to the exclusion of value to the owner as a factor in the assessment of real property. Application of a particular and highly favorable interpretation of "use value" to farmland is an example of its exceptional treatment.

Investment Value and Speculative Value

What is the value of agricultural land to a bona fide farmer? The benefit from current use is certainly one part of the property's value to the owner, but investment value is also a legitimate and crucial component. Failure to acknowledge this can distort the rationale and structure of agricultural assessment programs, leading to the assumption that farmers sell land for development only because of their property tax burden, and that preferential assessment is therefore the remedy for farmland loss.

In fact, the perceived unfairness of taxing land on the basis of its most profitable use is a complaint against all market value assessment and is not limited to agricultural concerns. A farmer's view, that "owning large tracts of farmland is not a measure of one's ability to pay property taxes, but merely a necessary part of producing safe, affordable food,"[8] is simply a variant of the complaint that a home's market value "is irrelevant to a property owner unless and until he or she sells."[9] Yet the sale value of their property is of enormous concern to all owners, and home equity loans and other financial instruments allow this potential to be realized even before sale.

Both homeowners and farmers are intensely concerned with their property as an investment, not only as a residence or workplace. It is not surprising that use-value assessment for farmland has led to suggestions for its application to other forms of property as well. In 2005 Maine voters approved a state constitutional amendment to allow use-value assessment for "working waterfront" property.[10] The governor then proposed extending use-value assessment to homestead residential property. That measure, which was not adopted, did not attempt to measure the value of current residential use. It would only have meant that assessments could not rise more rapidly than the rate of inflation.[11]

Homeowners and farmers often hold real estate with little or no current earnings but high sale value. Just as the owner of a uniquely useful but unsalable factory would not be compensated for its loss by a nominal insurance payment or eminent domain award, so a farmer losing property with development potential would not be fully compensated by a payment ignoring that land-value element. The farmer uses the land as a factor in agricultural production and also as a capital investment in its own right.

The pejorative connotations of "speculation" can confuse this point when that term is associated with absentee owners holding land idle in hopes of future profit. Speculation (or some less freighted synonym) can instead simply denote a purchase motivated by the hope of future gain. It is sometimes defined as the "practice of buying or selling with the motive of then selling or buying and thus making a profit if prices or exchange rates have changed."[12] Speculation can be one of a number of factors, including a love of the land and a commitment to agriculture, that may influence a farmer's real estate purchases. Use of land for crop production does not negate its simultaneous use as an investment.

Who Is a Farmer?

The difficulty of distinguishing between using property as farmland and using it as a capital asset is mirrored in attempts to identify "bona fide" farmers, as opposed to developers or other owners making interim agri-cultural use of land. Some state programs purchase development rights from farmers to prevent future nonagricultural use, but use-value assess-ment rarely requires a long-term commitment not to develop land. Bona fide farmers are often extremely hostile to governmental efforts to restrict their rights of use and sale. As researchers at the University of Wisconsin found, "In most public forums, it is often the nonfarm residents (many of whom had recently moved to their rural homes) that are the most ardent supporters of policies discouraging farmland conversion, while the older farmers who attend such meetings frequently seek to preserve their rights to sell their lands however they see fit as they plan for their own retire-ments."[13] But without restricting future use and sale, no long-term preser-vation of farmland is accomplished, and the farmer's right to develop the property prevents any simple exclusion of developers from the benefits of farmland assessment.

Defining Farm Activity

If current use assessment requires only modest farm activity, developers can legitimately reduce their taxes during the preconstruction period by leasing land to farmers or hiring workers to undertake minimal cultivation. Even statutes that limit agricultural assessment to lands "used primarily for bona fide agricultural purposes" cannot avoid this problem. Florida's pro-vision to this effect[14] has been held by courts not to bar agricultural as-sessment of land rezoned nonagricultural at the owner's request,[15] land purchased by a developer of an amusement park,[16] and farmland purchased "to develop the land as a commercial property or resell it for such pur-poses."[17] The court in the latter case found that although the primary goal of the owners was "to use all or part of the land for a shopping center . . . commitments for the requisite financing were not forthcoming. Thus, development remained only a hope or future expectancy. There was ab-solutely no nonagricultural commercial activity on the land."[18]

Other Florida cases have taken the same approach: "The fact that the land may have been purchased and was being held as a speculative in-vestment is of no consequence provided its actual use is for a bona fide agricultural purpose."[19] "As we interpret the statute, the intent of the title holder and his desire for capital gain are immaterial to the application of agricultural zoning."[20] Similarly, a Kansas court upheld agricultural assessment of otherwise vacant land whose owner had seeded it with grass and allowed a lessee to remove the hay free of charge. "The fact that the taxpayer's land is inside the city limits is irrelevant. . . . There is no minimum acreage requirement in the statute, nor is there a requirement that profit be made from the property. The fact that the parcel contains 2.26 acres is irrelevant, as is the fact that the taxpayer is not a farmer by occupation."[21] Or, as the Kansas Board of Tax Appeals succinctly concluded, "There is no statutory prohibition against the landowner planting grass in order to obtain a more favorable classification."[22]

At one time Florida law directed that sale of farmland for more than three times its agricultural assessment gave rise to a rebuttable presumption that the property was not in bona fide agricultural use.[23] The repeal of this provision in 2013 did not change assessment practice as much as might be expected, since the courts had interpreted it in an extremely lenient fashion. For example, it was not applied to a purchase of 350 acres of citrus grove at six times the agricultural assessment, because the court assumed that the entire excess price could be allocated to 25 acres that were developed into an amusement park, despite the lack of evidence that the grove was not purchased for a uniform price per acre.[24]

Office Parks, Developers, and Celebrity Farmers

Although much of the political and emotional appeal of use-value assessment stems from a desire to assist hard-pressed family farmers, many of these statutes do not distinguish among family farms, corporate farms, hobby farms, and even land being prepared for subdivision and development. News reports regularly highlight "millions of dollars in property tax breaks intended to preserve farmland are going instead to companies that bulldoze farms to build housing subdivisions, malls and industrial parks," such as a Des Moines commercial subdivision where planting of corn and soybeans reduced property taxes from $320,514 to $14,345; a Denver residential subdivision whose developer kept cows grazing on unbuilt lots, vi-

olating zoning ordinances but reducing property taxes from $22,000 to
$60; and a Mobile development on which pine seedlings reduced taxes
from $64,230 to $152.[25]

Some states explicitly extend current use assessment to land under development. The Illinois "developer's relief" statute[26] provides that platting,
subdividing, and developing farmland or vacant land of five acres or more
cannot lead to a new assessment before completion of construction. The
Indiana Tax Court was quite frank in considering the rationale for a similar provision in that state: "[T]he developer's discount was 'designed to
encourage developers to buy farmland, subdivide it into lots, and resell
the lots.'"[27]

New Jersey, a state with a strong commitment to agriculture and open-
space conservation, allows use-value assessments for lots as small as five
acres. Its requirement for $500 in annual agricultural earnings was raised
to $1,000 in 2013.[28] This increase was a response to concerns over "fake
farmers" and an attempt to limit its provisions to "working farmers."[29]
This change, however, was unlikely to affect the law's beneficiaries, which
included the King of Morocco, an heiress to the M&M candy fortune,
Bruce Springsteen, Steve Forbes, Exxon, Merck, and Merrill Lynch.[30]
The *New York Times* reported that an apple and peach orchard on the
20-acre headquarters of BMW North America in suburban New Jersey
reduced the taxes on the corporate campus to $373.52, while neighboring
homeowners paid $3,446.94 for 1.2 acres and $2,651.18 for three-quarters
of an acre.[31] Far from being an economically viable farm operation, the
orchard was tended by a tenant farmer who was paid by BMW and given
all the proceeds from the harvested crop. Agricultural assessment was
denied only after BMW requested and received rezoning of all its parcels
to allow multibuilding development. The new zoning ordinance for the
BMW parcels did not permit use of the property for orchard or farming
purposes.[32]

The New Jersey courts have long identified the primary goal of use-
value assessment to be "to preserve the 'family farm' by providing farmers
with some measure of economic relief by permitting farmland to be taxed
based on its value as a continuing farm and not on any other basis."[33] The
great confusion on this point was well illustrated by an official of the New

Jersey Division of Taxation who told the *New York Times*, "The law is blind in respect to who owns the land; it can be Exxon. The intent was to preserve the family farm in New Jersey."[34]

Just as full-time farmers may also be bona fide land speculators in hopes of profitably reselling their property at an appropriate time, so may full-time land developers undertake bona fide farming as an interim preconstruction activity. But tax subsidies for these activities are not consistent with support for preferential assessment measures based on a belief that they will help preserve family farms.

Moreover, at a time when farm households as a whole are wealthier than nonfarm households, even subsidies for family farmers require justification on grounds of need or as a means of achieving land planning objectives. The average income of farm households exceeded the average income of all U.S. households every year from 1996 to 2013.[35] Long ago the economist Henry Aaron wrote, "In the absence of evidence supporting artificial deferral, special farmland exemptions are inequitable and should be repealed. They specifically reduce taxes for owners of a rapidly appreciating asset and, hence, rapidly growing wealth."[36] Like all preferences, current use assessment should be considered a tax expenditure and evaluated in light of forgone revenue and the increased burden it places on remaining taxpayers. Because New Hampshire has neither a sales tax nor a broad-based income tax, it relies heavily on the property tax. In 2010 over half the total land area in the state was enrolled in its use-value assessment program,[37] contributing to effective rates on fully taxable property that are among the highest in the nation.

San Francisco's 2014 adoption of an "urban agriculture" tax incentive demonstrated the complexities attending such measures. A city with one of the most severe problems of housing affordability in the nation offered property tax reductions to owners of unbuilt lots who agreed to use their land for agriculture for at least five years. Qualifying property could be as small as one-tenth of an acre. The *San Francisco Chronicle* interviewed the owner of a double lot valued at two million dollars who planned to enroll in the program and so reduce its assessed value to $12,500 an acre. The owner anticipated that his children might want to build a house on the lot in the future, and until then was pleased to use it as a garden. "Hopefully there are other people like me that eventually might want to do some development on their land but aren't in a big rush, and meanwhile want to let it be used for this kind of public purpose."[38] A five-year commitment to gardening—agriculture does not seem the appropriate term when the area at issue could be one-tenth of an acre—achieves no long-term goal in exchange for the loss of tax revenue.

Where development pressure is greatest, the difference between the market value of agricultural land and the value based on agricultural income will also be greatest. Thus, use-value assessment by its nature is of least benefit to farmers outside the urban fringe. In truly rural areas, where farming is the most profitable use of the land, the current use is the highest and best use. Of course, formulas based on crop prices can still provide a current use value far below the sale price of land for agricultural purposes. However, an artificially low assessment may not benefit a taxpayer in a rural jurisdiction where all properties receive equally low assessments and tax rates must increase correspondingly to raise the needed revenue from the diminished base. An entirely rural area where all property qualified for agricultural assessment would have winners and losers from this tax shift, because current use formulas are not a simple percentage of full market value. But farmers would still bear the entire local tax burden.

Preserving Farmland and Open Space

Many supporters of use-value assessment view it as a tool for limiting sprawling suburban development. From this perspective, the forgone taxes, and the correspondingly higher taxes on other property owners, constitute an investment in landscape preservation. This raises questions about the durability of the protection thus achieved and its place within regional growth plans.

If agricultural owners are free to sell their land for development at any time, no long-term preservation is ensured. This would require legal limits on development, whether through zoning, agricultural preservation easements, sale or transfer of development rights, or outright public purchase of the land. In itself, use-value assessment does not ensure farmland preservation. In fact, only about half the states impose a penalty for withdrawal of farmland from use-value assessment programs, generally a "rollback" assessment reflecting the difference between the agricultural use taxes and the amount that would otherwise have been due for some number of years preceding the sale.[39] However, these are often a small percentage of the ultimate profit from farmland conversion. A minor penalty for a change in use will not have a decisive influence on a financial decision of this magnitude. An economist with the Wisconsin Department of Revenue reviewed studies of farmland preservation and concluded that "use value has a minimal impact on preserving farmland."[40]

Use-value assessment can produce enormous losses in property tax revenues without achieving long-term farmland preservation. The Indiana case allowing a "developer's discount" reduced the property's valuation from $2,237,300 to $15,684.[41] Professor Robert Glennon analyzed an Arizona case in which land purchased for $4,500,000 was assessed at $3,455 once the developer owning the property leased grazing rights to a neighboring rancher for five to seven head of cattle for $250 a year.[42] A 2012 Missouri case permitted agricultural taxation of 3.3 acres of commercially zoned land whose owners paid between $750 and $800 for hay baling annually and realized no profit on the sale of hay. Agricultural assessment reduced the taxable value of the property from $575,000 to $30.[43]

Maintaining any particular farm in agricultural use may or may not help avoid sprawl and promote desirable growth patterns. In the worst case, reducing taxes on land under the greatest development pressure, close to the urban fringe and served by existing infrastructure, may encourage "leapfrog" growth farther into the countryside—with the protected land simply developed for greater profit at a later time. Leapfrog development, and the consequent need for infrastructure expansion, may be the unintended consequences of efforts by individual communities to restrict growth near the urban perimeter.

The *Washington Post* found that the DC region's "war on sprawl," under which planning restrictions prohibit typical suburban housing developments on more than half the land in the metropolitan area, "accelerated the consumption of woods and fields and pushed developers outward in their search for home sites."[44] Bruce Katz of the Brookings Institution commented, "If you have each county limiting development, it's going to jump elsewhere."[45] At one time large-lot zoning was considered a significant instrument for preserving open space.[46] A quarter-century later, the director of the Boston Metropolitan Area Planning Council observed, "What those restrictions really do is encourage development in a land-hungry manner."[47]

Under the Massachusetts Agricultural Preservation Restriction (APR) program, the state purchases development rights from farmers who agree to continue agricultural use of their land. Even this outright transfer of development rights does not always preclude large-lot development. A former state commissioner of Food and Agriculture stated that he "has seen wealthy individuals with little interest in agriculture pay large sums for APR farms, demolish suitable, existing homes and build mansions. . . . The state's intent is to preserve farmland and keep it affordable for first-time buyers. A mansion surrounded by farmland is a perversion of the program. . . . 'We want to encourage farmers to have homes, but not $4 million homes,' he said."[48]

Suffolk County, New York, found that the public purchase of development rights to land in the Hamptons did not necessarily preserve agriculture there, as "it has become increasingly common for developers or neighbors to buy protected land and, preferring the patter of horses to the clatter of tractors, turn it into private equestrian complexes or simply giant lawns surrounded by hedges."[49] After similar sales in Vermont, a news article asked, "Would Vermonters be willing to continue spending tax dollars to protect farms that will end up as private estates?" The president of the Vermont Farm Bureau gave the alternate perspective: "We don't need the state to get into the business of telling farmers what they can and can't sell their farms for."[50]

The economists John E. Anderson and Seth H. Giertz concluded that the alliance between agricultural and environmental interests to favor use-value assessment might illustrate Bruce Yandle's "Bootleggers and Baptists" paradox, "which argues that regulations are often the result of alliances between groups with very different motivations. In Yandle's example, Baptists provide the moral case for prohibiting the sale of 'demon rum' on the Sabbath, whereas bootleggers lobby for the same goal because it protects them from competition. With use-value assessment, environmental groups may play the role of the 'Baptists,' making the public case for it, whereas the agriculture lobby represents the 'bootleggers,' working behind the scenes to influence the political process."[51]

Wisconsin's Adoption of Use-Value Taxation

The state of Wisconsin, known as "America's Dairyland," offers a particularly instructive example of the complexities involved in balancing farmland preservation, tax subsidies for family farms, and fair distribution of the property tax burden. As in most states, debate in Wisconsin combined all these elements, with use-value assessment seen as "a small price to pay to help farmers hang onto their land and help slow down urban sprawl."[52]

Wisconsin is also typical in its provision for uniformity in taxation, which required an amendment of the state constitution to permit use-value assessment. This measure was approved by the voters in 1974. However, Wisconsin then chose an atypical path and did not avail itself of this option for 20 years. Until 1996 Wisconsin farmland, like all other real property in the state, was assessed at market value based on highest and best use. The state provided tax assistance to farmers through state-funded income tax credits rather than preferential assessments that reduce local property tax collections.

These tax credits were available to farmers who entered contracts to preserve their land in agricultural use and whose land was located in counties with agricultural land use plans or exclusive agricultural zoning provisions.[53] Low-income, full-time farmers received the greatest assistance, with income measured by household earnings rather than farm income, to help distinguish full-time farmers from hobby farmers. These unconventional efforts to direct aid to the neediest farmers and to encourage local land use regulations were an innovative attempt to conserve farmland without indiscriminate subsidies to politically powerful constituencies.

However, a combination of factors led the legislature to introduce use-value assessment in 1995. The state-funded credit, an outright expenditure, could never reach the magnitude of tax expenditures achieved through reduced assessments, and by 1998 it averaged less than $1,000.[54] At the same time, the need for contractual agreements and land use plans imposed burdens on taxpayers and jurisdictions. The state revenue secretary told the Farmland Advisory Council, "With Wisconsin being a strong agricultural state, the fact that we are one of the last ag states in the country to have use-value, it's embarrassing."[55] The state embraced use-value assessment with such fervor that it was required to freeze agricultural values in 2003 when it became clear that its formula would result in negative assessments. As the Department of Revenue noted, this would lead to "the 'illogical conclusion' that farmers would be paid to own the land."[56]

The Challenge for Tax Policy

During the first decade of use-value assessment, Professor Donald Hagman wrote, "Too much of the present legislation constitutes a blatant tax favoritism, clothed for acceptance and respectability with land-use planning motives."[57] This sobering initial view provides cause for reflection on a half century's experience with use valuation. A program commanding enormous political support as a means of aiding needy farm families, preserving agricultural land, and preventing unchecked urban growth can lead to the unintended consequences of subsidizing development, encouraging "leapfrog" sprawl, and providing tax benefits that are not targeted according to need. A valuation method designed to reflect actual use rather than hypothetical highest and best use can produce arbitrary assessments unrelated to either value to the owner or value to the market.

Wisconsin's proud progressive heritage was consistent with its initial adoption of what many analysts would consider the right method for reducing the burden of agricultural property taxes: targeted state-funded credits tied to long-term contractual agreements for land preservation and countywide land use planning. The failure of that approach speaks to the gravity of its political challenges: adequately funding such a program, limiting benefits to areas under the greatest development pressure, and competing with the predominant use-value model.

Without the assurance of long-term preservation, use-value assessment can become simply a method of untaxing open space, with all its concomitant potential for perverse land use and distributional consequences. The tremendous nationwide support for use-value assessment challenges policy analysts to identify politically feasible methods for targeting its benefits and achieving its goals. Concretely, this means a legislative definition of eligibility that addresses the status of hobby farmers, developers, and agribusiness; an appropriate combination of incentives for covenants to retain land in agricultural use and penalties for withdrawal from the program; and a role for regional planning in identifying land whose long-term preservation offers the greatest public benefit.

Notes

1. Anderson and England (2014).
2. Newhouse (1984), 606.
3. Maryland Declaration of Rights, Art. 43.
4. *People ex rel. New York Stock Exchange Building Co. v. Cantor*, 221 A.D. 193, 223 N.Y.S. 64 (1st Dep't 1927), *aff'd*, 248 N.Y. 533, 162 N.E. 514 (1928).
5. *Dep't of Revenue v. BP Pipelines (Alaska) Inc.*, Alaska Supreme Court Nos. S-146 96/14705/14706/14716/14725, No. 7039 (August 28, 2015), 16–18.
6. *Borough of Fort Lee v. Hudson Terrace Apts.*, 175 N.J. Super. 221, 226; 417 A.2d 1124 (1980), *cert. denied*, 85 N.J. 459, 427 A.2d 559 (1980).
7. *F & M Schaeffer Brewing Co. v. Lehigh County Board of Appeals*, 530 Pa. 451, 457–458; 610 A.2d 1, 3–4 (1992).
8. *Buffalo News* (1995).
9. Hevesi (1982).
10. Me. Const. Art. IX, § 8(2)(D).
11. Rooks (2005).
12. Pearce (1992), 404.
13. Jackson-Smith and Bukovac (2000), 4.
14. Fla. Stat. § 193.461(3)(b).
15. *Harbor Ventures, Inc. v. Hutches*, 366 So. 2d 1173 (Fla. 1979).
16. *Roden v. K & K Land Management, Inc.*, 368 So. 2d 588 (Fla. 1978).
17. *Fischer v. Schooley*, 371 So. 2d 496 (Fla. Dist. Ct. App. 1979).
18. Ibid., 498.
19. *Smith v. Ring*, 250 So. 2d 913, 914 (Fla. Dist. Ct. App. 1971).
20. *Hausman v. Rudkin*, 268 So. 2d 407, 409 (Fla. Dist. Ct. App. 1972).
21. *Board of County Commissioners of Johnson County v. Smith*, 18 Kan. App. 2d 662, 666-667; 857 P.2d 1386 (1993).
22. Ibid., 667.
23. Fla. Stat. § 193.461(4)(c) (2012), repealed by H.B. 1193; Fla. Laws ch. 2013-95.
24. *Roden v. K & K Land Management, Inc.*, 368 So. 2d 588 (Fla. 1978).
25. Breed and Mendoza (2004).
26. 35 Ill. Comp. Stat. Ann. 200/10–30(a).

27. *Hamilton County Assessor v. Allison Road Development, LLC*, 988 N.E.2d 820, 823 (Ind. Tax Ct. 2013), quoting *Aboite Corp. v. State Bd. of Tax Comm'rs*, 762 N.E.2d 254, 257 (Ind. Tax Ct. 2001).

28. N. J. Stat. Ann. §§54:4-23.5, amended by S-489 (2013).

29. O'Dea (2013).

30. Ibid.; Friedman (1996).

31. Hanley (1997), Sec. 13 N.J., 1.

32. *BMW of North America, LLC v. Borough of Woodcliff Lake*, N.J. Tax Ct., Memorandum Opinion (December 17, 2013, unpublished).

33. *Hovbilt, Inc. v. Township of Howell*, 138 N.J. 598, 619, 651 A.2d 77, 88 (1994).

34. Gray (1993), 40.

35. Department of Agricultural and Consumer Economics, University of Illinois at Urbana-Champaign (2013).

36. Aaron (1975), 86.

37. Anderson and England (2014), 7, table 1.2.

38. Duggan (2014).

39. Anderson and England (2014), 26.

40. Boldt (2003), 679.

41. *Hamilton County Assessor v. Allison Road Development, LLC*, 988 N.E.2d 820, 823 (Ind. Tax Ct. 2013).

42. Glennon (1990), 305; *Stewart Title & Trust v. Pima County*, 156 Ariz. 236, 751 P.2d 552 (Ariz. Ct. App. 1987).

43. *Rinehart v. Bateman*, 363 S.W.3d 357 (Mo. Ct. App. 2012).

44. Whoriskey (2003a), A1.

45. Ibid.

46. Malone and Ayesh (1979), 437.

47. Whoriskey (2003a), A1.

48. De Leo (1999), B1.

49. Chaban (2014).

50. Page (2005), 1.

51. Anderson and Giertz (2015).

52. Rinard (1999), 2.

53. Jackson-Smith and Bukovac (2000), 4.

54. Timmerman (1999).

55. Rinard (1999), 2.

56. Berry (2003), 111.

57. Hagman (1964), 657.

9 The Valuation of Federally Subsidized Low-Income Housing

To those who have not previously dealt with this topic, the property tax treatment of federally subsidized low-income rental housing might seem a straightforward matter. Housing constructed under government programs to assist a needy population would appear to be a natural target for reduced taxation, if not an outright exemption. Moreover, familiar images of poorly maintained public housing projects hardly suggest that their value might greatly augment the local property tax base. However, many subsidized developments are not purely public housing in any simple sense. For many decades the federal government has offered incentives for private parties to own and operate low- and moderate-income rental apartments as a financial investment. These structures are generally not tax-exempt, and courts have struggled to characterize them for property tax purposes.

Federal housing incentives have taken many forms, including long-term, low-interest mortgages, payments to mortgage lenders to reduce the effective interest rate for construction loans, cash payments to supplement rent paid by qualified tenants, and, most recently, federal income tax credits. Property tax cases have considered all of these programs and their associated regulatory restrictions, particularly limitations on allowable rents. Subsidies provide the incentive to accept a restricted return, and courts must determine whether the financial benefit of the subsidies is to be considered in tandem with the financial burden of the rent restrictions. Courts have considered unprofitable developments and profitable investments, situations in which government supplements raised rents above market levels and the much more typical situations in which subsidies were granted in exchange for below-market rent. They have analyzed many valuation techniques and adopted a variety of interpretive principles.

As in the fable of the blind men and the elephant, this endeavor has given rise to sharply contrasting opinions. Is such housing a social good that deserves a reduced assessment? Is it the property of a private syndication whose wealthy investors take their profits in the form of tax benefits rather than cash income, with no claim to property tax relief on that account? Is it an investment gone bad, and, if so, should the owners receive the benefit of a tax reduction? Is it an investment expected to go bad even before construction, with capital knowingly placed into buildings not worth their cost because other subsidies made this investment profitable? This wide range of fundamental issues has implications far beyond the specific issue of rent-restricted property.

Operation of the Tax Credit: A Simplified Case

Early federal housing programs that offered reduced-interest mortgages, accelerated depreciation, or rent supplements contained many convoluted technical provisions, but these pale in comparison to the complexity of their successor, the Section 42 tax credit. The 1986 Tax Reform Act eliminated or restricted many Internal Revenue Code provisions that had supported earlier subsidies, such as accelerated depreciation and tax benefits from passive losses, but also added the new Section 42, the Low-Income Housing Tax Credit (LIHTC) program. This provision establishes an annual distribution of income tax credits to the states calculated as a dollar amount per capita. The states in turn allocate these credits among investors willing to provide funds for limited-income housing. Section 42 is now the primary form of federal assistance for subsidized rental housing. It is extremely complex, and is sometimes described as the longest provision of the Internal Revenue Code. As summarized by the Michigan Court of Appeals:

> In the section 42 program, the low-income housing developer is allocated tax credits for ten tax years, the developer generally uses the tax credits to recruit private investors, and the investors are assigned the

tax credits in exchange for the investors' contribution of capital to build or rehabilitate the housing project.

Generally, as here, the sale of the tax credits is structured as a limited partnership between the developer and the investors. The limited partner investors purchase the limited partner interests in the ownership of the development in return for the tax credit benefits expected to be realized in the ten-year period.[1]

The Tennessee Court of Appeals gave voice to the perplexity with which many tribunals first encounter Section 42 when it wrote, "Little is known about the LIHTC program outside of the circle of affordable housing developers, syndicators, and some investors who have waded through its sometimes oblique rules to take advantage of this rather unique incentive for the creation of affordable rental housing for lower income people. . . . [L]imited partner investors (many individuals or a single or several corporations) buy up to 99% of limited partner interests in the ownership of the development in return for an allocation of up to 90% of the tax credit benefits expected to be realized in the 10-year period."[2]

Because subsidized housing cases present a unified core set of issues, a simplified abstract case drawing on their common elements can identify the larger implications of these inherently fact-specific decisions. Such a case would consider the property tax valuation of low- and moderate-income rental housing whose owners receive a federal subsidy, whether in the form of cash assistance, mortgage reduction payments, income tax credits, or other transfers, in return for rent limitations and other restrictions on the property. Both the subsidies and the limitations would run for a set period of time, such as 10 to 20 years.[3]

These simplified facts allow consideration of an equally simplified tax dispute in which the owners challenge their assessment on the grounds that it does not adequately reflect the special burdens of ownership, primarily the restrictions on rent. They may also charge that the assessment overstates or incorrectly includes financial benefits, such as the Section 42 tax credits. Of course, in cases where government supplements have raised rents above market levels, the roles are often reversed, with taxing districts taking the position that government regulations enhance value and taxpayers arguing that this effect should be ignored.

These cases have required courts to consider many related issues, such as the taxability of the property, whether and how the income restrictions should affect its assessment, and the nature of the rent restrictions as a matter of property law. The resulting decisions are significant in themselves, but their greatest impact may lie in their contribution to understanding larger problems of property valuation.

General Valuation Questions

The most basic issue raised by these cases questions whether subsidized properties should be valued in the same manner as any other taxable real estate. Although these structures are rarely exempt from property tax under state law,[4] a sense that they serve the public good has plainly influenced courts and legislatures dealing with tax valuation. In some cases this consideration has led to what might be called a "quasi exemption," with the valuation process influenced by a desire to support housing policy goals.

For example, the Massachusetts Supreme Judicial Court distinguished the assessment of rent-restricted subsidized housing from that of property whose rent is limited by a private lease. It referred to the "unique status of a federally regulated low income housing project," finding that "federally funded projects are particularly vulnerable to changes in property taxes." Although the court had adopted the general rule that fair market rent, and not rent as limited by contract, sets the basis for assessment, it found subsidized housing to be an exception, noting that "there was evidence that the company would be forced to default on the mortgage" if its development were taxed in the same manner as private rental property.[5] This is a dramatic example of the way in which a seemingly technical choice among assessment methods can remove property value from the tax base even as the property itself remains on the tax rolls.

Other courts have taken the opposite position and refused special treatment for subsidized property. Some argue that the federal subsidies afforded these developments do not necessarily imply that they should receive favorable property tax treatment as well. The Michigan Supreme Court wrote, "To the extent that federal income tax receipts are utilized to subsidize the owners and tenants of Petitioner's property, the citizens of the City . . . are already contributing to the support of subject property, albeit indirectly."[6] Still other opinions have focused on the private and profit-motivated aspects of these projects, finding the rent restrictions simply a quid pro quo for other benefits: "This is nothing more than a financial arrangement voluntarily chosen by taxpayers, whereby taxpayers have substituted one income stream (higher rents) for another (lower rents and tax credits), because taxpayers believe that will maximize the return on their investment. . . . Had the legislature intended owners of property that qualified under IRC § 42 to be entitled to property tax relief on that basis, it surely would have provided for an explicit exemption or reduction."[7]

There are thoughtful arguments on both sides of this debate, although they are not often fully developed in a judicial context that does not explicitly recognize extralegislative exemptions. The political and social concerns underlying these assessment disputes are also particularly complex. The public responsibility to house the needy has always coexisted uneasily with the use of housing assistance funds to reduce wealthy investors' tax payments. A frequently quoted statement by the late Professor Stanley Surrey found "something terribly amiss when to provide low-income housing for the shelter of the poor, we at the same time shelter tax millionaires."[8] It can seem even more strange that the major federal program for subsidizing low-income rental housing is primarily overseen by the Internal Revenue Service rather than the Department of Housing and Urban Development.

At the same time, the inefficiencies and scandals that mark the history of publicly built and operated developments, often constructed on a massive scale, have lent support to efforts to enlist private investment and market discipline in the cause of housing assistance. The image of the Pruitt-Igoe towers being demolished in St. Louis, or the infamous Cabrini-Green apartments in Chicago, mirror the failure of similar enormous projects to the present day, "as public housing high-rise buildings have come tumbling down by the dozens across the country."[9] Even those who would prefer an entirely public commitment to low-income housing sometimes argue that private sector incentives can increase political support for these programs.

Another complexity concerns the economic incidence of the tax. Property owners stress that governmental limitations on rent cannot be changed during the life of the restrictions. That could also mean, however, that unsuccessful property tax appeals would not place a burden on the parties who are the object of the charitable endeavor, but rather would reduce the net income of the investors.[10]

A few states allow local governments to determine whether specific subsidized rental developments are to be assessed according to standard approaches or afforded some measure of exemption.[11] For example, under certain circumstances Texas permits local taxing units to "deny the exemption if the governing body determines that: (A) the taxing unit cannot afford the loss of ad valorem tax revenue that would result from approving the exemption; or (B) additional housing for individuals or families meeting the income eligibility requirements of this section is not needed in the territory of the taxing unit."[12]

For their part, developers often feel that governments at all levels look to them to provide affordable housing with insufficient subsidies. An architect writing in the *Washington Post* complained that the government "presumes that developers enjoy large profit margins, have access to unlimited capital and should willingly use some of that profit and capital to subsidize affordable units," while in fact "weak market demand, rental and pricing constraints, tight financing and cost overruns can result in slim, nonexistent, or negative profit margins." An accompanying cartoon shows public officials saying to developers, "Quit whining—you developers have plenty of money," while the developers respond, "Most of it borrowed!"[13]

The details of specific subsidy programs also complicate these arguments. For example, Section 42 is not designed to assist the neediest population, since its rents attempt to fit the budget of those earning approximately half the area median income. The income base for these calculations can include all households and not just renters, increasing the median figure. A study of several thousand LIHTC projects found average rents there to be 9 percent lower than average rents for the nation as a whole.[14] Although project sponsors may be mission-driven nonprofit entities, these buildings are almost always owned by partnerships or limited liability companies in which more than 99 percent of the interests are held by investors seeking tax shelter or banks seeking credit under the Community Reinvestment Act. Even official documents often refer to the investors as "buying tax credits," when in fact they are acquiring ownership interests in entities holding real estate.[15] Investors themselves are sometimes actually surprised to learn that they have essentially bought an interest in an apartment complex.

Developers, syndicators, and sponsors of subsidized housing have recognized the advantages of cutting this Gordian knot of legal analysis with special legislation. Over 20 states have addressed the taxation of subsidized housing by statute, often with very specific provisions favorable to taxpayers—for example, by prohibiting consideration of the Section 42 tax credits in the assessment process while requiring that value be set by reference to regulated rent limits. Other legislation has addressed more detailed valuation issues, such as income capitalization rates.

As would be expected when both financial interests and social advocates support highly technical legislation that the great majority of taxpayers would find incomprehensible, these measures generally have been approved easily. A 2006 study found most of them to have passed unanimously.[16] This trend follows a long history in which court decisions mandating uniformity in assessment have been met by legislative exceptions for property such as farmland or single-family residences. State legislatures are always more receptive to appeals for quasi exemptions that reduce the budgets of local governments than to those that affect the revenue of the states themselves.

The Significance of Construction Costs

The standard approaches to property valuation examine such measures as rental income, the market value of comparable realty, and depreciated construction cost. Of these, the cost approach is often the least relevant. The price of income-producing properties will clearly be affected by expected future net earnings, and an investor bidding on a structure will be extremely interested in recent sales of similar properties. But even recent construction cost may have limited influence on buyers who are not contemplating building a new structure themselves. James Bonbright wrote that a "hard-headed businessman . . . would hardly turn his finger" to discover the original cost of property.[17] Cost estimates for older buildings require adjustments for physical, economic, and functional depreciation that can rarely be estimated with precision in the absence of income or sales data. The cost approach is therefore generally used with special care.

Despite these limitations, construction cost can serve as a check on the results of the income and comparable sales approaches.[18] For example, a cost-based valuation of a successful and newly constructed building can challenge owners' claims that the property value is far below that figure. If owners argue that new property is not worth its cost, it is reasonable to require an explanation for their investment decision. In the *Seagram* cases,[19] New York courts found that Joseph E. Seagram & Sons had not met its burden in arguing for a reduced assessment of the renowned Seagram Building on Park Avenue. "Nowhere in the record is it explained how just two years before the period under review an experienced owner employing a reliable contractor and having the services of outstanding architects put $36,000,000 into a structure that was only worth $17,800,000. Such a startling result requires more than speculation before it can be accepted as fact."[20]

The cost approach can be particularly important in the valuation of subsidized housing, because there are few arm's-length sales, and the parties often disagree on the measure of income to be capitalized. At the same time, taxpayers have argued that special regulatory and prevailing wage requirements raise the cost of subsidized housing above that of comparable market-rental structures.[21] Analysts have also noted that "the basis for the tax credits in an LIHTC project is correlated to the reported construction costs, creating an incentive to show the highest cost possible" for the taxpayer's records.[22] Both considerations touch on a fundamental valuation challenge: whether special value to the owner, here in the form of tax credits and other financial benefits that made the initial investment worthwhile, should be considered in setting the taxable value. This issue arises in many cases dealing with special-purpose property. For example, the prestige value of name recognition and association with an architectural landmark such as the Seagram Building might or might not be transferable to another purchaser.

The question as to whether construction costs are evidence of value leads to another topic of intense dispute: whether the financial burdens of ownership can be taken into account without considering the corresponding tax benefits. Some analysts have argued that "[c]onstruction costs are known; but these overstate the market value of a project, since in the absence of subsidy the rental stream produced by the property would not justify the actual expenditure on construction."[23] But "in the absence of subsidy" begs the question of the basis for valuation. If both benefits and burdens are taken into account, as they were presumably taken into account by the investor, the actual expenditure could be justified by the combined return, including the subsidy.

If only the burdens are taken into account, the cost of a new and successful building could indeed be seen as overstating value. Ironically, the fear that tax incentives could distort investment decisions and lead to uneconomic construction was one of the concerns that led to the Tax Reform Act of 1986 and thus to the Section 42 credit. In discussing an earlier rental subsidy program, two analysts observed, "When a federal agency can guarantee a cash flow for twenty years and offer tax-exempt bond financing, accelerated depreciation, and other benefits, a marginal project can become feasible. Poor real estate decisions, based on misguided priorities, resulted in the construction of some poorly designed projects."[24]

Partnership Value and Real Estate Value

In appropriate circumstances, the sale of an entity holding real estate can be treated as a sale of the real estate itself for tax purposes. For example, real property transfer taxes are sometimes imposed on sales of controlling interests in corporations or partnerships that own real estate.[25] Could the recent sale price of partnership interests in syndicated subsidized housing be considered evidence of the value of the property itself? The details of the partnership's legal arrangements would complicate such an analysis, and the ownership interests may represent only a part of the project financing. One tax case referred to estimates that proceeds from the sale of partnership interests fund 50 to 70 percent of development costs.[26] However, these considerations bear on the computation of the price and the weight to be afforded it, not on the relevance of the sale itself. Such an investment is influenced by the purchaser's own tax situation and other individual considerations, but this can be the case with any sale, particularly one involving tax-favored property. This extension of the comparable sales approach has not been raised in property tax cases dealing with subsidized housing, and limited partnerships or limited liability companies could consider the price paid for their interests to be proprietary. But to the extent that limited partners or shareholders in limited liability companies are investing in real estate rather than simply "buying tax credits," this approach could shed light on the value of the underlying property.

Determining the relevance of the sale value of partnership interests is one facet of a larger challenge: distinguishing the value of property ownership from the value of a business conducted on that property. It would be erroneous, for example, to equate hotel occupancy revenue with property rent, for hotel charges constitute payment for many amenities and services, and they reflect the hotel's investment in such nontaxable assets as a trained workforce, a reservation system, and name recognition. Hotel valuation cases have long struggled to distinguish real property value from the value of the hotel enterprise—such as that reflected in the extra income attributable to the prestige of a premium hotel chain.[27]

Hotel owners have sometimes sought to enhance their valuations for mortgage appraisal purposes by attributing business value to the real property, only to find this information used against them in tax cases.[28] In a similar effort to strengthen mortgage financing of subsidized housing, a 1995 joint policy statement by the Office of Thrift Supervision, the Comptroller of the Currency, the Federal Deposit Insurance Corporation, and the Federal Reserve Board held that "lenders should ensure that appraisals of affordable housing projects identify, consider and discuss the effect of certain types of financial assistance, such as low-income housing tax credits, subsidies and grants, sometimes referred to as intangible items, on the estimate of market value for such projects."[29] This policy is especially significant for tax assessment disputes because mortgage lenders rely on the value of the real estate itself to secure their loans. The foreclosure value of the property would not be enhanced by an enterprise formerly operated there. The security for the mortgage loan lies in the real estate value that is the subject of the property tax.

Appropriate Treatment of Legal Restrictions

Restricted Rents and Market Rents

The problem of distinguishing property income from business income arises whenever rents set under a long-term lease diverge from current market levels. In most subsidized housing assessment disputes, the rents permitted to be charged to limited-income tenants are below the market rates that could be obtained for physically similar unregulated units. This situation can be considered analogous to the valuation of property burdened by below-market private leases, an area of lively differences of opinion among state courts, as discussed in chapter 3.

Many courts have concluded that a long-term private lease calling for rent that later falls below market levels does not provide the landlord with grounds for a reduction in the property's assessment. It is true that prospective purchasers seeking to buy the owner's interest will not pay as much for the right to collect below-market rents as they would bid for identical unencumbered property that could be leased at current market rates. But such a purchase would not convey all interests in the property—only the landlord's interest, the right to collect rents due under current leases. A true purchase of all rights in the property would also bid for the tenants' interests. This would mean acquiring the value of their right to pay below-market rent for the remainder of the lease term. Purchasing both sets of interests would transfer all rights in the property and place the new owner in a position to obtain full market rent. A rational buyer could choose instead to pay less, acquire only the owner's interest, and continue to collect below-market rents, but payment of that lower price for a partial interest does not establish that the property itself is worth less than an identical unencumbered parcel. These cases raise a truly fundamental issue. They demonstrate that the sale price of property can be estimated only after identifying the interests that constitute the property.

These arguments are mirrored in the subsidized housing cases. Courts basing assessments on actual rent point out that this is the amount that the landlord in fact receives. The opposite result obtains when courts focus instead on the private, voluntary, and profit-oriented motives for accepting below-market rent.

Subsidized housing cases have also considered the appropriate treatment of above-market rent. Section 8 of the 1937 Housing Act and its successor provisions, like some state subsidies for low-income housing, provide rental supplements that in some instances can provide building owners with "substantially higher rent than that received by comparable, nonparticipating apartments."[30] In such cases owners have urged courts to value the property without regard to these special provisions, "and to instead consider the rental income that the property would command in the open market of unsubsidized housing."[31] Courts that disagree have found it "obvious"[32] that "[a] willing buyer would most certainly consider the guaranteed income rate set by the Federal government when determining the fair cash value of the property."[33]

Courts that reach conflicting results in lease cases and subsidized housing disputes often fail to offer a convincing analytic basis for this distinction, whether it proves to be favorable or unfavorable to the taxpayer in any individual instance.[34] The Supreme Court of Ohio found the two situations to require a consistent approach, recognizing "economic rental value of commercial real property as an indicium of valuation for ad valorem real property taxation purposes."[35]

The Effect of Voluntary Restrictions

These disputes present a question as to whether below-market leases are sufficiently similar to subsidized housing rent limitations for the tax treatment of one to provide guidance with regard to the other. In both instances a property owner has entered an agreement to accept less than a market rate of return. In many cases, courts have allowed voluntary restraints on income to reduce property value only if the financial benefits that provide the incentive for accepting those restraints are taken into account as well.

In supporting consideration of both the benefits and burdens of subsidized status in assessment, the Indiana Tax Court commented, "Although a property owner can reduce a property's value by imprudently agreeing to deed restrictions and cause himself economic loss, a property owner should not be allowed to reduce the tax base in such a manner." The court found it reasonable to assume that the regulatory burdens were at least balanced by their benefits, for the taxpayer "would not have entered into the deed restrictions if the federal tax benefits did not adequately compensate [it] for the decreased rental income."[36]

Most publicly imposed restrictions governing the use of property must be considered in its assessment. A tax valuation cannot contemplate a hypothetical highest and best use for property that ignores legal limitations on development. The rental restrictions on subsidized property are similar in that they are publicly enforced and their breach would lead to heavy penalties. At the same time, these restrictions differ from zoning restrictions, wetlands protection, or public safety ordinances, because they have been voluntarily assumed by the owners. In fact, they may have been eagerly sought by syndicators in a competitive bidding process. As one expert wrote, "The important point about the rent restriction in LIHTC projects is that it is voluntarily imposed in return for special benefits. Restrictions are not imposed by the government, as with a zoning ordinance. The restrictions do not take something of value from the property owner for the benefit of the public at large or protect the public at large."[37]

The Supreme Court of North Carolina took a similar position in finding that Section 42 limitations on rental income did not necessarily govern the property tax assessment: "Unlike a governmental restriction such as zoning, section 42 restrictions do not diminish the property's value, but instead balance tax credits allowed to the developer against rent restrictions imposed on the developer."[38]

The Oregon Supreme Court took an opposing view when it interpreted the state's requirement that assessments take into account any "governmental restriction as to use" as being applicable to LIHTC rent limits. "[L]imits on what taxpayers may do with their properties, resulting from taxpayers' participation in the section 42 program, constitute 'governmental restrictions as to use.' . . . The most probable price depends on what the buyer will receive in exchange for that price; the buyer will pay only for what it will receive. Thus, the most probable price to be received for the properties at issue would not include the tax credits, because the record shows that the credits would be recaptured if the property were not maintained as low-income housing."[39]

The import of the last sentence is uncertain if a purchaser stepping into the shoes of the original owner could in fact succeed to the tax credits. The penalties for withdrawal from the subsidized housing program are designed to ensure that the property will be maintained as low-income housing. Note also how quickly additional issues become entwined in such analysis: whether the restrictions are considered publicly imposed, whether the benefits and burdens would carry over to a new purchaser, and whether the benefits and burdens can be separated for purposes of valuation.

In the Oregon case, a dissenting justice wrote, "This is nothing more than a financial arrangement voluntarily chosen by taxpayers, whereby taxpayers have substituted one income stream (higher rents) for another (lower rents and tax credits), because taxpayers believe that will maximize the return on their investment. The below-market rents charged by taxpayers are not the result of a 'governmental restriction'; rather, they are the result of a quid pro quo—federal income tax credits (a financial benefit) in return for charging the favored class below-market rents (a financial detriment)."[40]

Appropriate Treatment of Tax Benefits

The relevance of the tax benefits to valuation raises related questions concerning their characterization: whether they are an attribute personal to the owner rather than part of the taxable property, whether they are a "wasting asset," and whether they constitute intangible property that should not be included in the base of a real property tax.

A central issue raised by these cases questions whether the tax benefits to the individual investor are relevant to property valuation. If the recent construction cost or the price in an arm's-length sale were the basis for assessment, there would be no need to account for the tax considerations behind the decision to pay that specified amount, any more than the purchase price of a residence needs to be adjusted to account for the federal mortgage interest deduction. The existence of a market price obviates the need to construct an independent measure of value by reference to all the elements a potential purchaser might consider.

If, however, property is to be valued by reference to regulated rental income, or if those income limits are used as a basis for an obsolescence deduction from construction cost, it is not clear whether the limited rents permitted in exchange for tax benefits provide an accurate basis for valuation without consideration of the tax benefits themselves. As the Georgia Court of Appeals wrote, "[T]he tax credits go hand in hand with restrictive covenants that require the property to charge below-market rent. . . . If viewed in isolation, the rental restrictions would artificially depress the value of the property for tax valuation purposes."[41]

The Illinois Supreme Court took a similar position: "A valuation approach which considers the subsidy income, but does not consider the negative aspects of a subsidy agreement upon the earning capacity of the subsidized property, would be inappropriate."[42] This question has a long history in debate over the assessment of subsidized rental property. In a 1974 case the Supreme Court of Rhode Island observed, "The depreciation benefits were described as 'excellent' and the 6% return as the frosting on the cake."[43] In other words, the tax benefits were the true return, and the nominal rental income a welcome addition.

Taxpayers have responded that "[b]asing market value on the income tax benefits of ownership destroys uniformity because the tax consequences of ownership vary from person to person."[44] Courts that disagree consider that "there would be no market for private investment in low-income housing development were it not for these federal tax incentives. . . . [T]he appraised value of the property for property tax purposes would be artificially depressed if the value of the tax credits is not included."[45]

Some earlier programs, such as Section 236 of the National Housing Act, offered subsidies that reduced the effective mortgage interest rate to 1 percent. Many courts found that the reduced mortgage interest clearly affected the return to property ownership and so was relevant to an income-based valuation. "Certainly, the fact of lower mortgage payments decreases expenses and thereby increases the owner's potential income from the investment."[46] If the introduction of Section 42 were to change the mortgage subsidy to an economically equivalent tax credit, should that affect the valuation of the subsidized real property? Some courts have distinguished credits that affect the owner's individual after-tax income from items that affect property revenue,[47] but others have found "no legally cognizable distinction between low-income housing tax credits and these programs."[48]

Are Tax Attributes "Personal to the Owner"?

Property law distinguishes covenants personal to the owner from those that "run with the land" and bind future purchasers.[49] Although courts have sometimes referred to these categories in dealing with federally subsidized property, they do not necessarily apply with precision to the rent restrictions and tax benefits contained in a specific statute. However, in practical terms both run with the land if the legislative design includes incentives and penalties intended to make sure they will survive any change in ownership.

The Internal Revenue Code requires that owners seeking the low-income housing tax credit enter an agreement with the housing credit agency "which is binding on all successors of the taxpayer."[50] Section 42 provides a quid pro quo: financial penalties, including cancellation or recapture of tax credits, will be imposed if the taxpayers sell to future owners who do not abide by the restrictions, but purchasers who do abide by the restrictions can succeed to the credits as well as to the property ownership. The Michigan Court of Appeals wrote, "Though the low-income tax credits may not interest a 'typical' buyer of residential rental property, there is a specialized market for properties subject to § 42," because their foremost value "is found in the tax benefits they generate to the owner."[51] The Supreme Court of Idaho found that "a purchaser of creditworthy property steps into the seller's shoes with respect to the unused credits."[52] The benefits and burdens of ownership are intended to follow ownership of the property. This has strengthened the case for recognizing both in the assessment process.

Time-Limited Tax Benefits

Both the restrictions and tax benefits that accompany ownership of subsidized housing have limited lives. Section 42 credits generally extend over a 10-year period, while the rent limitations and other restrictions accompanying them often expire after 15 years. It is sometimes said that credits are earned over 15 years but paid out over 10 years. This discrepancy raises a question about how these time periods, and particularly the mismatch in their lengths, affect tax valuation. For some commentators, the final five-year period would be one in which prospective purchasers could assume only the burdens of subsidized housing, while the tax benefits, as a type of wasting asset, would have expired.[53] But the example of leased property suggests several complications in translating this situation into a nominal or even negative assessed value.

In states that do not equate taxable value with the sale price of the landlord's interest, a low sale value for the landlord's encumbered share does not set the taxable value of the real estate as a whole. Courts taking the opposite position and accepting low rents as evidence of property value still limit this approach in order to minimize the problem of identical properties bearing different property tax burdens. For example, no court would consider fraudulent or non-arm's-length agreements in the assessment—such as below-market rental terms accompanied by side payments not mentioned in the lease. Some courts have similarly attempted to distinguish prudent leases from those that were "improvident when made."[54]

A similar issue could arise if for valid business reasons a bona fide lease called for most of the rent to be paid early in the lease term. At the extreme, a completely legitimate lease might require an initial lump-sum payment equal to the discounted present value of a series of standard monthly payments for the duration of the tenancy, perhaps with provision for a bond or other means of securing the landlord's future performance. Could the landlord demand a nominal tax assessment after receipt of such a lump-sum payment, since no rent would remain to be paid for the term of the lease? It is highly unlikely that an unusual rent schedule would eliminate the owner's tax liability. Such questions might arise if a sale of subsidized housing were characterized as "buying only the restrictions without getting the benefit of the credits"[55] for tax purposes.

Are Tax Benefits a Nontaxable Intangible Asset?

Courts have disagreed over whether tax credits constitute intangible property not subject to a real estate tax.[56] Some of the states that have enacted special legislation addressing the assessment of subsidized housing have eliminated the value of the credits from the tax base by declaring them to be intangibles.[57] Of course, a tax benefit is intangible property, as are all types of financial interests and even currency itself—the paper and ink being tangible, but the claim on value that they represent being intangible. But this overlooks the distinction between imposing a tax on an intangible asset and imposing a tax on tangible property at a market value that reflects its intangible features. Many homes command a premium because buyers value intangible attributes such as historic significance, neighborhood reputation, or school quality. This situation periodically raises debate, as in the case of New Hampshire homeowners who protested that taking scenic settings into account in valuation amounted to a "view tax." The state explained that it had no view tax, but that tax assessments reflect tangible and intangible elements affecting market value.[58]

This debate echoes the distinction between taxing permits and licenses and recognizing their influence on property value. As the Michigan Court of Appeals wrote, "[I]ntangibles are not taxable in and of themselves, but they may be taken into account for purposes of assessing the value of tangible property."[59] Similarly, the Tennessee Court of Appeals stated, "The legislature clearly envisioned that intangible aspects of the property would be included in valuation. The potential to produce income in the future is itself an intangible."[60]

Lessons for Other Complex Valuation Questions

Although the legal and financial issues raised by the taxation of subsidized housing are extremely complex and sometimes arcane, these cases touch on controversies that arise in many tax disputes, and their lessons have wide application. Their attention to conceptual valuation problems has illuminated questions as diverse as the impact of voluntarily assumed restrictions and the intangible nature of tax benefits. In every instance, a determination of the interests that constitute the taxable property must precede a computation of value. Such a determination affects property tax valuation cases of every type.

The subsidized housing decisions examined here provide dramatic evidence of the importance of consistency in identifying the taxable interests to be valued. This concern has clearly motivated many courts that have required that both the benefits and burdens of regulation be considered in the assessment process. From this perspective, the fact that taxpayers seek the right to assume regulatory burdens in exchange for tax benefits means that both elements play a role in establishing the value of ownership. Consistency could also be achieved by disregarding both the benefits and burdens, on the assumption that they are roughly equivalent, as in the case of a cost-based approach to value. However, considering both the benefits and burdens has the advantage of recognizing the regulated status that is a central fact of these properties' economic reality. Even where statutory formulas or individual court decisions prescribe special treatment for the valuation of subsidized housing, the underlying importance of consistency in judicial interpretation remains a central lesson for other cases.

No set of decisions proceeding from such a wide array of factual situations, legislative enactments, and judicial precedent could be expected to provide a single conclusive resolution. However, a varied range of opinions allows stronger reasoning to emerge over time, in the best tradition of the common law.

Notes

1. *Huron Ridge L.P. v. Ypsilanti Township*, 275 Mich. App. 23, at 25 n. 1, 737 N.W.2d 187, at 188 n. 1 (2007).
2. *Spring Hill, L.P. v. Tennessee State Board of Equalization*, No. M2001-02683-COA-R3-CV (Tenn. Ct. App. 2003).
3. Note that many state and local programs support affordable owner-occupied housing and publicly owned housing, neither of which raises the specific tax issues considered here.

4. *Supervisor of Assessments v. Har Sinai West Corp.*, 95 Md. App. 631, at 642 n. 4, 622 A.2d 786, at 792 n. 4 (1993), discusses cases on this point. For an argument in favor of exemption, see Penna (2001).

5. *Community Development Co. of Gardner v. Board of Assessors*, 377 Mass. 351, at 354–355, n. 10, 385 N.E.2d 1376, at 1378, n. 10 (1979).

6. *Meadowlanes Limited Dividend Housing Associates v. City of Holland*, 437 Mich. 473, at 501 n. 51, 473 N.W.2d 636, at 650 n. 51 (1991) (quoting the Michigan Tax Tribunal in *Kentwood Apartments v Kentwood*, 1 MTTR 295, 301 [1977]).

7. *Bayridge Associates Limited Partnership v. Department of Revenue*, 321 Or. 21, at 40, 892 P.2d 1002, at 1012 (1995) (Van Hoomissen, J., dissenting).

8. Surrey (1973), 13.

9. Fernandez (2010).

10. Penna (2001).

11. E.g., Alaska Stat. § 29.45.110(d); Tex. Tax Code § 11.1825 (x)(3).

12. Tex. Tax Code § 11.1825 (x)(3).

13. Lewis (2010).

14. Cummings and DiPasquale (1999), 77, 82.

15. Maine Revenue Services (2007); *Rainbow Apartments v. Illinois Property Tax Appeal Board*, 326 Ill. App. 3d 1105, at 1108, 762 N.E.2d 534, at 537, 260 Ill. Dec. 875 (2001).

16. Rosenblum (2006).

17. Bonbright (1937), 146.

18. E.g., *Stone Brook Limited Partnership v. Sisinni*, 224 W.Va. 691, 688 S.E.2d 300 (2009).

19. *Joseph E. Seagram & Sons, Inc., Appellant, v. Tax Commission of the City of New York*, 18 A.D.2d 109, 238 N.Y.S.2d 228 (1963), *aff'd*, 14 N.Y.2d 314, 251 N.Y.S.2d 460, 200 N.E.2d 447 (1964).

20. 18 A.D.2d at 112, 238 N.Y.S.2d at 232–233.

21. Penna (2001).

22. Ibid., 56.

23. Peterson et al. (1973), 73, quoted in *Community Development Co. of Gardner v. Board of Assessors*, 377 Mass. 351, at 355, 385 N.E.2d 1376, at 1378 (1979).

24. Cummings and DiPasquale (1999), 53.

25. E.g., New York City Admin. Code § 11-2101(7).

26. *Schuyler Apartment Partners LLC v. Colfax County Board of Equalization*, Nebraska Tax Equalization and Review Commission, No. 06C-254 (June 2, 2009), *aff'd*, 279 Neb. 989, 783 N.W.2d 587 (2010).

27. E.g., *Chesapeake Hotel LP v. Saddle Brook Township*, 22 N.J. Tax 525 (2005).

28. Garippa (2006), 26–27.

29. Office of the Comptroller of the Currency (1995).

30. *Alta Pacific Associates, Ltd. v. Utah State Tax Commission*, 931 P.2d 103, at 104 (Utah 1997).

31. *Kankakee County Board of Review v. Property Tax Appeal Board*, 131 Ill. 2d 1, at 19, 544 N.E.2d 762, at 770, 136 Ill. Dec. 76 (1989).

32. *Alta Pacific Associates, Ltd. v. Utah State Tax Commission*, 931 P.2d 103, at 119 (Utah 1997) (concurring).

33. *Kankakee County Board of Review v. Property Tax Appeal Board*, 131 Ill. 2d 1, at 16, 544 N.E.2d 762, at 769, 136 Ill. Dec. 76 (1989). Other opinions taking this position include *Executive Square Limited Partnership v. Board of Tax Review*, 11 Conn. App. 566, 528 A.2d 409 (1987), and *Steele v. Town of Allenstown*, 124 N.H. 487, 471 A.2d 1179 (1984).

34. E.g., *Kankakee County Board of Review v. Property Tax Appeal Board*, 131 Ill. 2d 1, at 15–16, 544 N.E.2d 762, at 764, 136 Ill. Dec. 76 (1989); *Community Development Co. of Gardner v. Board of Assessors*, 377 Mass. 351, at 355, 385 N.E.2d 1376, at 1379 (1979).

35. *Canton Towers, Ltd. v. Board of Revision*, 3 Ohio St. 3d 4, 7, 444 N.E.2d 1027, 1030 (1983).

36. *Pedcor Investments-1990-XII, L.P. v. State Board of Tax Commissioners*, 715 N.E.2d 432, 437–439 (Ind. Tax Ct. 1999).

37. Collins (1999), 306.

38. *In the Matter of Appeal of the Greens of Pine Glen Ltd. Partnership*, 356 N.C. 642, at 651, 576 S.E.2d 316, at 322 (2003).

39. *Bayridge Associates Limited Partnership v. Department of Revenue*, 321 Or. 21, at 30–32, 892 P.2d 1002, at 1006–1007 (1995).

40. Ibid., 40 (Van Hoomissen, J., dissenting) (citations and footnotes omitted).

41. *Pine Pointe Housing, L.P. v. Lowndes County Board of Tax Assessors*, 254 Ga. App. 197, at 199, 561 S.E.2d 860, at 863 (2002).

42. *Kankakee County Board of Review v. Property Tax Appeal Board*, 131 Ill. 2d 1, at 16–17, 544 N.E.2d 762, at 764, 136 Ill. Dec. 76 (1989).

43. *Kargman v. Jacobs*, 113 R.I. 696, at 702, 325 A. 2d 543, at 546 (1974).

44. Penna (2001), 62.

45. *Huron Ridge, L.P. v. Township of Ypsilanti*, 275 Mich. App. 23, at 34, 737 N.W.2d 187, at 199 (2007).

46. *New Walnut Square Limited Partnership v. Louisiana Tax Commission*, 626 So. 2d 430, at 432 (La. Ct. App. 1993).

47. E.g., *Cottonwood Affordable Housing v. Yavapai County*, 205 Ariz. 427, at 429, 72 P.3d 357, at 359 (Ariz. 2003); *Maryville Properties, L.P. v. Nelson*, 83 S.W.3d 608, at 616 (Mo. Ct. App. 2002).

48. *Huron Ridge, L.P. v. Ypsilanti Township*, 275 Mich. App. 23, at 33, 737 N.W.2d 187, at 192 (2007).

49. Casner and Leach (1984), 988.

50. I.R.C. § 42 (h)(6)(B)(5).

51. *Huron Ridge L.P. v. Ypsilanti Township*, 275 Mich. App. 23, at 36, 737 N.W.2d 187, at 194 (2007) (quoting *Antisdale v. Galesburg*, 420 Mich. 265, 362 N.W.2d 632 [1984]).

52. *Brandon Bay Ltd. Partnership v. Payette County*, 142 Idaho 681, at 684, 132 P.3d 438, at 441 (2006), citing § 42(d)(7).

53. E.g., Tenenbaum (2003), 170.

54. E.g., *Merrick Holding Corp. v. Board of Assessors*, 58 A.D.2d 605, at 606, 395 N.Y.S.2d 233, at 234 (1977), *rev'd*, 45 N.Y.2d 538, 382 N.E.2d 1341, 410 N.Y.S.2d 565 (1978).

55. Tenenbaum (2003), 170.

56. E.g., *Woda Ivy Glen Limited Partnership v. Fayette County Board of Revision*, 121 Ohio St. 3d 175, at 183 n. 4, 902 N.E.2d 984, at 992 n. 4 (2009) ("[T]he tax credits qualify as intangible interests separable from the real property."); *Rainbow Apartments v. Illinois Property Tax Appeal Board*, 326 Ill. App. 3d 1105, at 1108; 762 N.E.2d 534, at 537; 260 Ill. Dec. 875 (2001) ("Section 42 tax credits are not intangible property because they do not constitute a right to a payment of money, have no independent value, and are not freely transferable upon receipt.") (citations omitted); *Cascade Court Ltd. Partnership v. Noble*, 105 Wash. App. 563, at 571, 20 P.3d 997, at 1002 (2001) ("Tax credits are intangible personal property and thus are not subject to real property taxation.").

57. N.H. Rev. Stat. Ann. § 75:1-a; Utah Code Ann. § 59-2-102(20)(b).

58. Kenyon (2007).

59. *Huron Ridge L.P. v. Ypsilanti*, 275 Mich. App. 23, at 37, 737 N.W.2d 187, at 195 (2007) (citations omitted).

60. *Spring Hill, L.P. v. Tennessee State Board of Equalization*, M2001-02683-COA-R3-CV, 2003 (Tenn. Ct. App. 2003).

10   Exemptions and Payments in Lieu of Taxes

A broad array of property tax disputes concern real estate that is not subject to taxation at all. State-mandated exemptions for charitable, educational, and philanthropic purposes often give rise to conflicting interpretations that change over time in response to the evolving nature of nonprofit operations and social attitudes. The resulting controversies touch on basic questions of tax structure and policy as well as the most practical aspects of political relationships between local officials and exempt organizations.

Elements of Controversy

Conflicts and ambiguities arise in connection with exemptions from any form of taxation. However, the nature of the property tax provides particularly fertile grounds for such controversies. There is no clear link between, for example, the federal income tax rate and the size of the nonprofit sector, but an elite university may represent the major portion of real estate value in a small municipality. The extent of its exemption may have a dramatic effect on other owners' tax bills. Unlike financial instruments or other intangible property, exempt real estate property holdings can be very evident to local taxpayers, and often are assumed to be signs of wealth and ability to pay.

Residents may feel a direct monetary loss from exemptions they consider wrongly granted. When the property tax functions as a residual tax, its rate is set annually after the local governing body has considered the total value of the taxable property base, its budget needs for the coming year, and other sources of revenue. In this situation, a reduction in taxable value due to exemptions may be seen as clearly connected to an increase in the rate imposed on the remaining property. This can lead local property owners to challenge an exemption, as in Princeton, New Jersey, where taxpayers brought a legal action contesting the exempt status of 19 university buildings.[1] By contrast, status as a federal taxpayer generally does not confer standing to challenge the constitutionality of governmental actions in federal court.[2] Overlapping jurisdictions such as special districts and school districts often may also challenge exemptions that reduce their tax base.[3]

Intergovernmental issues influence the debate on exemptions in a number of ways. While federal exemption determinations are based on federal law, the independent and often varying criteria for property tax exemptions among the states create additional uncertainty and divergent outcomes. YMCA and YWCA properties face many inconsistencies among state policies—an expected result of a system that values independent state authority, rather than consistency, in such matters.[4] Church-owned vacant land may be exempt[5] or taxable;[6] preschools may be considered seminaries of learning[7] or noneducational custodial institutions.[8]

Most property tax exemptions are conferred through state constitutional or statutory enactments, and localities often object to the loss of tax revenue from institutions such as schools, hospitals, and museums whose benefits extend far beyond their municipal boundaries. The clustering of such organizations in specific geographic regions has no effect on the federal income tax liabilities of residents in those areas, but property taxes will reflect this impact. In response, major institutions have become adept at highlighting their beneficial effects on local employment and economic development. For example, a 2013 report commissioned by 12 Philadelphia colleges and universities estimated that they collectively contribute $10.9 billion to the local economy, supplying 84,000 jobs and $211 million in tax revenue.[9]

The concern for benefits extended to nonresidents raises a question about the inverse phenomenon, tax exporting. This is sometimes the goal of limitations on homestead exemptions, which generally are not available to owners of second homes, vacation property, and time-share units.

Higher tax rates on commercial and industrial property are often seen as a means of placing some portion of the tax burden on parties such as shareholders who are not local voters. These exporting issues arose at the state level in a challenge to a Maine law denying a property tax exemption to a summer camp because it was not operated primarily for Maine residents. In a 5 to 4 decision the U.S. Supreme Court held that this violated the federal Commerce Clause, despite the taxing jurisdiction's argument that campers were not "articles of commerce." Interestingly, recognizing "the complexity of economic incidence analysis," the Supreme Court adopted the assumption of the lower courts that the burden of the tax fell at least in part on the campers.[10]

Some critics of this decision decried its equation of philanthropy with commerce. "The subsidized charitable sector is not comparable to business, regardless of how large a participant in interstate commerce it is. Charitable summer camps are not comparable to profit-seeking hotels; they are more like schools or orphanages."[11] In an article entitled "Hocking the Halo," Professor Evelyn Brody pointed out that the camp's successful appeal to the Commerce Clause added a new element of controversy, because the public is "uneasy about, if not hostile to, the increasing nonprofit commercialism."[12]

Professor Brody's comment touches on a major source of uncertainty with regard to the contours of the exemption. New methods of nonprofit management raise questions about the continuing validity of exemptions based on past practices. This has been most evident in the health care field, where rapidly changing business models have challenged courts, local officials, and hospital administrators to distinguish nonprofit and for-profit operations.

Not surprisingly, such evolving business practices have given rise to some of the most notable legal battles in the area of tax exemptions. In its 1985 *Hospital Utilization Project* decision the Pennsylvania Supreme Court opened an enormous and as yet unresolved debate in that state by determining that a "purely public charity" must donate or render gratuitously a substantial portion of its services, a criterion found not to be met in that case.[13] A 2010 decision of the Illinois Supreme Court similarly reverberated throughout the health care community when it denied a property tax exemption to a medical center for lack of sufficient unreimbursed care.[14] In 2015 the New Jersey Tax Court found that "the operation and function of modern non-profit hospitals do not meet the current criteria for property tax exemption."[15] Princeton taxpayers contended that the hundreds of millions of dollars in patent royalties paid to the university represented a commercial enterprise incompatible with exempt operations.[16] At the other end of the spectrum, new forms of spiritual practice can challenge the traditional understanding of exempt religious property, whether this takes the form of wetlands used for spiritual walks[17] or property deeded to the Universal Life Church.[18]

Property Value and Revenue Loss

Determining the amount of revenue lost due to exemptions can be complicated by the need to estimate the value of unusual or historic structures. Exempt property owners do not typically report the value of their land and buildings, and there is no significant incentive for assessors and other public officials to invest resources in valuing tax-exempt property. Some jurisdictions seek to appraise exempt property in the same manner as taxable parcels, but many do not. As one Dallas appraiser stated, "It makes no sense to waste time and effort on properties that don't produce taxes."[19]

It is possible to value complex and unusual properties according to standard appraisal procedures. In England, the Palace of Westminster and Buckingham Palace, to say nothing of Oxford and Cambridge Universities, are subject to assessment and taxation, although specific buildings such as churches and student residence halls may be exempt.[20] However, in the absence of valuation and assessment, the financial impact of property tax exemptions is unclear. An impressive physical plant owned by a university could yield a surprisingly low assessment in a vigorous contest over its actual market value. Churches challenging historic preservation restrictions may point to the unseen structural deficiencies, functional obsolescence, and financial burden of these architecturally significant structures.[21] Disputes involving specialized industrial property also show that assessed values of unusual structures may be substantially less than their cost.

Payments for Services

A tax exemption is sometimes viewed as a fundamental exclusion from the scope of the tax and sometimes as a subsidy extended in exchange for a specific public service.[22] These two perspectives suggest quite different concepts of the relationship between the taxing jurisdiction and the charitable entity. The first rests on the inherent status of a charitable enterprise; the second, on its ongoing provision of tangible social benefits as a type of quid pro quo for its exemption from taxation. The tension between these two views leads directly to practical political controversy when exempt institutions face local pressure to make cash contributions in lieu of taxes. The institutions generally consider their tax-free status to be conferred by law and not contingent on any additional payments.

Much of this debate centers on compensation for municipal services. Charitable organizations are generally not exempt from fees, and so one way to address this is to charge for such services. In fact, a number of municipalities have moved toward fee-based service provision, but for several reasons this is rarely undertaken as a means of obtaining payments from tax-exempt institutions.[23] A major impediment is the need to establish that fees are not in fact disguised taxes and so are not subject to exemptions, limitation measures, or other procedural requirements such as voter approval.

Emerson College successfully challenged a fire protection charge imposed by the City of Boston after passage of Proposition 2½ severely restricted property taxes there.[24] Although the Massachusetts legislature had authorized the charge, the state Supreme Judicial Court ruled that it constituted a property tax from which Emerson College was exempt. The court identified three characteristics that distinguish fees from taxes: they must constitute a charge for a specific service that benefits the party paying the fee in a manner "not shared by other members of society"; they must be voluntary, with the party paying the fee having the right to forgo the service and avoid the charge; and they must cover the cost of the specific service provision rather than contribute to general revenue.[25] In this case, the benefits of fire protection were not confined to the affected buildings, the charge was compulsory, and the revenues were used for general public safety purposes.

Other states have reached similar conclusions.[26] The attorney general of North Dakota cited the *Emerson College* case in concluding that "the cost of general city services available to all persons and entities alike, specifically including fire and police services, are paid by taxes and are not voluntary services that may be paid by charging fees."[27]

Although fees limited to certain exempt organizations may be vulnerable to characterization as a disguised tax, a general charge imposed on all users may be unpopular with taxpayers. In New Orleans, citizen opposition to two municipal service charges led to their repeal and to a charter amendment requiring voter approval for future charges and fees. Since that time, three proposed fees have been rejected by city voters.[28]

Payments in Lieu of Taxes

Uncertainties about the exact requirements for exempt status, together with difficulties in supplementing municipal revenue through direct service charges, have led to new interest in a hybrid instrument known as payments in lieu of taxes, or PILOTs. This tool is generally characterized as a means of recognizing the services provided to the exempt organization through a voluntary payment that does not constitute a tax. Many agreements between localities and nonprofits are truly voluntary and represent both parties' recognition of their mutual interest in the welfare of the organization and the municipality in which it is located.

In other situations, however, there is definitely an element of coercion to these requests for payment and sometimes an implied or even explicit challenge to the organization's exempt status. This raises a question about the voluntary nature of the payment. Critics argue that "taxpayers do not voluntarily turn over their earnings to the state without an impetus for doing so; the concept of 'voluntariness' in the context of taxes is more like a legal fiction."[29] However, there are many degrees of coercion, from moral suasion to outright extortion, and the limits of permissible pressure for voluntary payments are the subject of many controversies.

Coercion and Conflict

At one extreme, municipalities seeking payments from nonprofit institutions may threaten retaliation if no agreement is reached. In discussing voluntary payments, the former mayor of Ithaca, New York, told the city council of Evanston, Illinois, home of Northwestern University, "Most universities say that they legally are not required to do this, and so the position that we took is, 'OK, if you stick to every legal right that you have, we'll do the same. And [with] things like building permits and zoning law, we will adhere to every fine line of the law.' "[30] In Ithaca, he had blocked a $100 million Cornell renovation project on grounds that the university was not paying "its fair share for city services," asking it to contribute 10 percent of the city's budget.[31] In 2000 the long-standing tension between Evanston and Northwestern, which is exempt from taxation under its charter from the State of Illinois, took a dramatic turn when Northwestern filed suit in federal court charging that designation of 43 university buildings as historic properties subject to preservation restrictions constituted retaliation for failure to make voluntary payments.

The court refused to dismiss the case. Among other findings, it cited evidence that an alderman "engaged in a plan of extortion when he allegedly made a proposal . . . that conditioned exclusion of University property from the Local [Historic] District on the University's agreement to make contributions to the City."[32] Perhaps the most telling evidence of the degree of rancor in university-city relations was Evanston's argument in court "that any animus it may have toward Northwestern University is not in fact illegitimate. The City suggests it is perfectly rational to harbor animus for an institution which fails to pay for the provision of City services and which threatens to encroach on existing residential neighborhoods."[33]

This case was settled in 2004 by a consent decree that excluded 14 university properties from the historic district and established a university-city committee on land use issues. The university agreed to a building moratorium on specific sites and made a one-time payment of $700,000 to the city for street lighting improvements.[34]

Even in cases very far from this extreme, a coerced contribution could give rise to legal challenges, whether characterizing the payment as a tax or raising various state and federal constitutional issues of uniformity or due process.[35]

At the other end of the spectrum, amicably negotiated contributions have been in place in a number of cities for decades, the largest and most established involving major universities and medical centers. Six of the eight Ivy League universities make payments in lieu of taxes.[36] In most instances, however, PILOTs are not a significant source of local revenue. A 2012 study found that of 186 localities with information on PILOTs, 131 received less than one-quarter of 1 percent of their revenue from these arrangements. In only 21 localities was this figure above 1 percent.[37]

The proliferation of tax incentives and abatements to encourage businesses to locate in a jurisdiction provides a discordant background for efforts to promote payments by tax-exempt institutions.[38] Providence, which negotiated a major increase in PILOTs from Brown University in 2012,[39] undertakes legislatively authorized "tax treaties" with businesses that reduce their tax liabilities in whole or in part for up to 20 years.[40] At the same time that Cook County was successfully challenging the exempt status of Provena Hospital, the county assessor was unable to place a newly opened restaurant in Millennium Park on the tax rolls. The failure to tax a highly successful commercial venture whose investors had close ties to the Chicago mayor led to major investigations and protracted litigation, but the Illinois Supreme Court judged the business arrangement to constitute a nontaxable license rather than a lease.[41] One commentator labeled a Pittsburgh proposal the "Oddest PILOT Proposal to Date: Tax Nonprofits, Cut Business Taxes."[42] These initiatives come full circle when cities such as Atlanta, Columbus, and Orlando seek to encourage exempt organizations to locate within their borders with incentives that can range from free land to hundreds of millions of dollars in subsidies.[43]

Boston: Seeking a Uniform Policy

The city of Boston has long solicited PILOTs from its nonprofit sector. In 2009 Mayor Thomas Menino established a task force with representatives from the city council, business community, public employee unions, and nonprofit organizations to develop a uniform PILOT policy. The task force report recommended that nonprofit organizations with at least $15 million in real property should contribute an amount equal to 25 percent of the tax they would be liable for in the absence of the exemption. This reflected the fact that services such as police and fire protection, street cleaning, and snow removal accounted for approximately one-quarter of the city's budget.[44]

This initiative also elicited some negative reactions. When the city's Museum of Fine Arts was asked to increase its $55,000 contribution immediately to $250,000, and then to $1 million by 2015, its director calculated that the museum provided the city with $2.1 million in benefits, with no municipal funding.[45] In turn, his own salary became an issue, as often happens in these disputes. For example, former Philadelphia mayor Edward Rendell pointed to the $2.1 million compensation package for University of Pennsylvania president Amy Gutmann in concluding that "it's hard to say the University of Pennsylvania is a charity."[46]

In 2011 Boston sent letters to all nonprofit organizations covered by the new policy explaining its guidelines and calculating the indicated voluntary payment for each institution. The PILOT payments rose by more than one-quarter that year, to over $19 million.[47] However, PILOTs still yielded only a little over one-half of 1 percent of city revenue in 2012.[48] This is typical of municipal experience with voluntary payments. The 2012 survey found the top 10 localities receiving PILOT revenue—which accounted for nearly three-quarters of all reported PILOT payments—collectively received only $68 million.[49]

Pennsylvania: The Effect of Legal Uncertainty

Pennsylvania has been at the center of an energetic and multidecade legislative, judicial, and political debate over charitable exemptions, initiated in part because of the changing nature of the health care industry. The *Hospital Utilization Project* case, a 1985 decision by the state's Supreme Court, set forth a five-part test for exempt status as a "purely public charity," including gratuitous donation of a substantial part of its services and operating entirely free of a private profit motive.[50]

The resulting uncertainty about the tax status of many established charitable institutions led to numerous local efforts to elicit payments in lieu of taxes from these organizations. These could be viewed as payments to forestall legal challenges to a claimed exemption. The chair of the Philadelphia Board of Revision of Taxes described that city's Voluntary Contribution Program, a 1994 mayoral initiative, in this way: "Exemptions were provided for those nonprofits that met the test of a 'purely public charity.' . . . Other nonprofits were asked to make voluntary contributions of 40 percent of the annual property-tax payment they would owe if their property were fully taxable."[51]

Erie County notified all 600 nonprofit charities within its borders that they would be considered taxable unless they could prove they met the *Hospital Utilization Project* criteria.[52] Every major Pennsylvania city initiated some form of exemption review, and some nonprofits made payments in lieu of taxes rather than incur costs in what could become an annual challenge. One author wrote, "What began as an effort to summarize the definition of a 'purely public charity' has escalated into what some have called an 'open season' on nonprofit organizations."[53]

The Pennsylvania legislature responded with Act 55 of 1997, the Institutions of Purely Public Charity Act, designed to "reduce confusion and confrontation among traditionally tax-exempt institutions and ensure that charitable and public funds are not unnecessarily diverted from the public good to litigate eligibility for tax-exempt status."[54] As a result, PILOT payments diminished dramatically. Philadelphia, which had received $9 million in payments from approximately 50 nonprofits, including nearly $2 million from the University of Pennsylvania, collected less than a half million dollars in 2012.[55]

Meanwhile, the city official responsible for implementing Philadelphia's PILOT program became head of the board of trustees of the University of Pennsylvania. He told the *Philadelphia Inquirer*, "It's unfair—and grossly inaccurate—to measure Penn's contribution to the city only by cash, and absurd to measure it by cash PILOT payments. The in-kind value of Penn's contributions to the city represents millions and millions of dollars of additional value."[56]

The pendulum swung again in 2012, when the Pennsylvania Supreme Court held that Act 55 could not expand the judicial criteria for exemption. "The question is whether the General Assembly may, by statute, influence the definition of the constitutional phrase 'purely public charity.' . . . The General Assembly cannot displace our interpretation of the Constitution because 'the ultimate power and authority to interpret the Pennsylvania Constitution rests with the Judiciary, and in particular with this Court.'"[57]

The following year the City of Pittsburgh filed suit against the University of Pittsburgh Medical Center (UPMC) challenging its exempt status.[58] The Pennsylvania legislature also considered a constitutional amendment to grant itself authority to define institutions of purely public charity.[59] UPMC responded with a legal complaint alleging that the city's action was an attempt to deflect attention from corruption investigations involving the mayor's office, to "divert attention from scandalous public reports of his precarious legal predicament and to curry favor with parties intent on harming UPMC and capable of cushioning his political fall."[60] With the election of a new Pittsburgh mayor, both the city and UPMC ended these particular legal actions.[61] This case reflects the difficult history of relations between Pittsburgh and its exempt institutions, which also includes several attempts to impose special taxes, such as payroll taxes and tuition taxes, on them.[62]

Pennsylvania provides a window onto many of the elements of current exemption controversies, from the role of the legislature and the courts to the effect of changing patterns of nonprofit business operations to the use of PILOTs. One civic activist told the *Philadelphia Inquirer*, "The level of city services that the universities receive have value, and they are not taxpayers. They should have to do PILOTs to compensate for costs that taxpayers subsidize for them."[63] Should city services be financed by charges imposed on all users, or by taxes and PILOTs from tax-exempt organizations? If universities "have to do" PILOTs, are they truly voluntary contributions? Is the basic legislative or constitutional exemption consistent with a demand for payments to cover municipal expenses?

Alternate Viewpoints

New Orleans: A Recommendation against PILOTs

Louisiana has long been an example of expansive exemptions and lax administration. In part because of the Louisiana constitutional mandate for exemption of the first $75,000 in appraised value of homestead property, a 1996 report by the independent Bureau of Governmental Research (BGR) found 65 percent of all assessed value in Orleans Parish exempt from property taxation. It found "no requirement in law or practice that an applicant for an exemption specify the section of the Constitution under which the exemption is sought. . . . [t]he 'other' code used by Orleans Parish assessors includes one-fourth of the valuation of all exempt properties and includes properties ranging from hospitals to exemptions given as business incentives."[64]

A 2011 report found that the increase in exempt value in the intervening years could not be calculated because, as in many jurisdictions, no effort was made to appraise exempt property accurately. The BGR pointed to a parcel of exempt land owned by Loyola University on St. Charles Avenue that was assigned a zero value on the tax rolls, while an adjacent smaller parcel owned by Tulane University was valued at $58 million. In fact, official records showed an actual decrease in exempt value in the intervening period even as the number of exempt properties increased 60 percent.[65] The 2011 BGR report noted that the state "bestows exemptions on nonprofit entities with weak claims for public subsidy, exemption criteria are not defined, and the constitution does not possess a strong use requirement." The report recommended reform of exemptions and greater use of service fees rather than introduction of payments in lieu of taxes:

> As the experience of other cities demonstrates, however, PILOTs are generally an unfair and insubstantial revenue approach to offsetting the losses due to nonprofit exemptions. A small number of nonprofits would likely participate in such a program, leaving a great many nonprofit property owners off the hook for their share of public sector support. The participation of even that handful is not guaranteed, since PILOTs are voluntary. Furthermore, it is unlikely that the program would generate substantial funds. The city would be better served directing its energies toward other alternatives.[66]

The BGR's efforts to restrain the granting of exemptions in New Orleans seemed about to bear fruit in 2010 when the mayor established a Tax Fairness Commission to examine the equity, adequacy, and competitiveness of the city's tax structure. The BGR issued its report on nonprofit exemptions shortly thereafter, and in its presentation to the Tax Fairness Commission it emphasized the need to address these overly expansive, vague, and poorly administered provisions.[67] This led to news headlines such as "New Orleans Property Tax Exemptions for Nonprofit Groups Targeted,"[68] but a year later the BGR reported that a city official had "signaled to the public that the city would not pursue exemption reform for the time being," and that nonprofit groups "applauded state and local officials for 'generously' abandoning the reform effort."[69] The BGR commented, "While abandonment would indeed be generous to the beneficiaries of the current system, it would also be grossly unfair and ungenerous to the residents and businesses who foot the bill and live with substandard government services."

The Nonprofit Perspective

The situation in New Orleans, in which the BGR's meticulously researched critique of lax exemption practices failed to produce a policy response, illustrates many challenges facing such reform, including the difficulty of changing long-established practices and the continual mismatch between taxpayers bearing a cost that is cumulatively large but individually small and beneficiaries who are highly motivated to defend a subsidy that is extremely important to them. However, it also demonstrates the deep political support and goodwill enjoyed by the nonprofit sector. Even as municipal fiscal shortfalls and changing nonprofit operations place new stress on the nonprofit exemption, this underlying strength remains an important countervailing influence.

A number of nearly concurrent task force reports give evidence of this tension. Following the recession of 2007–2009, many states seeking increased revenue without tax increases established committees to study tax exemptions, and several of them considered drastic changes in the treatment of nonprofit entities.[70] In January 2014 a Vermont study committee recommended to the legislature that colleges and universities be required to enter into municipal service fee agreements.[71] The committee chair commented that he found "no particular reason that nonprofits shouldn't be contributing" toward the cost of local services.[72] The Association of Vermont Independent Colleges made clear its opposition, stating, "By mandating and monetizing that which is largely taking place in the spirit of volunteerism and cooperation, there is little question that community relationship would erode."

The following month the final report of the Maine Nonprofit Tax Review Task Force pointed to "respectful but clear disagreement" among its members on the feasibility and desirability of allowing municipalities to impose service charges on exempt organizations. It offered possible guidelines for future consideration, which were themselves the subject of dissent by nonprofit representatives, but made no recommendation. Its statement of the case against such charges summarized the perspective of these institutions: "The tax exempt organizations recognize and sympathize with the financial constraints that are bearing down on municipal government. . . . In fact, they are facing very similar constraints themselves. As a matter of principle, however, the imposition of service charges against the institutions only results in a further deterioration of the nonprofits' capacity to deliver the charitable and educational services which constitute their mission and which provide necessary and complementary benefits to the community and wider society, just as the local governments do."[73]

At the same time, a tax revision commission for the District of Columbia recommended against adoption of a program for payments in lieu of taxes by nonprofit organizations. The treatment of exempt property is of special importance to the District, home to the national government, international organizations and embassies, and numerous philanthropic headquarters. "The Commission did not recommend creating a PILOT program for the District. The Commission was concerned about the opaque and arbitrary nature of such programs and anticipated unnecessary administrative burdens for both nonprofit organizations and the DC Office of Tax and Revenue. Instead, the Commission recommended a local services fee as a simpler, more transparent, and less expensive means to achieve the same goals."[74] However, the local services fee was one of the recommendations that had "proven not to be very popular," and the mayor's budget made no mention of it.[75]

Municipalities and Nonprofits: An Evolving Relationship

Local government fiscal pressure, particularly in an environment in which it is difficult to raise tax rates, will always exist in tension with tax exemptions created at the state level. This may lead to direct challenges to the exemptions, whether through legal actions or efforts to encourage legislative change. It may result in requests for voluntary payments in lieu of taxes or in initiatives to impose fees for local services.

Each of these avenues is itself subject to instability. Direct challenges to exemptions must confront deep legal and political support for many philanthropic endeavors. Voluntary payments are inherently unpredictable. It is in the interest of exempt organizations to stress the nature of such transfers as gifts, while local governments seek ongoing reliable support. These difficulties mean that service charges will often seem the most favorable methods for cities seeking revenue from exempt organizations. However, the political difficulties in imposing jurisdiction-wide charges, seen in the DC and New Orleans examples, and the many instances in which charges limited to nonprofits have been characterized as impermissible taxes, show that this approach presents its own hurdles.

At the same time, changes in the nature of nonprofit operations require continual review to determine the appropriate application of sometimes very broad and historic legislative criteria for exempt status. Widespread awareness of the wealth of individual exempt organizations, such as universities with multibillion-dollar endowments, guarantees that all exemptions will receive scrutiny in times of fiscal constraint. The small amount of revenue raised by PILOTs, together with the inherent unpredictability of voluntary payments, prevent them from playing a major role in resolving this tension. But the important symbolic value of seeking revenue from every potential source in times of fiscal stress ensures that they will continue to be a factor in the evolving relationships between municipalities and the philanthropies that they host.

There is no question but that individual municipalities and exempt organizations can engage in respectful negotiations for PILOTs that benefit both parties, recognizing "that the success of the city depends on the nonprofits and vice versa, and that both sides benefit from economic development, nicer parks, and safer streets."[76] College towns and cities with wealthy medical centers and universities are best situated to obtain significant PILOT revenue from nonprofit organizations.

For other municipalities, it is likely that PILOTS may "generate some much needed revenue for local governments, but considering their ad-hoc and short-term nature, as well as the conflict associated with any arrangement, they do not appear to hold the key to resolving long-term issues."[77]

Creative steps toward resolving specific disputes could have wider implications. The property tax exemption touches on fundamental conceptual questions and immediate revenue needs, the appropriate spheres of charitable and state action, and the appropriate division of legislative and judicial decision making.

Notes

1. Blumenstyk (2013); Offredo (2013).
2. *Frothingham v. Mellon*, 262 U.S. 447, 43 S. Ct. 597, 67 L.Ed. 1078 (1923).
3. E.g., *Ashton Urban Renewal Agency v. Ashton Memorial Inc.*, 155 Id. 309, 311 P.3d 730 (2013).
4. Clotfelter (1989), 679.
5. *Mount Calvary Baptist Church, Inc. v. Dept. of Revenue*, 302 Ill. App. 3d 661, 706 N.E.2d 1008 (1998).
6. *Corporation of the Episcopal Church in Utah v. Utah State Tax Commission*, 919 P.2d 556 (Utah 1996).
7. *Kid's Korner Educare Center, Inc. v. County of Steele*, Nos. C7-97-258-R, C4-98-311-R, C2-98-565-R (Minn. Tax Ct. 1998).
8. *Circle C Child Development Center, Inc. v. Travis Central Appraisal District*, 981 S.W.2d 483 (Tex. App. 1998).
9. Econsult Solutions, Inc. (2013).
10. *Camps Newfound/Owatonna v. Town of Harrison*, 520 U.S. 564 (1997).
11. Sheppard (1997), 1666.
12. Brody (1997), 452.
13. *Hospitalization Utilization Project v. Commonwealth of Pennsylvania*, 507 Pa. 1, 487 A.2d 1306 (1985).
14. *Provena Covenant Medical Center v. Dep't of Revenue*, 236 Ill.2d 368, 925 N.E.2d 1131, 339 Ill. Dec. 10 (2010).
15. *ASA Hospital Corp. v. Town of Morristown*, 28 N.J. Tax 456, 536 (2015).
16. Blumenstyk (2013).
17. *Western Reserve Christian Church Inc. v. Testa*, No. 2011-Q-380 (Ohio Bd. Tax App. 2013).

18. *Dudley v. Kerwick*, 52 N.Y.2d 542, 439 N.Y.S.2d 305, 421 N.E.2d 797 (1981).
19. Lipman (2006).
20. McCluskey and Tretton (2013).
21. E.g., *Rector of St. Bartholomew's Church v. City of New York*, 914 F.2d 348 (2d Cir. 1990).
22. Brody (1998).
23. Leland (2002), 206.
24. *Emerson College v. City of Boston*, 391 Mass. 415; 462 N.E.2d 1098 (1984).
25. 391 Mass. at 424–425, 462 N.E.2d at 1105.
26. E.g., Office of the Attorney General of the State of South Carolina (2014).
27. Office of the Attorney General of the State of North Dakota (2001).
28. Bureau of Governmental Research (2011b), 14.
29. Di Miceli (2013), 851.
30. Spencer (1999), 1.
31. *New York Times* (1995), B9.
32. *Northwestern University v. City of Evanston*, No. 00 C 7309 (N.D. Ill. 2002).
33. Ibid.
34. Anzaldi (2004).
35. Di Miceli (2013).
36. Langley, Kenyon, and Bailin (2012).
37. Ibid.
38. Kenyon, Langley, and Paquin (2012).
39. Levitz (2012).
40. R. I. Gen. Laws § 44-3-9; Rhode Island Department of Administration (2006).
41. *Millennium Park Joint Venture, LLC v. Houlihan*, 241 Ill.2d 281, 948 N.E.2d 1, 349 Ill. Dec. 898 (2010).
42. Cohen (2013).
43. Sjoquist and Stoycheva (2010).
44. Rakow (2013), 5.
45. Di Miceli (2013), 848.
46. Snyder (2013).
47. Ibid., 6.
48. Langley, Kenyon, and Bailin (2012), 34.
49. Ibid., 5, table 3.
50. *Hospital Utilization Project v. Commonwealth of Pennsylvania*, 507 Pa. 1, 487 A.2d 1306 (1985).
51. Glancy (2002), 216.
52. Leland (1994).
53. Ibid.
54. 10 Pa. Stat. §372(b).
55. Snyder (2013).
56. Ibid.

57. *Mesivtah Eitz Chaim of Bobov, Inc. v. Pike County Board of Assessment Appeals,* 615 Pa. 463, 470, 44 A.3d 3, 9 (2012) (citations omitted).
58. Carr (2013a).
59. Carr (2013b).
60. Carr (2013c).
61. DePaul (2014b).
62. Blazina (2013); Urbina (2009).
63. Snyder (2013).
64. Bureau of Governmental Research (1996), 1, 10.
65. Ibid., 1; Bureau of Governmental Research (2011b), 1.
66. Bureau of Governmental Research (2011b), 13.
67. Bureau of Governmental Research (2011a), 5–7.
68. Eggler (2011).
69. Bureau of Governmental Research (2012), 3.
70. DePaul (2014a).
71. Vermont Property Tax Exemption Study Committee (2014).
72. DePaul (2014a).
73. Maine Nonprofit Tax Review Task Force (2014).
74. District of Columbia Tax Revision Commission (2014), 24.
75. Koklanaris (2014), 15.
76. Kenyon and Langley (2011), 176.
77. Sjoquist and Stoycheva (2010).

TAX LIMITATIONS AND MARKET VALUE ASSESSMENT

11 Tax Restrictions and Assessment Limits

M easures to restrict property taxation took on new political importance in the period following the passage of California's Proposition
13 in June 1978. Its influence was felt as early as November 1978, when
Michigan passed the Headlee Amendment on tax and expenditure limitations. The first five years after Proposition 13 saw more than 58 tax
limitation ballot measures.[1] Many dramatic enactments followed, such as
Colorado's Gallagher Amendment, which limited the percentage of assessed value represented by residential property statewide. A decade later
the Colorado Taxpayer Bill of Rights, or TABOR, restricted state and local
revenues and required taxpayer approval for tax rate increases. As the
movement spread, Oregon passed an assessment limit known as Measure
50, while Florida's was termed "Save Our Homes." In Massachusetts, Proposition 2½ contained both a levy limit and a rate limit. After the initial
Headlee Amendment, Michigan instituted Proposal A, an assessment limit
and a revision of its system of school finance.

These and other limitations can be divided into three major categories: assessment limits that restrict the amount by which a specific property's tax valuation can rise in a given year, no matter what the change in
its actual market value; limits that restrict the property tax rate; and levy
limits that restrict the amount by which the levy, or tax revenue collected,
may increase. Each approach has different effects and different potential
drawbacks. For example, an assessment limit may not prevent tax bills
from rising if tax rates are unconstrained; rate limitations will not address
shifting tax burdens across property classes; and levy limits will not restrict the growth of an individual taxpayer's annual bill.

The major standards for evaluating taxes often include such criteria as horizontal equity—the equitable treatment of similarly situated taxpayers; vertical equity—the equitable treatment of taxpayers in different situations; transparency; simplicity; predictability; administrative efficiency; and revenue adequacy. Limitation measures illustrate the choices that must be made when these goals conflict.

Some advocates of tax limits are acknowledged opponents of the property tax who see limitations as a step toward disabling it as a significant fiscal instrument. Others value the property tax as a stable source of autonomous local revenue but face the challenge of fashioning a response to political demands for tax constraints. For this group, it is troubling that some well-known limitations, such as Proposition 13 and the British Council Tax, have greatly eroded local government autonomy.

Assessment limits address the serious concern that dramatic changes in relative values may produce unexpected tax increases. But by undermining uniformity in taxation, they can reduce support for significant levels of property taxation. Thus, it is important to begin any analysis of assessment limits by considering the assessment and budget practices that may forestall tax revolts at the outset. In the late 1970s, many states, such as Massachusetts and New York, faced massive redistribution of their tax burdens when courts were prepared to order compliance with long-ignored requirements of full-value assessment. Failure to keep values up to date ensures taxpayer dissatisfaction when a delayed reassessment reflects years of market changes.

Of course, accurately tracking values in a rapidly increasing market will also burden taxpayers if tax rates are not correspondingly reduced. Although accurate assessments were blamed by some for Proposition 13, the failure to reduce tax rates was the cause of rising tax bills.[2] "Truth in Taxation" provisions seek to bring public attention to value-driven tax increases, where revenues rise while tax rates are held constant. These measures apply the same procedural requirements, such as notice and public hearings, to revenue increases due to increased values as to actual changes in tax rates.[3] There are also methods for assisting individual taxpayers, from "circuit breaker" relief based on income[4] to payment deferral for senior citizens. Adjustment of municipal budgets and tax rates to maintain stability requires consistent attention, and neglect of any of these elements sets the stage for disruptive change and unanticipated consequences.

Assessment Limits and Rate Limits

No tax is completely unconstrained, and the desirability of rate, assessment, or levy restrictions depends largely on assumptions about the method by which government spending is determined. These assumptions are central to understanding voter support for state tax limitations on local government. Local budget decisions can be analyzed as responses to voter preferences, with residents at the center of the political spectrum always holding the power to replace elected officials whose spending does not conform to their wishes. From this perspective, those seeking by majority vote to impose a tax limitation measure could instead exercise their ballot power and replace high-spending officials with more frugal political rivals.

At the other extreme, the Leviathan model, whose name harks back to Thomas Hobbes, considers government to operate, like any other monopolist, with the goal of maximizing revenue. As Professor Therese McGuire has written, "If the median-voter/benevolent-dictator model is operative, then property tax limits have little economic justification. If the budget maximizing/Leviathan model of local government behavior is operative, then property tax limits may be justified as a means to constrain inefficient, wasteful spending on the part of elected officials and bureaucrats."[5] Voters who do not feel empowered to replace local officials may support restrictions on local taxes and expenditures.[6]

This situation poses a critical empirical question: Is it possible for a property tax allocated according to accurate market values to respond to tax limitation pressure while remaining a significant source of independent local revenue? Assessment limits increase the predictability of future tax obligations, but sacrifice uniformity. Many tax limitation measures have the effect, intended or not, of greatly reducing local government autonomy. The Massachusetts experience discussed in the next chapter offers one example of a tax limitation that preserved both a market value tax base and the role of the property tax as a vital source of independent local revenue.

Although between 15 and 20 states now impose some form of assessment limit, the impact of these measures varies greatly.[7] It is the operation of the limit, rather than the form it takes, that determines the severity of the restriction. A levy limit that permits no growth in collections, as has been the case in Wisconsin, is far more restrictive than an assessment limit that allows an annual 10 percent growth in taxable value, as in Arizona or Maryland.[8] Many enactments combine several of these elements.

Assessment limits have been the most familiar form of property tax restrictions since Proposition 13 made purchase price, not market value, the basic standard for assessment in California. Proposition 13 also limited the tax rate to 1 percent, with additions for voter-approved debt and special assessments. The Massachusetts tax limit followed Proposition 13 and became known as Proposition 2½ because it restricted levy growth to 2½ percent annually—a severe restriction, particularly because at the time of its passage national inflation reached double-digit levels. But Proposition 2½ also limited the property tax rate to 2½ percent, a very high ceiling if applied to accurate assessed valuations. The fact that the rate limit was set at 2½ percent gives evidence of the extremely inaccurate assessments in place in Massachusetts at the time.

California's Proposition 13 set the pattern for a number of other state programs, such as the "Save Our Homes" amendment to the Florida constitution or Michigan's 1994 Proposal A. These assess a base-year value rather than current market value, with modest annual inflation adjustments (no more than 2 percent in California, 3 percent in Florida, and 5 percent in Michigan). The base-year value is then increased to market value upon a change in ownership. This approach solves the problem of uncertainty and "insurance value." California purchasers can predict their maximum future tax liability with precision.

A property's maximum assessment is rigidly constrained under an acquisition value system, but a drop in market values below that limit will generally cause assessed value to fall as well. The assessment cannot rise above the inflation-adjusted acquisition value, but in most cases it can fall by any amount—and rise by any amount—so long as it remains below that limit. It is a tribute to the optimism born of a long history of rising house prices in California that Proposition 13 did not even address potential declines in value when it was passed in 1978. Six months later this oversight was corrected by Proposition 8, which called for assessment upon the lower of a property's Proposition 13 value or its current market value. This means that in a period of declining prices tax revenue can drop precipitously.

As late as 2008, confidence in real estate values led analysts to predict that "in times of falling property values, assessment growth continues under an acquisition value system, because the new, substantially higher values from changes of ownership, new construction, and the 2 percent inflation factor are likely to exceed the Proposition 8 decline-in-value assessments."[9] In fact, areas of California hard hit by the subsequent housing downturn experienced considerable declines in their tax base, with one in four properties reassessed to market levels in 2010–2011.[10] The total assessed value of Riverside County declined 15 percent between 2008 and 2011.[11] Properties reassessed to market value can see their assessments rise by any amount in a given year, sometimes to the surprise of their owners, so long as the assessment does not exceed the Proposition 13 value.

An acquisition value system generally rewards longtime property owners at the expense of more recent purchasers. Los Angeles resident Stephanie Nordlinger based her ultimately unsuccessful U.S. Supreme Court challenge to Proposition 13 on the fact that the tax on her condominium was many times the amount paid by longtime owners of identical property.[12] As Justice John Paul Stevens wrote in his dissent, "The specific disparity that prompted petitioner to challenge the constitutionality of Proposition 13 is the fact that her annual property tax bill is almost 5 times as large as that of her neighbors who own comparable homes. . . . This disparity is not unusual under Proposition 13. Indeed, some homeowners pay 17 times as much in taxes as their neighbors with comparable property. For vacant land, the disparities may be as great as 500 to 1."[13]

By design, an assessment limit undermines the distribution of the tax burden according to property value. A Florida legislative study estimated that the 1995 assessment limit in that state had resulted in approximately one-quarter of total taxable value being taken off the tax rolls in a decade.[14] In 2012 the mayor of Columbus, Georgia, commented on the assessment freeze there: "Our tax freeze protects only those people who have lived in one house for a long time and not improved it since they bought it. It protects no one else. In fact, it disadvantages everyone else. So we see wildly disproportionate tax assessments. Nearly 27,500 homeowners in Muscogee County pay less than $500 in property taxes. Over 7,500 homeowners pay less than $50—and we mean way less. You may be paying $5,000 a year in property taxes, and your neighbor is paying one dollar. It's called 'horizontal inequity.'"[15] Considerations such as these have led Professor Keith Ihlanfeldt to conclude that the property tax cannot be a "good tax" unless it is based on accurate market values—leading again to the question of whether a market value system can respond to political pressure for tax limitations.[16]

A reduction in local autonomy may be one of the most serious effects of assessment limits, whether this is a direct goal of opponents of local taxation or an unintended consequence of reducing revenue under local control. To the extent decentralization permits greater flexibility, citizen involvement, and accountability in local taxation and service provision, diminished local autonomy is a loss to taxpayers and residents.

One California analyst observed that Proposition 13 "effectively transferred control of the property tax from local governments to the state government. . . . Proposition 13 required that the state become the final arbiter in deciding who receives local property tax revenues and how much they receive."[17] As the California Legislative Analyst's Office explains, "Unlike local communities in other states, California residents and local officials have virtually no control over the distribution of property tax revenue to local governments. Instead, all major decisions regarding property tax allocation are controlled by the state. Accordingly, if residents desire an enhanced level of a particular service, there is no local forum or mechanism to allow property taxes to be reallocated among local governments to finance this improvement."[18]

Pre–Proposition 13 tax receipts, and therefore 1970s local government service levels, serve as the starting point for California's property tax allocation system. A particularly dramatic example of the distortions that can ensue concerns the Los Trancos Water District in San Mateo County, which continues to receive a property tax allocation reflecting its services in the 1970s, even though the entire water distribution system was sold to a private company in 2005.[19] The allocation of tax revenue has been continually revised for such purposes as funding an "Educational Revenue Augmentation Fund" [ERAF], a "Second ERAF Shift," a "Triple Flip" in which the state used local sales tax revenue to repay bonds and reimbursed localities with ERAF payments, and a "VLF Swap," in which the state reduced localities' share of vehicle license fees and shifted further funds from ERAF. With admirable understatement, the Legislative Analyst's Office notes that this system "makes it difficult for taxpayers to see which entities receive their tax dollars."[20]

Other Types of Tax Limits

The basic models of assessment limits, rate limits, and levy limits by no means exhaust the potential for creative variation, particularly with regard to the share of the tax borne by different classes of property. Every form of tax limitation carries its own set of benefits and drawbacks, some of them unanticipated.

Colorado

In Colorado, the Gallagher Amendment sets an unusual restriction on the property tax base. It does not limit individual values or total values, but it permanently restricts the residential portion of the total property tax base *statewide* to 45 percent. After the Gallagher Amendment was approved in 1982, the assessment ratio for residential property, or the proportion of full market value represented by assessed value, was reduced from 30 percent to 21 percent, and the assessment ratio for nonresidential property was reduced to 29 percent. In every succeeding year the residential assessment ratio has been adjusted to maintain the residential percentage of total taxable value at 45 percent, while the nonresidential assessment ratio has remained at 29 percent. The residential assessment ratio dropped to 15 percent in 1990, fell below 10 percent in 2000, and reached 7.96 percent in 2011–2012.[21] A 2003 ballot measure to fix the residential rate permanently at 8 percent failed by more than a 3 to 1 margin.[22]

The 45 percent limit in Colorado considers only the total value of taxable residential and nonresidential property in the state as a whole.

Each individual county then applies the resulting assessment percentages to its own property values, and the fiscal impact there will depend on its combination of residential and nonresidential property. A largely residential county could see its tax base greatly reduced, with its residential property assessed at less than 10 percent of its value and with little nonresidential property available to be assessed at three times that amount. On the other hand, a largely nonresidential county can benefit from the higher nonresidential assessment ratio regardless of service demands or revenue needs. A decade after the Gallagher Amendment was passed, the Colorado Taxpayer's Bill of Rights, or TABOR, required advance voter approval for any tax rate increase, restricting both local governments' ability to adjust rates in response to this reduction in the local tax base and the state's ability to increase the residential assessment ratio.[23]

TABOR has been nationally influential and endlessly controversial. In 2011 a group of current and past legislators and local officials brought a legal challenge charging that by limiting the legislature's taxing powers TABOR violates the U.S. Constitution's guarantee clause, which requires that states be established with a "republican form of government." In 2014 the Court of Appeals for the Tenth Circuit held that the plaintiffs had legal standing to bring this action, a decision that was vacated and remanded by the U.S. Supreme Court in 2015.[24]

New York City and Nassau County

The New York State legislature responded to judicial rejection of a longstanding but unsanctioned system of fractional assessment[25] by acting to maintain the existing class shares of the property tax burden. Property in New York City and Nassau County was divided into four classes—basically, one-, two-, and three-family homes; apartment houses and other residential property; utilities; and all other property—with their proportion of the total tax collections preserved, changing only to reflect new construction. Individual Class One residential taxable values in New York City and Nassau County may grow no more than 6 percent annually and no more than 20 percent over five years.[26]

In addition to redistributing the tax burden, these complicated formulas also greatly reduce the transparency of the tax. In 2007 the city's commissioner of finance testified, "The law is far too complicated. New York City and Nassau County are the only places in the State with fractional assessments, which means people often have to do math just to understand the market value of their property. . . . The caps are incredibly confusing and most taxpayers don't understand that the caps limit the growth of assessments, not taxes or market values."[27] The tax rates themselves give evidence of this nontransparency. The rate for Class One residential property was 19.191 percent in 2013–2014, far above the 10.323 percent rate on Class Four commercial real estate.[28] But the Class One rate is applied against 6 percent of market value, while the rate for all other property is applied against 45 percent of market value.[29] Although the rate on Class One property appears to be almost twice that of the rate on Class Four property, the effective tax rate on Class Four property is more than four times the effective tax rate on Class One property.

A particularly important aspect of New York City property taxes concerns the manner in which valuation rules can function as relatively invisible assessment limits. For example, state law requires that condominiums and cooperatives be valued "at a sum not exceeding the assessment which would be placed upon such parcel were the parcel not owned or leased by a cooperative corporation or on a condominium basis."[30] This means that even extremely expensive luxury units are valued by reference to sometimes nonexistent comparable rental apartments. As a result, renters, who are generally less affluent than owners of cooperative and condominium units, bear a heavier tax burden. In 2015 the New York City Independent Budget Office reported that this valuation provision resulted in a citywide 83 percent reduction in the tax that would otherwise be payable on condominiums and cooperative apartments. "Apartments in Brooklyn (84.9 percent) receive the largest discount and apartments in the Bronx (68.4 percent) receive the smallest."[31]

In 1997 the effective tax rate for rental buildings was 1.8 times higher than for cooperatives; a decade later, the multiple had increased to 5.5.[32] In 2012 the New York Times reported that an apartment at the Plaza Hotel sold for $48 million but was valued for tax purposes at $1.7 million; one at Columbus Circle sold for $30.55 million but was valued at $2 million; and one on Central Park West sold for $88 million but was valued at $2.97 million.[33] Researchers at New York University identified 50 individual cooperative apartments that were sold in 2012 for amounts greater than the assessed market value of the entire building in which they were located.[34] This valuation provision would not be found under any survey of assessment limits, but its effects can be even more dramatic than recognized tax limitation measures.

Oregon

Oregon's constitution long required voter approval for levy increases exceeding 6 percent. In 1990 a ballot measure imposed rate limits of 0.5 percent for education taxes and 1 percent for general government purposes, with bond levies and some specific taxes exempt from these limits. An assessment limit patterned on Proposition 13 was approved by the voters in 1996 and reformulated as Measure 50 in 1997. Just as Proposition 13 turned back the initial base year for assessments to 1975–1976, Measure 50 established a similar base year of 1995–1996. However, the Oregon limitation is far more complex than Proposition 13, containing 19 sections and nearly 100 subsections. The standard concept of market value is now termed "real market value."[35] The initial maximum assessed value for the tax year 1997–1998 was set at the property's real market value for 1995–1996, reduced by 10 percent.[36] Thereafter, maximum assessed value is defined as the greater of 103 percent of the property's assessed value from the prior year, or 100 percent of the property's maximum assessed value from the prior year, with adjustments for new construction and other changes in the property.[37] This limit does not apply to taxes for pensions, bonds, or local option levies.[38]

A series of ballot measures and legislative enactments have given Oregon one of the nation's most complex property tax systems. A 2013 report by the City Club of Portland admitted, "This primer describes neither all the manipulations of Oregon's property tax system nor all of its features. The system is too complicated. . . . Neither experts nor members of your committee who studied it for eight months could answer significant questions about Oregon's property tax system. Its complexity appeared as one of the system's major weaknesses."[39] The report noted that the tax limitations could encourage the creation of new special districts as a means of diverting restricted revenue and that owners whose taxes were limited could nonetheless vote for tax increases that would only affect other properties. Two professors at Willamette University concluded: "Quick-witted financial officers in districts with approved levies soon realized that they could increase their share simply by raising their tax rates (as long as subsequent revenue was less than the approved levy)—which could be done without affecting their residents' tax payments. Instead, their gain came at the expense of other jurisdictions sharing the common tax base."[40]

Many Oregon taxpayers still anticipate that their assessments will reflect market value and that considerations of uniformity will govern valuation. But as the Oregon Tax Court has written, this is "fundamentally mistaken."[41] "Plaintiff's reliance on the assessed values assigned to his neighbors is also not persuasive. At one point, uniformity of assessment was an important consideration. . . . [W]ith Measure 50, the touchstone is the historical assessed value of the property. How those assessed values compare across properties over time, and their relative disparities, is not a cause for correcting the tax roll."[42] In other cases, taxpayers who purchased property at less than its assessed value have found no recourse,[43] and owners have been surprised by double-digit tax increases—a common situation in acquisition-value systems after a period of price declines.[44]

The most unusual feature of the Oregon system, and its greatest departure from the California model, lies in the absence of a reassessment to market value on a change in ownership. Reassessment on sale was fundamental to Proposition 13's underlying concept of fairness, since new purchasers took their property with full knowledge of future tax liabilities. Reassessment on sale also allows periodic calibration of assessments to market value, an adjustment no longer available in Oregon. Gentrified sections of Portland have experienced rapid price increases since 1995, far above 3 percent annually, while other areas have seen much less appreciation, leading to vastly different effective tax rates. As Portland commissioner Steve Novick wrote, "In some cases, the differences are startling:

you can literally have one property owner in the outer East Side paying $3,000 in taxes on a house that is actually worth $200,000, and someone in inner Northeast paying $600 in taxes on a house worth $300,000."[45] This was in a comment entitled, "Our Goofy Property Tax System."

Any system that freezes assessed values without regard to future changes in market price presents the most serious problem of nonuniformity in property taxation. Basing taxes on past values ensures that areas in economic decline will bear a heavier effective tax rate than affluent neighborhoods. Because the New York State legislature shielded Nassau County from implementing court-ordered revaluation, for decades the county used 1938 construction costs and 1964 land prices as the basis for its assessments. However, as noted in chapter 3, it was forced to undertake a revaluation in 2003 in the face of civil rights actions charging that decades of failure to reassess placed a disproportionate tax burden on largely minority neighborhoods with declining values relative to more prosperous areas experiencing rising home prices.[46]

This situation demonstrated the unintended consequences of explicit and unacknowledged assessment limits, both those enacted by the legislature and those resulting from administrative neglect. As described in chapter 6, the 2003 reassessment caused residential assessments to rise far above the 6 percent allowed in New York City and Nassau County. When taxpayers challenged these new values, New York's highest court was faced with the choice of impeding the legislative assessment limit or blocking the settlement of the civil rights action. It found that by using a fractional assessment ratio of 1 percent, that is, reducing the new assessments to 1 percent of the new values and correspondingly adjusting the tax rate, Nassau County could comply with the assessment limits, since the nominal increases were less than 6 percent of the prior year's unadjusted values.[47] A dissenting opinion argued, "To uphold what the county has done the majority must first decide that 'assessment' in the statute does not mean 'assessed value'—the actual value of the property as determined by the assessor—but 'fractional assessment'—the amount obtained after assessed value is multiplied by a percentage. The key, of course, is that the assessed value cannot be changed arbitrarily, but the percentage used to multiply it, and thus the fractional assessment, can be."[48]

Cook County, Illinois

In Illinois, the Cook County assessor, whose jurisdiction includes the city of Chicago, obtained legislative authorization in 2003 to limit annual assessment increases on qualifying owner-occupied property to 7 percent, with a maximum value reduction in any one year of $20,000.[49] Restriction of the "seven percent solution" to homesteads shifted a portion of the Chicago levy to commercial, industrial, and rental properties. But where this shift was permitted in New York City on a permanent basis, the politically active and well-organized business taxpayers in Chicago succeeded in restricting this provision to a series of three-year periods, with its last effects to expire in 2014.

The Institute of Government and Public Affairs (IGPA) at the University of Illinois prepared an exhaustive analysis of the effects of this limit in 2006.[50] It found that eligible homeowners saved an average of 14.2 percent on their tax bills, with correspondingly higher taxes on business property and apartment buildings. As a policy matter, it questioned the assessor's emphasis on the proportion of the total tax paid by homestead property and by business property before and after imposition of the cap.[51] The report took the position that "there is nothing in Illinois tax law or, as we read it, principles of tax policy concerning aggregate tax shares by class."[52]

This is a core challenge to efforts to maintain stable class shares of total property tax payments despite changes in the relative values of different property classes. If commercial and industrial property values rise at a lower rate than residences, should class shares change to reflect that difference? A limit on assessment increases addresses the problem of unpredictable rises in the tax bills of individual homeowners. Restricting the share of the total tax base contributed by any class of property, as the Colorado experience demonstrates, is far more problematic. It does not respond to any particular index of need and may favor property owners who least require assistance.

The report noted that "Illinois politicians and journalists sometimes refer to the assessment cap as 'the seven percent solution.'" The authors pointed out that this phrase has its origin in a Sherlock Holmes story referring to cocaine use and make this provocative observation: "Special tax provisions have an addictive quality, in that they create distortion and in-equities, which create a case for other special provisions, which begs for even more."[53]

Great Britain: "Banding" of Residential Property

The property tax in Britain can be traced to Elizabethan times, but residential property taxes, or rates, were in fact terminated there in 1990. Although Prime Minister Margaret Thatcher had a deep and well-known animus toward the property tax, the immediate cause for this upheaval was a long delay in revaluation. The last general revaluation of property in Britain before Mrs. Thatcher took office was conducted in 1973. In 1979, she responded to the political problem of updating values with the statement, "There's no problem. We're not doing it."[54] Another decade of rapid value increases for homes in southeast England only increased fear that a shift to accurate market values would be so disruptive as to be unacceptable.

While appreciating the difficulties of maintaining a value-based tax, many observers found Mrs. Thatcher's insistence on replacing it with a per-person charge, or poll tax, nothing short of astonishing. As the nineteenth-century American economist Edwin Seligman had observed, "[A]s the social conscience develops, more stress is laid on other elements of ability to pay than on mere number. . . . The poll tax becomes unjust and is gradually abolished."[55] Public reaction to the poll tax, officially known as the Community Charge, paralleled the rejection of a poll tax instituted by Richard II more than 600 years earlier. One commentator wrote, "Surely no modern tax has created such rancour, cost so much to collect and also not to collect, contributed so greatly to the unpopularity and eventual downfall of a prime minister and temporarily shaken a government's confidence through by-election failure."[56] This dispute over local property taxes actually helped end the term of office of the century's longest serving British prime minister.

The poll tax was quickly replaced by a "Council Tax," a residential property tax that is not based on exact values. Instead, each home is assigned to a class or band of value, and all properties in a given band pay

TABLE 2

Valuation Bands for Great Britain

Band	Value	Percent of Band D Tax
A	Under £40,000	66.6
B	£40,001–£52,000	77.7
C	£52,001–£68,000	88.8
D	£68,001–£88,000	100
E	£88,001–£120,000	122.2
F	£120,001–£160,000	144.4
G	£160,001–£320,000	166.6
H	Over £320,000	200

SOURCE: Valuation Office Agency (2014), Section 1.2.

the same amount of tax. Homes of lowest value are assigned to Band A, and homes of the highest value to Band H. Band D is intended to represent the average tax, with all other bands taxed in proportion to the amount paid on a Band D house (see Table 2).

The most expensive homes in Britain are worth enormously more than the top band value of £320,000, but their tax is limited to twice the amount paid by a Band D home worth £88,000 or less. Within each band, the tax declines as a percentage of market value as values increase, and this phenomenon accelerates dramatically as values rise above £320,000. Scotland and Wales also divide residential property into bands, with slight variations in the numerical values assigned to each band.

The great political drama surrounding the poll tax to some extent obscured the impact of these changes on local fiscal autonomy. When residential property taxes were abolished, business property taxes were retained but nationalized. The central government set a uniform tax rate and distributed tax proceeds on the basis of population.[57] Replacement of the poll tax by the Council Tax was accompanied by another blow to local autonomy.

> A few days before announcing the structure of the new council tax, the Government announced . . . that all local tax bills were to be reduced retrospectively by about one third, and grants increased from central

government to compensate, financed by an increase from 15 to 17.5% in the national rate of value added tax. At a stroke therefore the whole balance between central and local government services was altered ... and all pretence at promoting "accountability" through a close correlation between increases in expenditure on local services and the level of the local tax has been dropped.[58]

The Council Tax was therefore an instrument of tax reduction, redistribution—some of it perhaps unintended—and centralization of financial control.

Thoughtful commentators have suggested that the banding may be "a reasonable compromise between ability-to-pay and benefits-received criteria ... a system that preserves relative stability in relative property tax valuations, thereby eliminating one degree of individual taxpayer uncertainty."[59] Yet it is not clear if political acceptance of the banding approach is sufficiently strong in Britain to allow even one revaluation. Although Wales completed a successful revaluation in 2005,[60] Britain has been politically unable to take this step. A complete absence of revaluation is one form of insurance against unexpected changes in assessment, but at the price of increasingly arbitrary tax burdens. A reassessment would result in some properties being reassigned to higher bands, a change potentially more disruptive in individual cases than an increase in tax based on discrete assessed values.

The first update to the 1991 valuations on which the Council Tax is based was planned for 2005. Of course, 14 years is far too long for a change in values to be politically acceptable—the 1973 general revaluation was only six years old when Mrs. Thatcher first refused to undertake a reassessment. After investing tens of millions of pounds in drawing up new valuation rolls, the government announced in September 2005 that revaluation would be postponed until 2009 at the earliest. The U.K. Institute of Revenues Rating and Valuation (IRRV) expressed deep disappointment with this delay. In his annual address, the IRRV president stated, "The last postponement led to the discrediting of a perfectly sound system of local taxation and the introduction of the ill-fated poll tax."[61] A member of the IRRV Council called the postponement "a triumph of ignorance and political expediency over reason and fairness."[62] The next step in this sequence was predictable: in September 2010 the government announced that no revaluation would be undertaken during the current Parliament.[63] In 2011 the Mirrlees Review of the U.K. tax system by a set of international experts concluded, "Part of the problem now is that a revaluation has been avoided for so long that changes in relative tax liabilities would be very substantial. But as council tax valuations have passed the milestone of being 20 years out of date, the absurdity of the status quo becomes ever more apparent. Any property tax requires regular revaluations, and this process should begin as soon as possible."[64]

The Council Tax reduced property taxes and effectively quelled the revolt incited by the poll tax. However, its acceptance has been accompanied by a freeze on banded values, with accompanying distributional problems, and by a reduction in local fiscal autonomy. Implementation of the Council Tax in Britain cannot be considered a success if its stability rests on assessments that have not changed in more than two decades.

Assessment Limits: Winners and Losers

Many researchers have noted that assessment limits produce "winners" and "losers" among affected taxpayers. This is not surprising when limits are restricted to particular property classes, such as homestead property, and do not affect other taxpayers, such as business property owners. What is often unexpected is the existence of winners and losers even within the favored classes eligible for the limited assessments. As researchers at the University of Illinois noted, "If expenditures remain constant, the limits should lower taxes for favored groups such as homestead properties by raising taxes for groups whose assessments are not restricted—an expected result that comes as no surprise. The surprise is that taxes also go up for many property owners in the favored groups."[65]

Higher tax rates are needed to compensate for the limited tax base if revenues are to stay level. All properties pay the higher tax rate, and for those not subject to the assessment limit this clearly produces a heavier tax bill—the product of a higher rate with no reduction in the base. But even among properties whose assessments are lowered, the increase in the tax rate will offset some of the benefit of a decreased tax base. Low-value properties experiencing appreciation that is only slightly above the assessment limit may owe more taxes as a result of the limit if the reduction in the assessment of high-value properties is dramatic enough to require an increase in the tax rate. For example, Chicago senior citizens whose assessed values were "frozen"[66] received no benefit from the Cook County assessment limit but were subject to the resulting higher tax rate.

The phenomenon of winners and losers even among the favored classes has been observed in other states. In New York City, the commissioner of finance wrote, "If you were to scan the *New York Times* Real Estate Section on any Sunday, you could probably find an owner of a $1 million brownstone in Park Slope, one of the wealthiest neighborhoods in Brooklyn, paying less tax than the owner of a $1 million home in Bedford-Stuyvesant, one of Brooklyn's less wealthy neighborhoods. Why? The limits on assessment increases tend to provide larger benefits in neighborhoods where sales prices are rising fast and smaller benefits in those neighborhoods where values are rising modestly."[67] The Minnesota Department of Revenue studied the effect of that state's limits on assessment increases and found that more than one-third of the properties in the favored categories and more than 84 percent of all residential homesteads across the state faced higher tax bills as a result.[68]

The lack of transparency in limited assessment systems can leave even winners feeling that they are losers. As noted, a limitation measure that allows specific capped value increases each year, such as Proposition 13, can surprise taxpayers who see their assessments rise sharply, although not above the inflation-adjusted limit, after a period of market decline. When this occurred in Michigan after the 2007–2009 recession, a lawmaker introduced a proposed constitutional amendment to limit assessments when values rise but freeze them when values fall.[69] Similarly, some homes in New York City covered by the assessment cap saw values rise even after damage from Hurricane Sandy in 2012. News reports attacked these increases as "cruel," "totally insensitive," "heartless," and "unconscionable," while a Finance Department spokesman explained that "any tax hikes are part of a capped, state-approved five-year formula for setting assessment levels."[70]

Winners can also feel that they are losers when their situations change. The initial effort to reduce taxes by limiting assessment increases can give rise to different pressure when property owners face a lock-in effect, a disincentive to move if a change in ownership leads to assessment at the sale value of their new home, as in California. Tax provisions that impede mobility may reduce the efficiency of housing markets and ill serve taxpayers who would benefit from different living arrangements. This led Florida to introduce "portability" for the tax reductions enjoyed by owners under the state's assessment limit, as fear of being taxed out of a home was replaced by fear of being locked into a home.[71] California offers a more limited form of portability, in some circumstances allowing owners to carry a portion of their tax savings to a new residence. The danger of lock-in can be real, with estimates of the average increase in ownership duration because of assessment limits rising as high as 7.5 years.[72] But portability illustrates the addictive quality of special tax provisions, as the problems raised by one limitation give rise to new complexities in which assessed value represents neither market value nor purchase price but carries over tax benefits enjoyed on an earlier residence.

Assessment limits address the problem of volatility in property taxation, but at a heavy price. They can undermine the distribution of the tax according to property value, providing the greatest benefit to the most expensive property experiencing the most rapid price appreciation. Their complexity diminishes the transparency and accountability that are among the greatest strengths of the property tax. When tax limitations are under consideration as necessary responses to pressure for tax relief, alternative approaches that maintain the integrity of the valuation rolls should be considered first. These would include restrictions on tax rates, deferrals and other extended payment options, "circuit breaker" relief for owners whose taxes are disproportionate to their income, and limitations on collections, which are the subject of the case study in the next chapter.

Notes

1. O'Sullivan, Sexton, and Sheffrin (1995), 1.
2. Schrag (1998).
3. Cornia and Walters (2005).
4. Bowman et al. (2009).
5. McGuire (1999), 130.
6. Brooks and Phillips (2009).
7. Haveman and Sexton (2008), 11, table 1.
8. Wisc. Stat. § 66.0602 (This levy may grow to reflect net new construction.); Ariz. Rev. Stat. § 42-13301 (Increases in assessed value are limited to the greater of either: [1] 10 percent of prior year's limited property value or [2] 25 percent of the difference between last year's limited property value and current fair market value.); Md. Code Ann. Tax-Property § 9-105.
9. Doerr (2008), 312–313.
10. California Legislative Analyst's Office (2012), 29.
11. Ibid., 30.
12. *Nordlinger v. Hahn*, 505 U.S. 1, 112 S. Ct. 2326, 120 L.Ed.2d 1 (1992).
13. Ibid., 505 U.S. 29, 112 S. Ct. 2341–2342, 120 L.Ed. 24 (1992) (dissenting) (citations omitted).
14. Florida Legislative Office of Economic and Demographic Research (2007).
15. Tomlinson (2012).
16. Ihlanfeldt (2013).
17. Shires (1999), 7–8.
18. California Legislative Analyst's Office (2012), 24.
19. Ibid., 25.
20. Ibid., 24.
21. Colorado Department of Local Affairs, Division of Property Taxation (2013).
22. Bunch (2003).
23. Colo. Const. Art. X, § 20 (4).
24. *Kerr v. Hickenlooper*, 744 F.3d 1156 (10th Cir. 2014), *vacated and remanded, Hickenlooper v. Kerr*, 135 S. Ct. 2927 (2015).
25. *Hellerstein v. Assessor of Islip*, 37 N.Y.2d 1, 332 N.E.2d 279, 271 N.Y.S.2d 388 (1975).
26. N. Y. Real Prop. Tax Law § 1805 (1).
27. Stark (2007), 2–3.
28. New York City Department of Finance (2014b).
29. New York City Department of Finance (2014a).
30. N.Y. Real Prop. Tax Law § 581 (1)(a).
31. New York City Independent Budget Office (2015), 3.
32. New York City Independent Budget Office (2006), 25.
33. Harris (2012).
34. Furman Center for Real Estate and Urban Policy (2013), 3.
35. Or. Const. Art. XI, § 11(2)(a).

36. Or. Const. Art. XI, § 11(1)(b).
37. Or. Const. Art. XI, § 11(1)(b); Or. Rev. Stat. § 308.146.
38. Or. Const. Art. XI, § 11 (11).
39. City Club of Portland (2013), 36.
40. Thompson and Walker (2014), 274.
41. *Gall v. Dep't of Revenue*, 17 O.T.R. 268, 270 (2003).
42. *McKee v. Clackamas County Assessor*, TC-MD 050249A (Or. Tax Ct., Magistrate Div., November 18, 2005).
43. *McCollum v. Multnomah County Assessor*, TC-MD 050483A (Or. Tax Ct., Magistrate Div., November 18, 2005).
44. *Kirkpatrick v. Lane County Assessor*, TC-MD 050346A (Or. Tax Ct., Magistrate Div., November 18, 2005).
45. Novick, "Our Goofy Property Tax System."
46. *Coleman v. County of Nassau*, Index No. 97-30380 (Sup. Ct. Nassau Co., March 29, 2000); Lambert (2003).
47. *O'Shea v. Board of Assessors of Nassau County*, 8 N.Y.3d 249, 864 N.E.2d 1261, 832 N.Y.S.2d 862 (2007).
48. Ibid., 8 N.Y.3d 249, 261–262, 864 N.E.2d 1268, 832 N.Y.S.2d 870 (dissenting).
49. Ill. P.L. 93-715.
50. Dye, McMillen, and Merriman (2006).
51. Cook County Assessor's Office (2005), 9–10.
52. Dye, McMillen, and Merriman (2006), 712.
53. Ibid., 715.
54. Butler, Adonis, and Travers (1994), 61.
55. Seligman (1939), 10.
56. Thomas (2002).
57. Slack (2004).
58. Farrington (1992), 191.
59. Sheffrin (2010a), 259. See also Sheffrin (2013), ch. 3.
60. Sheffrin (2013), 100–109.
61. Institute of Revenues, Rating and Valuation (2005), 22.
62. Dixon (2005), 11.
63. Siddique (2010).
64. Mirrlees et al. (2011), 383.
65. Dye and McMillen (2007), 9.
66. 35 Ill. Comp. Stat. 200/15-170.
67. Stark (2007), 3–4.
68. Minnesota Department of Revenue (2007), 15.
69. Hart (2009); Cornish (2008).
70. Calder (2013).
71. Cheung and Cunningham (2011).
72. Hodge, Sands, and Skidmore (2015).

12 Tax Limitations and Accurate Assessments: The Massachusetts Experience

The limitation measures that followed Proposition 13 took many forms, with different effects on the structure of the property tax. Some, such as assessment limits, deliberately change the market value basis for taxation. Others, including rate limits and procedural requirements for public approval of tax increases, can preserve an accurate system of property assessment. One approach limits the tax levy, or overall revenue, without distorting individual assessments. In 2010, New Jersey enacted a measure designed to restrict increases in property tax collections to 2 percent annually, and one year later New York State adopted a similar ceiling on property tax revenues.[1] In this way two extremely influential states have chosen a fundamentally different approach to property tax limitations than the one introduced by California's Proposition 13 more than 30 years ago. Proposition 13 limited annual increases in taxable property values, while New York and New Jersey have limited property tax revenues. Massachusetts enacted a stringent levy limit in 1980, and its experience provides an example of a tax restriction built on a system of accurate assessments.

The Property Tax in Massachusetts

Many observers were surprised that Massachusetts joined the post–Proposition 13 property tax revolt, because high property taxes were a long-established feature of its fiscal landscape. For more than 20 years it ranked among the four top states in property taxes per capita.[2] However, this history did not inoculate it from the "perfect storm" of extremely high property tax rates, outdated assessments, and a court-ordered revaluation that threatened to shift tax burdens dramatically from business property to residences. In this respect the Massachusetts situation resembled that of New York State, where literally centuries of judicial willingness to condone fractional assessment systems were replaced with a new activism supporting legal requirements of full-value assessment.

The Massachusetts requirement of "proportional and reasonable assessments," with no provision for different effective tax rates on different classes of property, is even older than its 1780 constitution, dating back to the provincial charter granted by William and Mary in 1691.[3] However, as in most states, courts long held to the fiction that assessments at a fraction of full market value could also be uniform, if it was assumed that all properties were assessed at the same ratio of full value. The nominal tax rate might rise as a result, but actual tax bills could still be accurate. In fact, as discussed in chapter 6, unauthorized fractional assessments were never designed to replicate a full-value distribution of the tax burden, but to favor specific taxpayers, to avoid the effort and controversy of revaluation, or both.

Again as in most states, nineteenth-century Massachusetts law held that a taxpayer whose property was assessed at less than its market value but at a higher percentage of value than other property in the jurisdiction could not require that this assessment be reduced to the common level, even though the property bore a higher burden than others of similar value. In 1890 the Massachusetts Supreme Judicial Court held that the relevant legal question was "whether the property has been valued at more than its fair cash value, and not whether it has been valued relatively more or less than similar property of other persons."[4] This result was overturned by the U.S. Supreme Court in 1923,[5] but unequal fractional assessment continued to be widespread, both as a result of failure to maintain accurate tax values and as a means of extending benefits to favored classes of property, particularly single-family residences.

The 1960s and 1970s saw increased judicial willingness to challenge these practices. In 1961 the Massachusetts court held that relative underassessment of single-family residences and overassessment of commercial, industrial, and utility property violated the state's constitutional and statutory requirements of uniformity.[6] In 1972 a number of jurisdictions striving for accurate assessments brought an action to require the state to enforce full market valuation, pointing out that they were disadvantaged by distribution of state aid in part according to municipalities' property wealth. Under that approach, cities with the most inaccurate assessments appeared the most in need. The court ruled that the state had the power to require local assessors to value property accurately.[7] Subsequent legislation authorized the state itself to contract directly with revaluation firms and to deduct the cost of those contracts from state aid to municipalities that refused to update their assessments.[8]

In its new willingness to challenge established "extra-legal" classification, the Supreme Judicial Court held that taxpayers in disadvantaged classes had the right to have their valuations lowered, not simply to the jurisdiction-wide average assessment ratio but to the average ratio of the most favored property class.[9] Where the 1890 court found no legal remedy for relative overassessment except revaluation of all other property, by 1979 the same court recognized that even requiring proof of disproportionate assessment "imposes on the taxpayer a wasteful burden of proving the assessed values and the fair cash values of a great number of properties other than his own. To require the taxpayer to revalue even a substantial fraction of the property of a large city may be tantamount to a denial of relief."[10]

Among the localities ignoring the legal requirement of uniformity in taxation, the capital city of Boston was a particularly egregious example, having had no full citywide reassessment since the 1920s. In the 1970s its residential property was assessed at a ratio to full value far below that of business property, and utilities were assessed at a ratio far above that of businesses. Within those classes there were enormous differences across properties and neighborhoods. Residential property in the largely minority Boston neighborhood of Roxbury, for example, was assessed at approximately 40 percent of market value, while the comparable figure for the traditionally Irish neighborhood of Charlestown was approximately 16 percent.[11] The extent of underassessment was evidenced by Boston's 1980 nominal tax rate of over 25 percent—a level that would be completely unsupportable if assessments were at all close to market values. The 1981 rate was even higher, above 27 percent. The 1981 rate in Somerville was above 29 percent and in Billerica above 31 percent.[12]

Proposition 2½

In many ways the 1980 Massachusetts tax limitation was an inverted image of Proposition 13, even as its name proclaimed its California heritage.[13] Both expressed political opposition to uniform full-value assessment. Proposition 13 was in part a response to a highly accurate assessment system, reformed in the wake of corruption scandals, that tracked a dramatic increase in housing prices in the 1970s. In fact, some commentators felt that the unreformed system was preferable. "In government one should not rely too heavily on rules to replace political discretion. Had California's assessors retained some of their pre-1965 authority to set assessments, they could have mediated at least some of the housing inflation."[14]

Proposition 2½ was passed as Massachusetts courts were moving to enforce the legal requirement of full-value assessment, with its potential for significant tax shifts across property classes. Where Proposition 13 set tax rates at 1 percent and changed the basis for assessment from market value to acquisition value, Proposition 2½ took a radically different path. It did not alter the market value basis for the property tax, and it limited tax rates to only 2½ percent—a very high rate for a market value system, but less than one-tenth the Boston rate in 1980. In fact, limiting tax rates to 2½ percent encouraged localities to comply with the law and reassess properties whose taxable value was far below market levels.[15]

In 1981 the Department of Revenue had judged fewer than 100 of the state's 351 cities and towns to have implemented market value assessment; by 1985, all but 12 had met that standard.[16] Boston completed its revaluation in 1983, after Proposition 2½ had been in effect for one year. The dramatic rise in the property tax base meant that for many localities the most significant limit in Proposition 2½ was its restriction of the growth in property tax collections to 2½ percent annually. In an era of high inflation this appeared to run the risk of completely destabilizing municipal finances, and the Department of Revenue estimated first year revenue losses at more than $300 million.[17] This nearly 10 percent fall in property tax collections led to more than an 11 percent decrease in public employment.[18]

The severity of this transition was mitigated by a number of factors: (1) state aid rose to cover more than two-thirds of the lost property tax revenue;[19] (2) new tax rates were phased in, with jurisdictions whose tax rates exceeded 2½ percent—areas accounting for 79 percent of the state's population[20]—required to reduce their collections by 15 percent annually; and (3) local voters could choose to increase collections through override ballots. However, one of the most dramatic mitigating factors was not in fact a part of Proposition 2½, a state constitutional amendment permitting tax rates to vary by property class.

Classification

Implementation of Proposition 2½ received assistance from a most unexpected source: passage of a constitutional amendment explicitly allowing higher tax rates on business and commercial property than on residences. Popular support for this measure reflected the expectation that court-ordered reassessment would result in a redistribution of the tax burden, particularly if the extremely high tax rates prevailing in older urban areas went unchanged. These fears were inflamed by local politicians, led by Boston mayor Kevin White, who distributed a pamphlet warning homeowners that they would face an effective tax rate of 10 percent under full-value assessment. "I'm not about to sit still and let 100% valuation destroy Boston," he wrote. "That's why I'm opposing it with every legal means available." The classification amendment approved in 1978 and the 1979 legislation implementing it permitted differential taxation of four classes of property: residential, open space, commercial, and industrial.[21]

By 1987, 85 of the state's 351 taxing jurisdictions had adopted classification, reducing the residential share of the property tax by an average of 8 percentage points.[22] Thus Massachusetts joined New York and a number of other states in which a judicial decision overturning unauthorized classification was followed by enactment of an explicit and legal system of classification.[23] This step was disturbing to those who valued uniformity in taxation, but the constitutional requirement of uniformity had long been ignored in favor of de facto classification.

The 1979 legislation provided a minimum residential factor of 65 percent of the tax burden under a uniform system, and a maximum shift to commercial and industrial property of 150 percent of a uniform tax, with allowance for reduced taxation of commercial properties of modest value.[24] The new classification program was far different than the prior regime, under which outdated assessments and the individual assessor's judgment could produce a system with nearly as many classes as taxable properties. Crucially, no locality could institute differential rates until the state Department of Revenue had certified that its assessments were at full and fair market value. All jurisdictions are required to revalue their property on at least a three-year cycle and to be certified by the Department of Revenue as assessing property accurately.[25]

These classification limits have been periodically and sometimes temporarily adjusted in response to homeowner pressure for tax relief during periods of dramatically rising residential values. Like classification itself, this response represented a political compromise to market value taxation. The challenge from the analysts at the Institute of Government and Public Affairs at the University of Illinois discussed in chapter 6—why should not a class's rising share of property value be reflected in a rising share of the property tax base for that class?—still stands.[26]

Other Mitigating Factors

A number of important changes to the initial provisions of Proposition 2½ enhanced local jurisdictions' ability to adjust their budgets and tax rates. Initially, a jurisdiction that did not tax to the full amount of its levy capacity was limited to 2½ percent growth on that restricted base in the next year. This served as an incentive to tax to the maximum levy capacity whether that was needed in a given year or not—an example of the unintended consequences of complex limitation provisions. After 1982, unused tax capacity was also allowed to be "banked" for the future, and the levy limit was increased to reflect the value of new construction.

Local voters may also take action to suspend the levy limit in a number of ways. An override increases the levy limit through majority approval of a ballot question specifying the dollar amount and the spending purpose. Between 2002 and 2008, overrides added more than $30 million annually to the aggregate levy limit, with at least 35 successful votes in each of these years.[27] Communities may also request voter approval of a temporary increase in the levy ceiling to retire municipal debt incurred for a specific purpose. A 1987 amendment permitted a third option—a one-year exclusion from the levy limit to pay for specific capital expenditures. Between 1999 and 2008, more than 340 overrides raised the levy limit in the communities approving them. Smaller communities were more likely to approve overrides, as were jurisdictions with greater property wealth per capita and those with high public school enrollment.[28]

An extremely important factor in this transition was the state Department of Revenue's active role in maintaining updated assessments, first through its triennial certification of each taxing jurisdiction as assessing taxable property at full and fair cash value, and then by requiring assessors to submit annual reports demonstrating compliance with full-value assessment and uniform treatment of all classes of property.[29] This oversight avoids lengthy intervals without updated assessments, which would ensure political resistance to the resulting tax shifts, particularly in periods of rapid property inflation.

A Changing but Significant Revenue Source

Proposition 2½ caused enormous changes in the Massachusetts system of property taxation, and the limitations it imposed continue to constrain local spending. A 2007 report stated, "Massachusetts towns have had to lay off school and municipal employees (including firefighters and police), freeze wages, close town libraries and senior centers, and stop funding infrastructure projects to comply with the state's severe property tax cap."[30] At the same time, the property tax continued to function as a major local revenue source. In 1978 it provided 55.6 percent of general local revenue in the state; 30 years later, this figure was 43 percent.[31]

State aid to localities rose dramatically again in the 1990s as part of a program of school finance reform. However, reductions in aid following economic downturns showed the importance of maintaining an independent revenue source for local government.

The Massachusetts property tax did not fall in absolute terms between 1979 and 2009, but it rose much more slowly than in the country as a whole. Adjusted for inflation, per capita property taxes were approximately 14 percent higher in Massachusetts at the end of that 30-year period, while the national figure rose over 60 percent.[32] The Department of Revenue noted that the increase in average residential tax bills began to slow after the housing downturn, increasing only 3.3 percent in fiscal 2010, after rising an average of 5.5 percent each year in the previous decade.[33] The Department found the diminished rise of residential tax bills to reflect "leaner budgets, reduced excess levy capacity, and Proposition 2½ override fatigue."

Conclusion

The search for practical methods to address political demands for property tax limitations has led to many types of responses, each with its own consequences. The most familiar limitations copy California's Proposition 13 and divorce assessed values from current market prices, a serious blow to uniformity in taxation and a possible source of weakened support for using a nonuniform tax as a source of significant autonomous local revenue.

Proposition 2½ proudly highlighted its California heritage, but in fact its provisions are in many ways the inverse of Proposition 13. Its rate limit encouraged improved assessment accuracy, and a new classification option required state certification of full-value assessment. It presents a test case for a tax limit that does not sacrifice market value assessments.

Proposition 2½ has been the subject of much legitimate criticism. It does not require uniformity in taxation, and the ability of localities to increase the burden on business property by half, or even to double it, reflects the diminished but continuing practice of favoring single-family homeowners. Those who find its limitations too severe note the random nature of any limits on revenue increases that do not take into account inflation, changes in demands for public services, and the availability of state aid. They point to the problems of increased local dependence on state aid, widened disparities between communities on the basis of wealth, and cuts to valued services.[34] At the same time, others note that property taxes continue to rise even when home prices have declined,[35] providing a rising share of local revenue as state aid was reduced in the latest recession.[36]

Every tax limitation has drawbacks, some extremely serious. However, no tax is unconstrained, and it is important to understand the comparative effects of alternate limitation measures.

Massachusetts offers an example of a populist limitation measure designed to reduce tax rates and tax collections rather than to shift to a non-market value tax base. In fact, its aftermath saw the introduction of assessments based on full market value in a state that had tolerated many decades of egregiously inaccurate assessments. This in itself was an extraordinary accomplishment, and for it to have taken place in the context of a citizen-initiated tax revolt is nothing short of astonishing.

No property tax system will ever be uncontroversial or free of pressure, but the Massachusetts structure has remained relatively stable for over 30 years. This achievement represents an effective tax limitation that succeeded in preserving accurate market value assessments.

Notes

1. White (2010); Setze (2011b) (This measure does not apply to New York City.).
2. Bradbury and Ladd, with Christopherson (1982).
3. Cobb (1999).
4. *City of Lowell v. County Commissioners of Middlesex*, 152 Mass. 372, 375; 25 N.E. 469, 470 (1890).
5. *Sioux City Bridge Company v. Dakota County*, 260 U.S. 441 (1923).
6. *Bettigole v. Assessors of Springfield*, 343 Mass. 223, 178 N.E.2d 10 (1961).
7. *Town of Sudbury v. Commissioner of Corporations & Taxation*, 366 Mass. 558, 321 N.E.2d 641 (1974).
8. Mass. Gen. Laws, ch. 58, §§ 4A–4C.
9. *Tregor v. Board of Assessors,* 377 Mass. 602, 387 N.E.2d 538 (1979).
10. Ibid., 377 Mass. 609, 387 N.E.2d 543.
11. Engle (1975).
12. Commerce Clearing House (1982), ¶ 71-001.

13. The Massachusetts Supreme Judicial Court wrote, "The characterization of the initiative proposal as 'Proposition 2½' is a blatant colloquialism. The word 'proposition' is derived from a well-known tax limitation measure submitted to the people of California in 1978 as Proposition 13. . . . In Massachusetts we simply call them questions. The reference to '2½' is not based on an offbeat numbering system. Proposition 2½ was in fact the second question on the 1980 ballot." *Massachusetts Teachers Association v. Secretary of the Commonwealth*, 384 Mass. 209, 212 n. 4, 424 N.E.2d 469, 472 n. 4 (1981).
14. Levy (1979), 89.
15. O'Sullivan, Sexton, and Sheffrin (1995).
16. Ibid., 37.
17. Bradbury and Ladd, with Christopherson (1982), 15.
18. Wallin (2004), 41.
19. Ibid.
20. Bradbury and Ladd, with Christopherson (1982), 4.
21. Mass. Const. Art. CXII; Mass. Gen. Laws. ch. 40, § 56, and ch. 59, § 2A(b).
22. Bradbury (1988), 42.
23. Beebe and Sinnott (1979 a–c).
24. Mass. Gen. Laws ch. 59, § 51.
25. Mass. Gen. Laws ch. 40, § 56; Massachusetts Department of Revenue (2010b).
26. Dye, McMillen, and Merriman (2006), 712.
27. Kingsley (2008).
28. Ibid., 7.
29. Massachusetts Department of Revenue (2004).
30. Lyons and Lav (2007), 430.
31. Advisory Commission on Intergovernmental Relations (1980), 86; Lincoln Institute of Land Policy (2008).
32. The per capita property tax in Massachusetts in 2009 was $1,845; the U.S. figure was $1,339. In 1979 the per capita figure for Massachusetts was $549 in nominal terms, and $1,622 in 2009 dollars. The 1979 figures for the United States are $278 in nominal terms and $822 in 2009 dollars. *State & Local Government Finance Data Query System*, http://www.taxpolicycenter.org/index.cfm. The Urban Institute–Brookings Institution Tax Policy Center. Data from U.S. Census Bureau, Annual Survey of State and Local Government Finances, Government Finances, and Census of Governments.
33. This followed the downturn in residential property values. After rising every year since 1994, assessed values fell in 2008, and in 2010 statewide single-family property values decreased 4.61 percent. Massachusetts Department of Revenue, "Fiscal 2010 Average Single-Family Tax Bills and Assessed Values," *City & Town*, 2010.
34. Oliff and Lav (2010).
35. Carroll (2011).
36. Riley (2011).

References

Aaron, Henry. 1975. *Who Pays the Property Tax?* Washington, DC: Brookings Institution.

Advisory Commission on Intergovernmental Relations. 1963. *The Role of the States in Strengthening the Property Tax*, vol. 1. Washington, DC: U.S. Government Printing Office.

———. 1980. *Significant Features of Fiscal Federalism*, 1979–1980 edition. Washington, DC: U.S. Government Printing Office.

Anderson, John E. 2012. *Public Finance*, 2nd ed. Mason, OH: South-Western.

Anderson, John E., and Richard W. England. 2014. *Use-Value Assessment of Rural Land in the United States*. Cambridge, MA: Lincoln Institute of Land Policy.

Anderson, John E., and Seth H. Giertz. 2015. "Farm Follies." *U.S. News & World Report*, Economic Intelligence (August 24). http://www.usnews.com/opinion/economic-intelligence/2015/08/24/taxpayers-shortchanged-by-agriculture-use-value-assessment.

Anuta, Joe. 2013. "De Blasio Tells Lot Owners to Put Up or Pay Up." *Crain's New York Business*, November 24.

Anzaldi, Stephen. 2004. "Northwestern, Evanston Settle Lawsuit." *Northwestern University Observer*, February 19.

Arsen, David, and David N. Plank. 2004. "Michigan School Finance under Proposal A: State Control, Local Consequences." *State Tax Notes* (March 15): 903–922.

Bahney, Anna. 2003. "Greetings from . . . Wyotana, 'Home of the Second Home.'" *New York Times*, January 17: F1.

Banzhaf, H. Spencer, Wallace E. Oates, and James N. Sanchirico. 2010. "Success and Design of Local Referenda for Land Conservation." *Journal of Policy Analysis and Management* 29(4): 769–798.

Becker, Sidney. 1997. Letter to the Editor. *New York Newsday*, Queens Edition, October 14: A39.

Beebe, Robert L., and Richard J. Sinnott. 1979a. "In the Wake of *Hellerstein*: Whither New York? (Part One)." *Albany Law Review* 43(2): 203–293.

———. 1979b. "In the Wake of *Hellerstein*: Whither New York? (Part Two)." *Albany Law Review* 43(3): 411–486.

———. 1979c. "In the Wake of *Hellerstein*: Whither New York? (Part Three)." *Albany Law Review* 43(4): 777–860.

Berman, Dennis. 2011. "When States Default: 2011, Meet 1841." *Wall Street Journal*, January 4. http://www.wsj.com/articles/SB10001424052748704835504576060193029215716.

Berry, Todd A. 2003. "Farmland Council Freezes Agricultural Use Value." *State Tax Notes* (October 13): 111.

Blanding, Michael. 2006. "Buyer's Market." *Boston Magazine*, May, 123–128.

Blazina, Ed. 2013. "Payroll Tax Would Elicit Some Cash from Large Pittsburgh Nonprofits." *Pittsburgh Post-Gazette*, January 15.

Blumenstyk, Goldie. 2013. "Princeton's Royalty Windfall Leads to Challenge of Its Tax-Exempt Status." *Chronicle of Higher Education*, July 8.

Bogart, William T., and David F. Bradford. 1990. "Incidence and Allocation Effects of the Property Tax and a Proposal for Reform." *Research in Urban Economics* 8: 59–82.

Boldt, Rebecca. 2003. "Impact of Use Valuation of Agricultural Land: Evidence from Wisconsin." *State Tax Notes* (February 24): 677–686.

Bonbright, James C. 1937. *The Valuation of Property*, vol. 1. New York: McGraw-Hill.

Booth, Philip A. 2012. "The Unearned Increment: Property and the Capture of Betterment Value in Britain and France." In *Value Capture and Land Policies*, ed. Gregory K. Ingram and Yu-Hung Hong. Cambridge, MA: Lincoln Institute of Land Policy.

Boston Globe. 2014. "On Open Space, a Gloomy Tale Turns Rosy." Editorial, August 17.

Bourassa, Steven C. 2009a. "The Political Economy of Land Value Taxation." In *Land Value Taxation: Theory, Evidence, Practice*, ed. Richard F. Dye and Richard W. England. Cambridge, MA: Lincoln Institute of Land Policy.

———. 2009b. "The U.S. Experience." In *Land Value Taxation: Theory, Evidence, and Practice*, ed. Richard F. Dye and Richard W. England. Cambridge, MA: Lincoln Institute of Land Policy.

Bowman, John H., Daphne A. Kenyon, Adam Langley, and Bethany P. Paquin. 2009. *Property Tax Circuit Breakers: Fair and Cost-Effective Relief for Taxpayers*. Cambridge, MA: Lincoln Institute of Land Policy.

Bowman, Karlyn, and Andrew Rugg. 2011. *Public Opinion on Taxes: 1937 to Today*. AEI Public Opinion Studies. Washington, DC: American Enterprise Institute for Public Policy Research.

Bradbury, Katharine L. 1988. "Shifting Property Tax Burdens in Massachusetts." *New England Economic Review* (September-October): 36–48.

Bradbury, Katharine L., and Helen Ladd, with Claire Christopherson. 1982. "Proposition 2½: Initial Impacts." Stanford University Institute for Research on Educational Finance and Governance Report IFG-PR-82-A12 (June).

Breed, Allen G., and Martha Mendoza. 2004. "Loopholes Limiting Land-Preservation Efforts?" *Telegraph Herald* (Dubuque, Iowa), April 4: B7.

Briffault, Richard. 2010. "The Most Popular Tool: Tax Increment Financing and the Political Economy of Local Government." *University of Chicago Law Review* 77: 65–95.

Brody, Evelyn. 1997. "Hocking the Halo: Implications of the Charities' Winning Briefs in *Camps Newfound/Owatonna, Inc*." *Stetson Law Review* 27: 433–456.

———. 1998. "Of Sovereignty and Subsidy: Conceptualizing the Charity Tax Exemption." *Journal of Corporation Law* 23: 585–629.

Brooks, Leah, and Justin Phillips. 2009. "Municipally Imposed Tax and Expenditure Limits." *Land Lines* 21(2) (April): 8–13.

Brunner, Eric J., and Jon Sonstelie. 2006. "California's School Finance Reform: An Experiment in Fiscal Federalism." In *The Tiebout Model at Fifty: Essays in Public Economics in Honor of Wallace Oates*, ed. William A. Fischel. Cambridge, MA: Lincoln Institute of Land Policy.

Brunori, David. 1999. "Interview: Steven M. Sheffrin on the 'Worst Tax,' Local Options, and Prop 13." *State Tax Notes* (December 27): 1721–1723.

———. 2011. "Schizophrenia around the Country." *State Tax Notes* (February 28): 625.

———. 2015. "Good Politics, Bad Policy." *State Tax Notes* (July 6): 49–50.

Buchanan, James M. 1993. "The Political Efficiency of General Taxation." *National Tax Journal* 46(4): 401–410.

Buffalo News. 1995. "New York Taxes Farm Property Too Heavily." November 27: 2B.

Buhl, John. 2010. "Governor Signs TIF Expansion for Distressed Localities." *State Tax Notes* (May 24): 576.

Bunch, Joey. 2003. "Colorado Voters in 'No' Mood." *Denver Post*, November 5: A1.

Bureau of Governmental Research. 1996. *Property Taxes in New Orleans*. New Orleans: Bureau of Governmental Research.

———. 2011a. "Taxation in New Orleans: BGR Presentation to the Tax Fairness Commission" (February).

———. 2011b. "The Nonprofit Margin: Addressing the Costs of the Nonprofit Exemption in New Orleans." New Orleans: BGR Fiscal Issues Series (March).

———. 2012. "The Nonprofit Exemption: Bad News for Taxpayers." BGR NOW: Spotlight on Local Government Issues (January).

Butler, David, Andrew Adonis, and Tony Travers. 1994. *Failure in British Government: The Politics of the Poll Tax*. Oxford: Oxford University Press.

Byrne, Paul F. 2006. "Determinants of Property Value Growth for Tax Increment Financing Districts." *Economic Development Quarterly* 20(4): 317–329.

Cabral, Marika, and Caroline Hoxby. 2012. "The Hated Property Tax: Salience, Tax Rates, and Tax Revolts." Working Paper No. 18514. Cambridge, MA: National Bureau of Economic Research.

Calder, Rich. 2013. "City Hikes Taxes on Sandy-Hit Houses." *New York Post*, February 11.

California Consortium of Educational Foundations. 2014. "About Us." http://cceflink.org/wpnew/about-us-2/.

California Department of Education. 2008. "School District Revenue Limit." http://www.cde.ca.gov/fg/fo/profile.asp?id=1296.

———. 2013. *Comparison of Per-Pupil Spending Calculations*. Sacramento: California Department of Education.

California Legislative Analyst's Office. 2012. *Understanding California's Property Taxes*. Sacramento: Legislative Analyst's Office.

Carr, Jennifer. 2013a. "Pittsburgh Sues Healthcare Organization for Payroll Tax." *State Tax Notes* (April 1): 26–27.

———. 2013b. "Lawmakers May Amend Charitable Exemption Criteria." *State Tax Notes* (April 8): 113.

———. 2013c. "Pittsburgh Hospital Payroll Tax Suit Takes a Nasty Turn." *State Tax Notes* (June 24): 967.

Carr, Jennifer, and Cara Griffith. 2007. "Florida's TIF Ruling—A Hard Pill for Local Governments to Swallow." *State Tax Notes* (October 8): 117.

Carroll, Matt. 2011. "Falling Home Prices, Rising Taxes Squeeze Towns." *Boston Globe*, December 15.

Casner, A. James, and W. Barton Leach. 1984. *Cases and Text on Property*, 3rd ed. Boston: Little, Brown.

Chaban, Matt A. V. 2014. "Amid Preservation Efforts, Farmland in the Hamptons Goes for Other Uses." *New York Times*, August 4.

Cheung, Ron, and Chris Cunningham. 2011. "Who Supports Portable Assessment Caps: The Role of Lock-in, Tax Share and Mobility." *Regional Science and Urban Economics* 41(3): 173–186.

Chicago Tribune. 2013. "Another Ratings Agency Downgrades Illinois Credit." June 6.

———. 2015. "Tough TIF Talk." July 20.

Citizens Research Council of Michigan. 2010. *State and Local Revenues for Public Education in Michigan*, Report 363 (September). Livonia: Citizens Research Council of Michigan.

City Club of Portland. 2013. "Reconstructing Oregon's Frankentax: Improving the Equity, Financial Sustainability, and Efficiency of Property Taxes." *City Club of Portland Bulletin* 95(8) (November 7).

Clotfelter, Charles T. "Tax-Induced Distortions in the Voluntary Sector." 1989. *Case Western Reserve Law Review* 39: 663–704.

Cobb, Charles K. 1999. *Tax Law in Massachusetts 1629–2000*. All Seasons Books.

Coffman, Jennifer. 2012. "AAPS Mulls Suing State Over School Aid Fund." *Ann Arbor Chronicle*, January 22.

Cohen, Felix S. 1935. "Transcendental Nonsense and the Functional Approach." *Columbia Law Review* 35(6): 808–849.

Cohen, Rick. 2013. "Oddest PILOT Proposal to Date: Tax Nonprofits, Cut Business Taxes." *Nonprofit Quarterly, Policy/Social Context* (January 24).

Collins, Michael W. 1999. "Another Ad Valorem View of Low-Income Housing Tax Credit Properties." *Appraisal Journal* 67 (July): 306–308.

Colorado Department of Local Affairs. Division of Property Taxation. 2013. "Estimated Residential Assessment Rate for 2013–2014." Report to the State Board of Equalization and the General Assembly (January 14).

Commerce Clearing House. 1982. *Massachusetts Tax Reports*. Chicago: Commerce Clearing House.

Cook County, Illinois, Assessor's Virtual Office. 2013. http://www.cookcountyassessor .com.

Cook County Assessor's Office. 2005. *The Impact of the 7% Expanded Homeowner Exemption: City of Chicago Tax Years 2003 & 2004, North District Tax Year 2004, South District Projected Tax Year 2005.* Chicago: Office of the Cook County Assessor.

Corcoran, Sean P., and William N. Evans. 2015. "Equity, Adequacy, and the Evolving State Role in Education Finance." In *Handbook of Research in Education Finance and Policy,* ed. Helen F. Ladd and Margaret E. Goertz. 2nd edition. New York: Routledge.

Corkery, Michael, and Jeannette Neumann. 2011. "Illinois Bond Sale Gets Done at a Cost." *Wall Street Journal,* February 24: C1.

Cornia, Gary C., and Lawrence C. Walters. 2005. "Full Disclosure: Unanticipated Improvements in Property Tax Uniformity." *Public Budgeting & Finance* 25(2): 106–123.

Cornish, Bill. 2008. "Market Down, Property Taxes Up." *Saginaw News,* February 23.

Coupal, Jon. 2013. "California Commentary: The Shameful History of Parcel Taxes" (February 10). http://www.hjta.org/california-commentary/shameful-history -parcel-taxes.

Cribbet, John E. 1975. *Principles of the Law of Property,* 2nd ed. Mineola, NY: Foundation Press.

Cummings, Jean L., and Denise DiPasquale. 1999. "The Low-Income Housing Tax Credit: An Analysis of the First Ten Years." Fannie Mae Foundation, *Housing Policy Debate* 10(2): 251–307. Reprinted in Thomas A. Jaconetty, ed., *The Valuation of Subsidized Housing.* Chicago: International Association of Assessing Officers (2003).

Davis, Christopher West. 2003. "Pushing the Sprawl Back: Landowners Turn to Trusts." *New York Times,* October 12: 14WC, 1.

Dearborn, Philip M. 1993. "ACIR 1993 Poll Takes Public Pulse on Taxes." *State Tax Notes* (October 4): 780–782.

De Leo, Dan. 1999. "Farmers, State at Odds." *Worcester Telegram & Gazette,* December 12: B1.

Department of Agricultural and Consumer Economics, University of Illinois at Urbana-Champaign. 2013. "Farm Policy Background: Income of U.S. Farm versus Nonfarm Population." *FarmDoc Daily* (July 3). http://farmdocdaily.illinois .edu/2013/07/Farm-Policy-Income-Farm-Nonfarm.html.

DePaul, Jennifer. 2014a. "Short on Revenue, State and Local Governments Turn to Nonprofits." *State Tax Notes* (January 27): 205–207.

———. 2014b. "Pittsburgh Drops Suit against UPMC over Tax-Exempt Status." *State Tax Notes* (August 4): 329–330.

Di Miceli, Maria. 2013. "Drive Your Own PILOT: Federal and State Constitutional Challenges to the Imposition of Payments in Lieu of Taxes on Tax-Exempt Entities." *Tax Lawyer* 66(4): 835–872.

District of Columbia Tax Revision Commission. 1977. *Financing an Urban Government.* Washington, DC.

———. 1998. *Taxing Simply, Taxing Fairly*. Washington, DC.

———. 2014. "Recommendations." *State Tax Today*. 2014 STT 29-11 (February 12).

Dixon, Tom. 2005. "Counting the Cost." *Insight* 11 (November). London: Institute of Revenues Rating and Valuation.

Dodge, Joseph M. 2009. "What Federal Taxes Are Subject to the Rule of Apportionment under the Constitution?" *University of Pennsylvania Journal of Constitutional Law* 11: 839–956.

Doerr, David R. 2008. "The Evolution of Proposition 13." *State Tax Notes* (August 4): 305–314.

Doherty, Patrick. 1999. "Collection of Local Taxes." *Journal of Property Tax Assessment & Administration* 4: 31–36.

Duggan, Tara. 2014. "S.F. Property Owners to Get Tax Break from Creating Urban Farms." *San Francisco Chronicle*, September 1. http://www.sfgate.com/bayarea/article/S-F-property-owners-to-get-tax-break-from-5725876.php.

Dye, Richard F., and Richard W. England, eds. 2009. *Land Value Taxation: Theory, Evidence, and Practice*. Cambridge, MA: Lincoln Institute of Land Policy.

Dye, Richard F., Nancy W. Hudspeth, and David Merriman. 2011. "Titanic and Sinking: The Illinois Budget Disaster." In *The Illinois Report 2011*. Chicago: Institute of Government and Public Affairs, University of Illinois.

Dye, Richard F., and Daniel P. McMillen. 2007. "Surprise! An Unintended Consequence of Assessment Limitations." *Land Lines* (July): 8–13.

Dye, Richard F., Daniel P. McMillen, and David F. Merriman. 2006. "Illinois' Response to Rising Residential Property Values: An Assessment Growth Cap in Cook County." *National Tax Journal* 59 (September): 707–716.

Dye, Richard F., and David F. Merriman. 2000. "The Effects of Tax Increment Financing on Economic Development." *Journal of Urban Economics* 47: 306–328.

———. 2003. "The Effect of Tax Increment Financing on Land Use." In *The Property Tax, Land Use and Land Use Regulation*, ed. Dick Netzer. Cheltenham: Edward Elgar, 37–61.

———. 2006. "Tax Increment Financing: A Tool for Local Economic Development." *Land Lines* (January): 2–7.

Dye, Richard F., and Jeffrey O. Sundberg. 1998. "A Model of Tax Increment Financing Adoption Incentives." *Growth and Change* 29 (Winter): 90–110.

Ebke, Werner F. 1997. "Company Law and the European Union." *International Lawyer* 31: 961–986.

Econsult Solutions, Inc. 2013. "The City of Philadelphia and Its Higher Eds: Shared Goals, Shared Missions, Shared Results." http://www.econsultsolutions.com/report/35740/.

Eggler, Bruce. 2011. "New Orleans Tax Exemptions for Nonprofit Groups Targeted." *Times-Picayune*, March 15.

Eitel, Michael R. 2004. "Comment: Wyoming's Trepidation toward Conservation Easement Legislation." *Wyoming Law Review* 4: 57–111.

Engle, Robert F. 1975. "De Facto Discrimination in Residential Assessments: Boston." *National Tax Journal* 28: 445–451.

Farrington, Colin. 1992. "Development in the United Kingdom." *Review of Urban and Regional Development Studies* 4: 179–192.

Fernandez, Manny. 2010. "New York City Plans to Topple Public Housing Towers." *New York Times,* February 6. http://www.nytimes.com/2010/02/06/nyregion/06demolish.html?_r=0.

Fischel, William A. 1989. "Did *Serrano* Cause Proposition 13?" *National Tax Journal* 42(4): 465–473.

———. 1996. "How *Serrano* Caused Proposition 13." *Journal of Law and Politics* 12(Fall): 607–636.

———. 2001a. *The Homevoter Hypothesis.* Cambridge, MA: Harvard University Press.

———. 2001b. "Municipal Corporations, Homeowners and the Benefit View of the Property Tax." In *Property Taxation and Local Government Finance,* ed. Wallace E. Oates. Cambridge, MA: Lincoln Institute of Land Policy.

Fisher, Ronald C. 2007. *State and Local Public Finance,* 3rd ed. Mason, OH: Thompson South-Western.

Flint, Anthony. 2003. "Report Assails Growth/Cost Formula Need to Gauge Project Impact." *Boston Globe,* March 11: B3.

Florida Legislative Office of Economic and Demographic Research. 2007. *Florida's Property Tax Study Interim Report.* Tallahassee: Florida Legislature, Office of Economic and Demographic Research.

Follick, Joe. 2008. "State Supreme Court Reverses Tax Increment Finance Ruling." *State Tax Notes* (September 29): 860.

Freedberg, Louis, and Stephen K. Doig. 2011. "Spending Far from Equal among State's School Districts, Analysis Finds." *California Watch,* June 2.

Friedman, Jeffrey A. 1996. "Comment: New Jersey's Farmland Assessment: Welfare for New Jersey's Landed Gentry or Beneficial Open Space Program?" *Temple Environmental Law & Technology Journal* 15: 83–100.

Furman Center for Real Estate and Urban Policy of New York University School of Law and Wagner School of Public Service. 2013. "Shifting the Burden: Examining the Undertaxation of Some of the Most Valuable Properties in New York City."

Gainer, Bridget. 2010. *A Citizens' Guide to Your Property Tax Bill.* Cook County Commissioner, 10th District, Illinois.

Galle, Brian. 2009. "Hidden Taxes." *Washington University Law Review* 87: 59–113.

Garippa, John. 2006. "The Other Side of the *Marriott v. Saddle Brook* Decision." *Fair & Equitable* (April): 26–29.

Geheb, Phillip J. F. 2009. "Tax Increment Financing Bonds as 'Debt' under State Constitutional Debt Limits." *Urban Lawyer* 41 (Fall): 725–753.

Gelfand, M. David. 1979. "Seeking Local Government Financial Integrity through Debt Ceilings, Tax Limitations, and Expenditure Limitations: The New York City

Fiscal Crisis, the Taxpayer's Revolt, and Beyond." *Minnesota Law Review* 63: 545–608.

George, Henry. 1879. *Progress and Poverty*. San Francisco: D. Appleton.

Glaeser, Edward L., and Bryce A. Ward. 2009. "The Causes and Consequences of Land Use Regulation: Evidence from Greater Boston." *Journal of Urban Economics* 65(3): 265–278.

Glancy, David B. 2002. "PILOTs: Philadelphia and Pennsylvania." In *Property Tax Exemption for Charity*, ed. Evelyn Brody. Washington, DC: Urban Institute Press.

Glennon, Robert. 1990. "Taxation and Equal Protection." *George Washington Law Review* 58: 261–307.

Gómez-Ibáñez, José A. 2010. "Prospects for Private Infrastructure in the United States: The Case of Toll Roads." In *Municipal Revenues and Land Policies*, ed. Gregory K. Ingram and Yu-Hung Hong. Cambridge, MA: Lincoln Institute of Land Policy.

Gordon, Tracy. 2011. "A Funny Thing Happened on the Way to the Coliseum . . ." TaxVox, The Tax Policy Center Blog. Washington, DC: Urban Institute and Brookings Institution Tax Policy Center, January 21. http://taxvox.taxpolicycenter .org/2011/01/21/a-funny-thing-happened-on-the-way-to-the-coliseum/.

Governor's Property Tax Reform Study. 1974. *Reforming the Virginia Property Tax.* Vol. II, *Recommendations to the Governor and Appended Consultants' Reports*. Richmond, VA.

Gray, Jerry. 1993. "Whitman Sold Wood to Trim Farm Taxes." *New York Times*, August 15: sec. 1, 40.

Greenberger, Scott S. 2006. "Study Says Regulations Raising Home Prices." *Boston Globe*, January 1.

Grimes, Katy. 2011. "Big-City Mayors Bulldoze Gov. Jerry Brown's Redevelopment Plan." *San Francisco Examiner*, January 26.

Hagman, Donald. 1964. "Open Space Planning and Property Taxation—Some Suggestions." *Wisconsin Law Review* 1964: 628ff.

Hamilton, Bruce. 1975. "Property Taxes and the Tiebout Hypothesis: Some Empirical Evidence." In *Fiscal Zoning and Land Use Controls: The Economic Issues*, ed. Edwin S. Mills and Wallace E. Oates. Lexington, MA: Lexington Books.

Hanley, Robert. 1997. "Five Acres, and a Tax Break?" *New York Times*, January 12.

Harris, Elizabeth A. 2012. "As Prices Soar to Buy a Luxury Address, the Tax Bills Don't." *New York Times*, October 15.

Hart, Jerry. 2009. "Homeowners See Taxes Rise as Property Values Sink Amid Deficits." *Bloomberg News*, March 12.

Harvard Law School International Program in Taxation. 1963. *Taxation in the United States*. Chicago: Commerce Clearing House, Inc.

Haughwout, Andrew, Robert Inman, Steven Craig, and Thomas Luce. 2004. "Local Revenue Hills: Evidence from Four U.S. Cities." *Review of Economics and Statistics* 86(2): 570–585.

Haveman, Mark, and Terri A. Sexton. 2008. *Property Tax Assessment Limits: Lessons from Thirty Years of Experience.* Cambridge, MA: Lincoln Institute of Land Policy.

Hevesi, Alan G. 1982. "100% Market Value as Assessment Basis for Homes Is Unfair." *Newsday,* January 29.

Hicks, Ursula. 1961. *Development from Below: Local Government and Finance in Developing Countries of the Commonwealth.* London: Oxford University Press.

Hodge, Timothy R., Gary Sands, and Mark Skidmore. 2015. "Assessment Growth Limits and Mobility: Evidence from Home Sale Data in Detroit, Michigan." *National Tax Journal* 68: 573–600.

Hughes, Mark Alan. 2007. "Why So Little Georgism in America? Using the Pennsylvania Case Files to Understand the Slow, Uneven Progress of Land Value Taxation." Working Paper. Cambridge, MA: Lincoln Institute of Land Policy.

Hutchinson, Mike. 2008. "Direct Debit Health Check." *Insight.* London: Institute of Revenues Rating and Valuation (February): 10.

Ihlanfeldt, Keith R. 2013. "The Property Tax Is a Bad Tax, but It Need Not Be." *Cityscape: A Journal of Policy Development and Research* 15(1): 255–259.

Indiana Fiscal Policy Institute. 2010. *Income Taxation in Indiana: Concepts and Issues.* Indianapolis: Indiana Fiscal Policy Institute.

Institute of Revenues Rating and Valuation. 2005. "Rewind to Manchester." *Insight* 22 (November). London: Institute of Revenues Rating and Valuation.

Institute on Taxation and Economic Policy. 2012. "Tax Principles: Building Blocks of a Sound Tax System." Policy Brief. Washington, DC (December).

Jackson-Smith, Douglas, and Jill Bukovac. 2000. "Limitation of Agricultural Land Use Planning Tools in Rural Wisconsin." Program on Agricultural Technology Studies, Paper No. 3. Madison: University of Wisconsin.

Jeane, Stephanie S. 2013. "The Façade of Valuation." *Tax Lawyer* 66(2): 501–517.

Jensen, Jens P. 1931. *Property Taxation in the United States.* Chicago: University of Chicago Press.

Johnson, Calvin H. 1998. "Apportionment of Direct Taxes: The Foul-Up in the Core of the Constitution." *William & Mary Bill of Rights Journal* 7: 1–103.

Jones, Paul. 2015. "State Revives Improvement Tax Increment Finance Districts." *State Tax Notes* (October 26): 278–279.

Joravsky, Ben. 2009. "October Surprise." *Chicago Reader,* November 5.

———. 2013. "Rahm's New TIF Program Looks a Lot Like the Old TIF Program." *Chicago Reader,* May 28.

Joravsky, Ben, and Mick Dumke. 2009. "The Shadow Budget." *Chicago Reader,* October 22.

Kauai County. 2013. "2013 Tax Rates." http://www.kauai.gov/Government/Departments-Agencies/Finance/Real-Property/Tax-Rates.

Kell, Karl. 2006. "Group Touts Benefits of Land Conservation." *New Orleans Times-Picayune,* June 29: 1.

Kenyon, Daphne A. 2007. "Seeing Through the 'View Tax' Myth." *State Tax Notes* (September 3): 641–645.

Kenyon, Daphne A., and Adam H. Langley. 2011. "Payments in Lieu of Taxes by Nonprofits: Case Studies." *State Tax Notes* (July 18): 171–181.

Kenyon, Daphne A., Adam Langley, and Bethany P. Paquin. 2012. *Rethinking Property Tax Incentives for Business*. Cambridge, MA: Lincoln Institute of Land Policy.

Kingsley, Rick. 2008. "A Ten-Year Perspective on Proposition 2½ Overrides." Massachusetts Department of Revenue, *City & Town* (August).

Koklanaris, Maria. 2014. "D.C. Mayor Presents Budget with Switch to Single Sales Factor." *State Tax Notes* (April 7): 15.

Kruimel, Jan Paul. 1999. "Property Tax Systems in the Netherlands." In *Property Tax: An International Comparative Review*, ed. William McCluskey. Ipswich, Suffolk: Ashgate.

Lambert, Bruce. 2003. "Accusations Flying in Nassau over Reassessments of Property." *New York Times*, June 11: B5.

Langley, Adam H., Daphne A. Kenyon, and Patricia C. Bailin. 2012. "Payments in Lieu of Taxes by Nonprofits: Which Nonprofits Make PILOTs and Which Localities Receive Them." Working Paper. Cambridge MA: Lincoln Institute of Land Policy.

Lawson, Frederic H. 1958. *Introduction to the Law of Property*. Oxford: Clarendon Press.

Layfield, Frank. 1976. *Local Government Finance: Report of the Committee of Enquiry*. London: Her Majesty's Stationery Office.

Lefcoe, George. 2008. "After *Kelo*, Curbing Opportunistic TIF-Driven Economic Development: Forgoing Ineffectual Blight Tests; Empowering Property Owners and School Districts." *Tulane Law Review* 83 (November): 45–110.

———. 2011. "Competing for the Next Hundred Million Americans: The Uses and Abuses of Tax Increment Financing." *Urban Lawyer* 43: 427–482.

Leland, Pamela J. 1994. "Responding to a Property Tax Challenge: Lessons Learned in Pennsylvania." *State Tax Notes* (October 3): 927ff.

———. 2002. "PILOTs: The Large City Experience." In *Property Tax Exemption for Charity*, ed. Evelyn Brody. Washington, DC: Urban Institute Press.

LeRoy, Greg. 2008. "TIF, Greenfields, and Sprawl: How an Incentive Created to Alleviate Slums Has Come to Subsidize Upscale Malls and New Urbanist Developments." *Planning & Environmental Law* 60(2): 3–11.

Levitz, Jennifer. 2012. "Ivy League School to Pay City Millions." *Wall Street Journal*, May 1.

Levy, Frank. 1979. "On Understanding Proposition 13." *Public Interest* 56: 66–89.

Lewis, Paul. 2013. "Empty Home Owners' Council Tax Shock." *BBC News Business* (March 16). http://www.bbc.co.uk/news/business-21814039.

Lewis, Roger K. 2010. "Affordable Housing Needs Public Funding." *Washington Post*, March 13: E4.

Lin, Judy. 2011. "Audit Faults California Redevelopment Agencies." *San Diego Union-Tribune*, March 7.

Lincoln Institute of Land Policy. 2008. "Property Taxes as a Percent of State and Local Total General Revenue." *Significant Features of the Property Tax.* www .lincolninst.edu/subcenters/significant-features-property-tax/census.

Lipman, Harvy. 2006. "Cities Take Many Approaches to Valuing Tax-Exempt Property." *Chronicle of Philanthropy* 19(4): 13 (November 23).

Long, Ray, and Monique Garcia. 2013. "Illinois Credit Rating Sinks to Worst in Nation." *Chicago Tribune*, January 25.

Lyons, Karen J., and Iris J. Lav. 2007. "The Problems with Property Tax Revenue Caps." *State Tax Notes* (August 13): 429–443.

Madden, Janet L. 1983. "Tax Incentives for Land Conservation: The Charitable Contribution Deduction for Gifts of Conservation Easements." *Boston College Environmental Affairs Law Review* 11(Fall): 105–148.

Maine Nonprofit Tax Review Task Force. 2014. Final Report. *State Tax Today.* 2014 STT 25–27 (February 4).

Maine Revenue Services. 2007. "Factors to Be Considered in Determining the Just Value of Property Acquired, Rehabilitated or Constructed Pursuant to Federal Laws Related to Affordable Housing." Report Prepared for the Joint Standing Committee on Taxation by the Department of Administrative and Financial Services, Maine Revenue Services, Property Tax Division.

Malone, Clarence J., and Mark Ayesh. 1979. "Comprehensive Land Use Controls through Differential Assessment and Supplemental Regulation." *Washburn Law Journal* 18: 432ff.

Martin, Isaac. 2006. "Does School Finance Litigation Cause Taxpayer Revolt? *Serrano* and Proposition 13." *Law and Society Review* 40 (September): 525–557.

Massachusetts Department of Revenue. 2004. *Tax Classification Report.* Boston: Division of Local Services.

———. 2010a. "Fiscal 2010 Average Single-Family Tax Bills and Assessed Values." *City & Town.*

———. 2010b. "Fiscal Year 2011 Guidelines for Annual Assessment and Allocation of Tax Levy." Information Guideline Release No. 10-401 (September).

McCluskey, William, and David Tretton. 2013. "Valuing and Taxing Iconic Properties: A Perspective from the United Kingdom." *Land Lines* 25(2) (April): 2–7.

McGhee, Eric, and Margaret Weston. 2013. "Parcel Taxes for Education in California." *At Issue* (September). Public Policy Institute of California.

McGuire, Therese J. 1999. "Proposition 13 and Its Offspring: For Good or for Evil?" *National Tax Journal* 52: 129–138.

McQuiston, John T. 1999. "Long Island Land Taxes Are Called Biased." *New York Times*, March 9.

Merriman, David F. 2010. "Does TIF Make It More Difficult to Manage Municipal Budgets? A Simulation Model and Directions for Future Research." In *Municipal Revenues and Land Policies*, ed. Gregory K. Ingram and Yu-Hung Hong. Cambridge, MA: Lincoln Institute of Land Policy.

Mikesell, John L. 2010. "The Contribution of Local Sales and Income Taxes to Fiscal Autonomy." In *Municipal Revenues and Land Policies*, ed. Gregory K. Ingram and Yu-Hung Hong. Cambridge, MA: Lincoln Institute of Land Policy.

———. 2012. "The Disappearing Retail Sales Tax." *State Tax Notes* 63 (March 5): 777–791.

Mill, John Stuart. 1848. *The Principles of Political Economy*. Book V, Ch. IV, §1. Reprinted in *The Collected Works of John Stuart Mill*, ed. John M. Robson. 1965. Toronto: University of Toronto Press, and London: Routledge and Kegan Paul.

Minnesota Department of Revenue. 2007. *Limited Market Value Report: 2006 Assessment Year*.

Minnesota Property Tax Working Group. 2012. Final Report Submitted to the Minnesota State Legislature (November 30).

Minorini, Paul A., and Stephen D. Sugarman. 1999a. "Educational Adequacy and the Courts: The Promise and Problems of Moving to a New Paradigm." In *Equity and Adequacy in Education Finance*, ed. Helen F. Ladd, Rosemary Chalk, and Janet S. Hansen. Washington, DC: National Academy Press.

———. 1999b. "School Finance Litigation in the Name of Educational Equity: Its Evolution, Impact, and Future." In *Equity and Adequacy in Education Finance*, ed. Helen F. Ladd, Rosemary Chalk, and Janet S. Hansen. Washington, DC: National Academy Press.

Mirrlees, James, Stuart Adam, Tim Besley, Richard Blundell, Steve Bond, Robert Chote, Malcolm Gammie, Paul Johnson, Gareth Myles, and James Poterba. 2011. *Tax by Design*. London: Institute for Fiscal Studies.

Morriss, Andrew P. 2004. "Private Conservation Literature: A Survey." *Natural Resources Journal* 44(2): 621–651.

Murray, Sheila E., William N. Evans, and Robert M. Schwab. 1998. "Education-finance Reform and the Distribution of Education Resources." *American Economic Review* 88(4): 789–812.

Musgrave, Richard A., and Peggy B. Musgrave. 1984. *Public Finance in Theory and Practice*, 4th ed. New York: McGraw-Hill.

National Center for Education Statistics. 2013. *Digest of Education Statistics*. Washington, DC.

National Conference of Commissioners on Uniform State Laws. 1981. "Uniform Conservation Easement Act." *Uniform Laws Annotated*, vol. 12. St. Paul, MN: West Publishing Co.

Netzer, Dick, ed. 1998. *Land Value Taxation: Can It and Will It Work Today?* Cambridge, MA: Lincoln Institute of Land Policy.

Newhouse, Wade. 1984. *Constitutional Uniformity and Equality in State Taxation*, vol. 1, 2nd ed. Buffalo, NY: William S. Hein.

New York City Department of Finance. 2014a. "Determining Your Assessed Value."

———. 2014b. "Property Tax Rates."

New York City Independent Budget Office. 2006. "Twenty-Five Years After S7000A: How Property Tax Burdens Have Shifted in New York City."

———. 2014. *New York City by the Numbers: New York City Public Schools: Have Per Pupil Budgets Changed since 2010–2011?* New York: New York City Independent Budget Office.

———. 2015. "From Tax Breaks to Affordable Housing: Examining the 421—A Tax Exemption for One57."

New York City Office of Tax Policy. 2009. *Summary of 2008 New York State and New York City Legislation Affecting City Taxes and Department of Finance Programs.* New York: New York City Department of Finance.

New York Office of State Aid, State Education Department. 2011. *2011–2012 State Aid Handbook.* Albany, NY: Office of State Aid.

New York State Board of Equalization and Assessment. 1983. *Report on Special Franchise Assessment Administration.* Albany, NY.

New York Times. 1994. "Rich Are Wary of Michigan's Revolt." March 23: A19.

———. 1995. "Ithaca's Mayor Blocks Cornell Construction Projects." May 3: B9.

———. 2013. "Why Other Countries Teach Better." Editorial, December 18: A22.

Novick, Steve. "Our Goofy Property Tax System." http://www.portlandoregon.gov/novick/article/428020.

Oates, Wallace E. 1969. "The Effect of Property Taxes and Local Public Spending on Property Values: An Empirical Study of Tax Capitalization and the Tiebout Hypothesis." *Journal of Political Economy* 77: 957–971.

———. 2001. "An Overview and Some Reflections." In *Property Taxation and Local Government Finance*, ed. Wallace E. Oates. Cambridge, MA: Lincoln Institute of Land Policy.

———. 2005. "Property Taxation and Local Public Spending: The Renter Effect." *Journal of Urban Economics* 57(3): 419–431.

———. 2006. "The Many Faces of the Tiebout Model." In *The Tiebout Model at Fifty: Essays in Public Economics in Honor of Wallace Oates*, ed. William A. Fischel. Cambridge, MA: Lincoln Institute of Land Policy.

Oates, Wallace E., and Robert M. Schwab. 2014. "The Window Tax: A Transparent Case of Excess Burden." *Land Lines* (April): 10–14.

———. 2015. "The Window Tax: A Case Study in Excess Burden." *Journal of Economic Perspectives* 29(1): 163–180.

Obhof, Larry J. 2004. "Rethinking Judicial Activism and Restraint in State School Finance Litigation." *Harvard Journal of Law and Public Policy* 27: 569–607.

O'Dea, Colleen. 2013. "Lawmakers Look to Restrict Farmland Tax Break to Working Farmers." *NJ Spotlight*, March 8.

Office of the Attorney General of the State of North Dakota. 2001. Opinion 2001-F-09 (November 2).

Office of the Attorney General of the State of South Carolina. 2014. Opinion (January 15).

Office of the Comptroller of the Currency, Federal Deposit Insurance Corporation, Federal Reserve Board Office of Thrift Supervision. 1995. "Appraised Market Value Clarified for Affordable Housing Loans" (March 10). http://www.occ.treas .gov/ftp/bulletin/95-16a.htm.

Offredo, Jon. 2013. "Lawsuit Challenging Princeton University's Tax-Exempt Status Won't Be Dismissed." www.NJ.com (June 29).

Oliff, Phil, and Iris J. Lav. 2010. "Hidden Consequences: Lessons from Massachusetts for State Considering a Property Tax Cap." Center for Budget and Policy Priorities (May 25).

Ortega, J. M. 2012. "Contractors Push for Overhaul of Municipal Taxes." *State Tax Notes* 65 (July 2): 517.

O'Sullivan, Arthur, Terri A. Sexton, and Steven M. Sheffrin. 1995. *Property Taxes & Tax Revolts: The Legacy of Proposition 13.* Cambridge: Cambridge University Press.

Page, Candace. 2005. "Critics Worry Some Vermont Farmland Is Being Conserved for the Wealthy." *Burlington Free Press,* January 26: 1.

Pearce, David W., ed. 1992. *The MIT Dictionary of Modern Economics,* 4th ed. Cambridge, MA: MIT Press.

Penna, Jonathan. 2001. "Fairness in Valuation of Low-Income Housing Tax Credit Properties: An Argument for Tax Exemption." *Journal of Affordable Housing and Community Development Law* 11(1): 53–77.

Peterson, George E., Arthur P. Solomon, Hadi Madjid, and William C. Apgar Jr. 1973. *Property Taxes, Housing and the Cities.* Lexington, MA: D. C. Heath.

Pidd, Helen. 2009. "Unoccupied, Unloved: London Mansions Left to Crumble by Elusive Offshore Owners." *Guardian,* October 16.

Pidot, Jeff. 2005. *Reinventing Conservation Easements: A Critical Examination and Ideas for Reform.* Cambridge MA: Lincoln Institute of Land Policy.

Quigley, William P. 1996. "Five Hundred Years of English Poor Laws, 1349–1834." *Akron Law Review* 30 (Fall): 73–128.

Rakow, Ronald W. 2013. "Payments in Lieu of Taxes: The Boston Experience." *Land Lines* 25(1): 2–7 (January).

Reschovsky, Andrew. 1998. "The Progressivity of State Tax Systems." In *The Future of State Taxation,* ed. David Brunori. Washington, DC: Urban Institute Press.

Reschovsky, Andrew, and Paul Waldhart. 2012. "Property Tax Delinquency and the Number of Payment Installments." *Public Finance and Management* 12(4): 316–330.

Restatement of Property. 1944. Philadelphia: American Law Institute.

Rhode Island Department of Administration. 2006. *Report on Municipal Tax Exemptions and Tax Treaties.* Providence, RI: Office of Municipal Affairs.

Rikoski, Jennifer Anne. 2006. "Comment: Reform but Preserve the Federal Tax Deduction for Charitable Contributions of Historic Facade Easements." *Tax Lawyer* 59(2): 563–588.

Riley, David. 2011. "Taxes Soar in Past 10 Years." *MetroWest Daily News,* April 17.

Rinard, Amy. 1999. "Hastening Use-Value Would Let Farmers Reap Big Benefits." *Milwaukee Journal Sentinel*, October 24: 2.

Rooks, Douglas. 2005. "Amendment to Freeze Homestead Values Stalls in Senate." *State Tax Notes* (February 14): 436.

Rosen, Harvey S. 1985. *Public Finance*, 1st ed. Homewood, IL: R. D. Irwin.

———. 1999. *Public Finance*, 5th ed. Boston: Irwin/McGraw-Hill.

Rosenblum, Joseph. 2006. "Assessing the Value of Affordability: Ad Valorem Taxation of Properties Participating in the Low Income Housing Tax Credit Program." *John Marshall Law School Fair and Affordable Housing Commentary* 2: 32–59.

Schrag, Peter. 1998. *Paradise Lost: California's Experience, America's Future*. New York: New Press.

Seipel, Tracy. 2011. "California Redevelopment Agencies Blasted in State Review." *San Jose Mercury News*, March 7.

Seligman, Edwin R. A. 1931. "The Development of Taxation." In *Essays in Taxation*, 10th ed. New York: Macmillan.

———. 1939. *Essays in Taxation*, 10th ed. New York: Macmillan.

Seligman, Katherine. 1988. "Creative Fund-Raisers for Schools Keep Affluent Districts Humming." *San Diego Union-Tribune*, November 18.

Setze, Karen. 2011a. "Governor Plans Tax Reform Commission, Spending Cuts." *State Tax Notes* (February 21): 531.

———. 2011b. "New York Governor Signs Property Tax Cap" *State Tax Notes* (July 4): 9.

Sheffrin, Steven M. 2010a. "Fairness and Market Value Property Taxation." In *Challenging the Conventional Wisdom on the Property Tax*, ed. Roy Bahl, Jorge Martinez-Vasquez, and Joan Youngman. Cambridge, MA: Lincoln Institute of Land Policy.

———. 2010b. "Tax Reform Commissions in the Sweep of California's Fiscal History." *Hastings Constitutional Law Quarterly* 37 (Summer): 661–688.

———. 2013. *Tax Fairness and Folk Justice*. New York: Cambridge University Press.

Sheppard, Lee A. 1997. "Supreme Court Overextends the Negative Commerce Clause." *State Tax Notes* (June 2): 1665–1667.

Shires, Michael A. 1999. *Patterns in California Government Revenues since Proposition 13*. San Francisco: Public Policy Institute of California.

Shobe, Gladriel. 2015. "Ending the Local Tax Deduction." *State Tax Notes* (November 16): 551–557.

Siddique, Haroon. 2010. "No Council Tax Revaluations, Say Tories." *Guardian*, September 23.

Significant Features of the Property Tax. http://www.lincolninst.edu/subcenters /significant-features-property-tax/. Lincoln Institute of Land Policy and George Washington Institute of Public Policy.

Simmons, Melody, and Joan Jacobson. "A Dream Derailed." *Daily Record* (Maryland) January 31: 1A.

Sjoquist, David L., and Rayna Stoycheva. 2010. "The Property Tax Exemption for Nonprofits." In *Handbook of Research on Nonprofit Economics and Management*, ed. Bruce A. Seaman and Dennis R. Young. Cheltenham, and Northampton, MA: Edward Elgar.

Slack, Enid. 2004. "Property Taxation in the United Kingdom." In *International Handbook of Land and Property Taxation*, ed. Richard Bird and Enid Slack. Cheltenham: Edward Elgar.

Slemrod, Joel. 1999. "Professional Opinions about Tax Policy: 1994 and 1934." In *Tax Policy in the Real World*, ed. Joel Slemrod. Cambridge: Cambridge University Press.

———. 2006. "The Role of Misconceptions in Support for Regressive Tax Reform." *National Tax Journal* 59(1): 57–75.

Smith, Henry E. 2012. "Property as the Law of Things." *Harvard Law Review* 125(7): 1691–1726.

Snyder, Susan. 2013. "A Debate on Raising Funds from City's Universities and Non-profits." *Philadelphia Inquirer*, September 27. http://articles.philly.com/2013-09 -27/news/42430184_1_penn-alexander-nonprofits-property-taxes.

Sonstelie, Jon. 2015. "Parcel Taxes as a Local Revenue Source in California." Public Policy Institute of California (April).

Spencer, LeAnn. 1999. "City Looks Jealously at Campus Tax Status." *Chicago Tribune*, March 9: sec. 2, p. 1.

Spielman, Fran. 2009. "Chicago's 2010 Budget Devours Asset-Sale Windfall." *SouthtownStar* (Chicago), December 3.

Stark, Kirk, and Jonathan Zasloff. 2003. "Tiebout and Tax Revolts: Did *Serrano* Really Cause Proposition 13?" *UCLA Law Review* 50 (February): 801–858.

Stark, Martha E., Commissioner, New York City Department of Finance. 2007. Testimony before the Assembly Real Property Taxation Committee (April 17).

Stephens, Joe. 2004. "For Owners of Upscale Homes, Loophole Pays: Pledging to Retain the Facade Affords a Charitable Deduction." *Washington Post*, December 12: A1.

Stephens, Joe, and David B. Ottaway. 2003a. "Developers Find Payoff in Preservation: Donors Reap Tax Incentive by Giving to Land Trusts, but Critics Fear Abuse of System." *Washington Post*, December 21: A1.

———. 2003b. "Nonprofit Sells Scenic Acreage to Allies at a Loss: Buyers Gain Tax Breaks with Few Curbs on Land Use." *Washington Post*, May 6: A1.

Steuerle, C. Eugene. 2002. "And Equal (Tax) Justice for All?" In *Tax Justice: The Ongoing Debate*, ed. Joseph J. Thorndike and Dennis J. Ventry Jr. Washington, DC: Urban Institute Press.

Stockford, Daniel C. 1990. "Comment: Property Tax Assessment of Conservation Easements." *Boston College Environmental Affairs Law Review* 17 (Summer): 823–853.

Stringer, Scott M. 2007. *No Vacancy? The Role of Underutilized Properties in Meeting Manhattan's Affordable Housing Needs*. New York: Office of the Manhattan Borough President.

Surrey, Stanley S. 1973. Comments. Panel Discussion on Tax Reform, Committee on Ways and Means, 93rd Congress, 1st Session (February 5).

Tenenbaum, Wayne A. 2003. "Fitting a Square Peg into a Round Hole: The Difficulty in Valuing Section 42 Low Income Housing Tax Credit Properties for Ad Valorem Tax Purposes." In *The Valuation of Subsidized Housing*, ed. Thomas A. Jaconetty. Chicago: International Association of Assessing Officers.

Thiel, Craig. 2012. "Rising School Retirement Contribution Rate Erodes Value of Foundation Grant." Citizens Research Council of Michigan, *CRC Column*, February 21. http://www.crcmich.org/column/?p=233.

Thomas, Philip A. 2002. "From McKenzie Friend to Leicester Assistant: The Impact of the Poll Tax." *Public Law* (Summer): 208–220.

Thompson, Fred, and Robert Walker. 2014. "A Tale of Two Cities: Learning from Oregon's Property Tax Administration." *State Tax Notes* (November 3): 273–284.

Thompson, Jeremy, Jason Liechty, and Mike Quigley. 2007. *A Tale of Two Cities: Reinventing Tax Increment Financing*. Chicago: Cook County Commissioner Mike Quigley.

Tiebout, Charles M. 1956. "A Pure Theory of Local Expenditures." *Journal of Political Economy* 64: 416–424.

Timmerman, Luke. 1999. "Losing Ground." *Capital Times* (Madison, WI), October 16: 1A.

Tomlinson, Teresa. 2012. "Structural Defect: Mayor Tomlinson Offers Case for Phasing Out the Freeze in Columbus." *Ledger-Enquirer* (Columbus, GA), February 4.

Urbina, Ian. 2009. "Pittsburgh Sets Vote on Adding Tax on Tuition." *New York Times*, December 16.

U.S. Census Bureau. 2013. "Per Student Public Education Spending Decreases in 2011 for First Time in Nearly Four Decades, Census Bureau Reports." Press Release. May 21.

U.S. Census Bureau, Education Finance Branch. 2015. *Public Education Finances: 2013*.

U.S. Department of the Treasury. 1984. *Report to the President on Tax Simplification and Reform*. Commerce Clearing House Standard Federal Tax Reports, Vol. 71, No. 52 (November 27).

U.S. Endowment for Forestry and Communities. 2014. National Conservation Easement Database. http://conservationeasement.us/.

Valuation Office Agency (UK). 2014. *Council Tax Manual*.

Vermont Property Tax Exemption Study Committee. 2014. Final Report. *State Tax Today*, 2014 STT 14-29 (January 15).

Wallin, Bruce A. 2004. "The Tax Revolt in Massachusetts: Revolution and Reason." *Public Budgeting & Finance* 24: 34–50.

Walsh, Michael J., and Jonathan D. Jones. 1988. "More Evidence on the 'Border Tax' Effect: The Case of West Virginia, 1979–1984." *National Tax Journal* 41(2): 261–265.

Wasson, Dave. 2011. "Washington Senate Votes to End Property Tax Deferrals." *State Tax Today*, 2011 STT 98-28 (May 20).

Weber, Rachel, and Laura Goddeeris. 2007. "Tax Increment Financing: Process and Planning Issues." Working Paper. Cambridge, MA: Lincoln Institute of Land Policy.

Weston, Margaret. 2010. *Funding California Schools: The Revenue Limit System*. San Francisco: Public Policy Institute of California.

——. 2015. *Voluntary Contributions to California's Public Schools*. San Francisco: Public Policy Institute of California.

White, Nicola M. 2010. "New Jersey Governor Signs Property Tax Cap." *State Tax Notes* (July 19): 137.

Whoriskey, Peter. 2003a. "Density Limits Only Add to Sprawl; Large Lots Eat Up Area Countryside." *Washington Post*, March 9: A1.

——. 2003b. "No Kids? That's No Problem: Falls Church's Deal with Builder Highlights Area School Crowding." *Washington Post*, May 25: A1.

York, Anthony. 2013. "Jerry Brown Signs School Funding Overhaul." *Los Angeles Times*, July 1.

Zodrow, George R. 2001. "Reflections on the New View and the Benefit View of the Property Tax." In *Property Taxation and Local Government Finance*, ed. Wallace E. Oates. Cambridge, MA: Lincoln Institute of Land Policy.

Legal Cases

Aboite Corp. v. State Bd. of Tax Comm'rs, 762 N.E.2d 254 (Ind. Tax Ct., 2001).

Allegheny Pittsburgh Coal Co. v. Webster County, 488 U.S. 336, 109 S. Ct. 633, 102 L.Ed.2d 688 (1989).

Alta Pacific Associates, Ltd. v. Utah State Tax Commission, 931 P.2d 103 (Utah 1997).

ASA Hospital Corp. v. Town of Morristown, 28 N.J. Tax 456 (2015).

Ashton Urban Renewal Agency v. Ashton Memorial Inc., 155 Id. 309, 311 P.3d 730 (2013).

Assessors of Weymouth v. Curtis, 375 Mass. 493, 375 N.E.2d 493 (1978).

Bay County v. Town of Cedar Grove, 992 So. 2d 164 (Fla. 2008).

Bayridge Associates Limited Partnership v. Department of Revenue, 321 Or. 21, 892 P.2d 1002 (1995).

Bettigole v. Assessors of Springfield, 343 Mass. 223, 178 N.E.2d 10 (1961).

BMW of North America, LLC v. Borough of Woodcliff Lake, N.J. Tax Ct., Memorandum Opinion (December 17, 2013, unpublished).

Board of Assessment Appeals v. Colorado Arlberg Club, 762 P.2d 146 (Colo. 1988).

Board of County Commissioners of Johnson County v. Smith, 18 Kan. App. 2d 662, 857 P.2d 1386 (1993).

Borough of Fort Lee v. Hudson Terrace Apts, 175 N.J. Super. 221, 417 A.2d 1124 (1980).

Brandon Bay Ltd. Partnership v. Payette County, 142 Id. 681, 132 P.3d 438 (2006).

Brigham v. State, 166 Vt. 246, 692 A.2d 384 (1997).

C.A.F. Investment Co. v. Township of Saginaw, 410 Mich. 428, 302 N.W.2d 164 (1981).

Caldwell v. Department of Revenue, 122 Ariz. 519, 596 P.2d 45 (1979).

California Redevelopment Association v. Matosantos, 53 Cal. 4th 231, 267 P.3d 580; 135 Cal. Rptr. 3d 683 (2011).

Camps Newfound/Owatonna v. Town of Harrison, 520 U.S. 564, 117 S. Ct. 1590, 137 L. Ed. 2d 852 (1997).

Canton Towers, Ltd. v. Board of Revision, 3 Ohio St. 3d 4, 444 N.E.2d 1027 (1983).

Carr v. Assessors of Springfield, 339 Mass. 89, 157 N.E.2d 880 (1959).

Cascade Court Ltd. Partnership v. Noble, 105 Wash. App. 563, 20 P.3d 997 (2001).

Chesapeake Hotel LP v. Saddle Brook Township, 22 N.J. Tax 525 (2005).

Circle C Child Development Center, Inc. v. Travis Central Appraisal District, 981 S.W.2d 483 (Tex. App. 1998).

City of Lowell v. County Commissioners, 152 Mass. 372, 25 N.E. 469 (1890).

Claremont School District. v. Governor, 142 N.H. 462, 703 A.2d 1353 (1997).

Clarke Associates v. County of Arlington, 235 Va. 624, 369 S.E.2d 414 (1988).

Clayton v. County of Los Angeles, 26 Cal. App. 3d 390, 102 Cal.Rptr. 687 (1972).

Clifton v. Allegheny County, 600 Pa. 662, 969 A.2d 1197 (2009).

Coleman v. County of Nassau, Index No. 97-30380 (Sup. Ct. Nassau County, March 29, 2000).

Communauté Urbaine de Montréal c. Avor Realty Corp. et Crédit Foncier et Ville de Montréal, 57 Q.A.C. 302 (Québec 1993).

Community Development Co. of Gardner v. Board of Assessors, 377 Mass. 351, 385 N.E.2d 1376 (1979).

Corporation of the Episcopal Church in Utah v. Utah State Tax Commission, 919 P.2d 556 (Utah 1996).

Cottonwood Affordable Housing v. Yavapai County, 205 Ariz. 427, 72 P.3d 357 (2003).

Cox Cable San Diego, Inc. v. County of San Diego, 185 Cal. App. 3d 368, 229 Cal. Rptr. 839 (1986).

Darcel, Inc. v. City of Manitowoc Board of Review, 137 Wis. 2d 623, 405 N.W.2d 344 (1987).

Demoulas v. Town of Salem, 116 N.H. 775, 367 A.2d 588 (1976).

Dep't of Revenue v. BP Pipelines (Alaska) Inc., Alaska Supreme Court Nos. S-14696/1 4705/14706/14716/14725, No. 7039 (August 28, 2015).

Donovan v. City of Haverhill, 247 Mass. 69, 141 N.E. 564 (1923).

Dressler v. County of Alpine, 64 Cal. App. 3d 557, 134 Cal. Rptr. 554 (1976).

Dudley v. Kerwick, 52 N.Y.2d 542, 439 N.Y.S.2d 305, 421 N.E.2d 797 (1981).

Ed Guth Realty, Inc. v. Gingold, 34 N.Y.2d 440, 358 N.Y.S.2d 367, 315 N.E.2d 441 (1974).

Emerson College v. City of Boston, 391 Mass. 415, 462 N.E.2d 1098 (1984).

Englewood Cliffs v. Estate of Allison, 69 N.J. Super. 514, 174 A.2d 631 (App. Div. 1961).

Executive Square Limited Partnership v. Board of Tax Review, 11 Conn. App. 566, 528 A.2d 409 (1987).

Fischer v. Schooley, 371 So. 2d 496 (Fla. Dist. Ct. App. 1979).

F & M Schaeffer Brewing Co. v. Lehigh County Board of Appeals, 530 Pa. 451, 610 A.2d 1 (1992).

Folsom v. County of Spokane, 111 Wash. 2d 256, 759 P.2d 1196 (1988).

Francis Small Heritage Trust, Inc. v. Town of Limington, 2014 Me. 102, 98 A. 3d 1012 (2014).

Freeman v. County of Fresno, 126 Cal. App. 3d 459, 178 Cal. Rptr. 764 (1981).

Frothingham v. Mellon, 262 U.S. 447, 43 S. Ct. 597, 67. L.Ed. 1078 (1923).

Gall v. Dep't of Revenue, 17 O.T.R. 268 (2003).

Hamilton County Assessor v. Allison Road Development, LLC, 988 N.E.2d 820 (Ind. Tax Ct. 2013).

Harbor Ventures, Inc. v. Hutches, 366 So. 2d 1173 (Fla. 1979).

Hausman v. Rudkin, 268 So. 2d 407 (Fla. Dist. Ct. App. 1972).

Hellerstein v. Assessor of Islip, 37 N.Y.2d 1, 371 N.Y.S.2d 388, 332 N.E.2d 279 (1975).

Hilborn v. Commissioner, 85 T.C. 677 (1985).

Holbrook Island Sanctuary v. Inhabitants of the Town of Brooksville, 161 Me. 476, 214 A. 2d 660 (1965).

Hospitalization Utilization Project v. Commonwealth of Pennsylvania, 507 Pa. 1, 487 A.2d 1306 (1985).

Hovbilt, Inc. v. Township of Howell, 138 N.J. 598, 651 A.2d 77 (1994).

Huron Ridge L.P. v. Ypsilanti Township, 275 Mich. App. 23, 737 N.W.2d 187 (2007).

In re Appeal of Marple Springfield Center, Inc., 530 Pa. 122, 607 A.2d 708 (1992).

In the Matter of Appeal of the Greens of Pine Glen Ltd. Partnership, 356 N.C. 642, 576 S.E.2d 316 (2003).

In the Matter of the Trans-Alaska Pipeline System, Alaska State Assessment Review Board OAH No. 15-3060-TAX (June 1, 2015).

Joseph E. Seagram & Sons, Inc., Appellant, v. Tax Commission of the City of New York, 18 A.D.2d 109, 238 N.Y.S.2d 228 (1963), *aff'd*, 14 N.Y.2d 314, 251 N.Y.S.2d 460, 200 N.E.2d 447 (1964).

Kaiser Co. v. Reid, 30 Cal. 2d 610, 184 P.2d 879 (1947).

Kankakee County Board of Review v. Property Tax Appeal Board, 131 Ill. 2d 1, 544 N.E.2d 762, 136 Ill. Dec. 76 (1989).

Kargman v. Jacobs, 113 R.I. 696, 325 A. 2d 543 (1974).

Kelo v. City of New London, 545 U.S. 469, 125 S. Ct. 2655, 162 L.Ed. 2d 439 (2005).

Keniston v. Board of Assessors, 380 Mass. 888, 407 N.E.2d 1275 (1980).

Kerr v. Hickenlooper, 744 F.3d 1156 (10th Cir. 2014), *vacated and remanded, Hickenlooper v. Kerr*, 135 S. Ct. 2927 (2015).

Kid's Korner Educare Center, Inc. v. County of Steele, Nos. C7-97-258-R, C4-98-311-R, C2-98-565-R (Minn. Tax Ct. 1998).

Kirkpatrick v. Lane County Assessor, TC-MD 050346A (Or. Tax Ct., Magistrate Div. November 18, 2005).

Lehnhausen v. Lake Shore Auto Parts Co., 410 U.S. 356, 93 S. Ct. 1001, 35 L.Ed. 2d 351 (1973).

Martin v. Liberty County Board of Tax Assessors, 152 Ga. App. 340, 262 S.E. 2d 609 (1979).

Maryville Properties, L.P., v. Nelson, 83 S.W.3d 608 (Mo. Ct. App. 2002).

Massachusetts Teachers Association v. Secretary of the Commonwealth, 384 Mass. 209, 424 N.E.2d 469 (1981).

McCollum v. Multnomah County Assessor, TC-MD 050483A (Or. Tax Ct., Magistrate Div., November 18, 2005).

McKee v. Clackamas County Assessor, TC-MD 050249A (Or. Tax Ct., Magistrate Div., November 18, 2005).

Meadowlanes Limited Dividend Housing Associates v. City of Holland, 437 Mich. 473, 473 N.W.2d 636 (1991).

Merrick Holding Corp. v. Board of Assessors, 58 A.D.2d 605, 395 N.Y.S.2d 233 (1977), *rev'd,* 45 N.Y.2d 538, 382 N.E.2d 1341, 410 N.Y.S.2d 565 (1978).

Mesivtah Eitz Chaim of Bobov, Inc. v. Pike County Board of Assessment Appeals, 615 Pa. 463, 44 A.3d 3 (2012).

Michael Todd Co. v. County of Los Angeles, 57 Cal.2d 684, 371 P.2d 340, 21 Cal. Rptr. 604 (1962).

Michels v. Watson, 229 Cal. App. 2d 404, 40 Cal. Rptr. 464 (1964).

Millennium Park Joint Venture, LLC v. Houlihan, 241 Ill.2d 281, 948 N.E.2d 1, 349 Ill. Dec. 898 (2010).

Mount Calvary Baptist Church, Inc. v. Dep't of Revenue, 302 Ill. App.3d 661, 706 N.E.2d 1008 (1998).

Nassif v. Board of Supervisors, 231 Va. 472, 345 S.E.2d 520 (1986).

New England Forestry Foundation, Inc. v. Board of Assessors of Hawley, 468 Mass. 138, 9 N.E.3d 310 (2014).

New Walnut Square Limited Partnership v. Louisiana Tax Commission, 626 So. 2d 430 (La. Ct. App. 1993).

Nicoladis v. Commissioner, 55 T.C.M. 624 (1988).

Nordlinger v. Hahn, 505 U.S. 1, 112 S. Ct. 2326, 120 L.Ed. 2d 1 (1992).

Northwestern University v. City of Evanston, No. 00 C 7309 (N.D. Ill. 2002).

O'Shea v. Board of Assessors, 8 N.Y.3d 249, 864 N.E.2d 1261, 832 N.Y.S.2d 862 (2007).

Pedcor Investments-1990-XII, L.P. v. State Board of Tax Commissioners, 715 N.E.2d 432 (Ind. Tax Ct. 1999).

People ex rel. Manhattan Railway Co. v. Barker, 146 N.Y. 304, 40 N.E. 996 (1895).

People ex rel. New York Stock Exchange Building Co. v. Cantor, 221 A.D. 193, 223 N.Y.S. 64 (1st Dep't 1927), *aff'd,* 248 N.Y. 533, 162 N.E. 514 (1928).

People v. Shearer, 30 Cal. 645 (1866).

Pine Pointe Housing, L.P. v. Lowndes County Board of Tax Assessors, 254 Ga. App. 197, 561 S.E.2d 860 (2002).

Pollock v. Farmers' Loan and Trust Co., 158 U.S. 601, 15 S. Ct. 912, 39 L.Ed. 1108 (1895).

Provena Covenant Medical Center v. Dep't of Revenue, 236 Ill.2d 368; 925 N.E.2d 1131, 339 Ill. Dec. 10 (2010).

Rainbow Apartments v. Illinois Property Tax Appeal Board, 326 Ill. App. 3d 1105, 762 N.E.2d 534, 260 Ill. Dec. 875 (2001).

Rector of St. Bartholomew's Church v. City of New York, 914 F.2d 348 (2d Cir. 1990).

Rinehart v. Bateman, 363 S.W.3d 357 (Mo. Ct. App. 2012).

Robinson v. City of New York, slip op. 30623(U), Docket No. 151679/2014 (Sup. Ct. N.Y. County, April 20, 2015).

Roden v. K & K Land Management, Inc., 368 So. 2d 588 (Fla. 1978).

Rose v. Council for Better Education, 790 S.W.2d 186 (Ky. 1989).

San Antonio Independent School District v. Rodriguez, 411 U.S. 1, 93 S. Ct. 1278, 36 L.Ed. 2d 16 (1973).

Schuyler Apartment Partners LLC v. Colfax County Board of Equalization, Nebraska Tax Equalization and Review Commission, No. 06C-254 (June 2, 2009), *aff'd*, 279 Neb. 989, 783 N.W.2d 587 (2010).

Serrano v. Priest, 5 Cal. 3d 584, 487 P.2d 1241, 96 Cal. Rptr. 601 (1971).

Serrano v. Priest, 200 Cal. App. 3d 897, 226 Cal. Rptr. 584 (1986).

Sioux City Bridge Co. v. Dakota County, 105 Neb. 843, 182 N.W. 485 (1921), *rev'd*, 260 U.S. 441, 43 S. Ct. 190, 67 L.Ed. 340 (1923).

Sirrell v. New Hampshire (Rockingham Superior Court, January 17, 2001).

Sirrell v. New Hampshire, 146 N.H. 364, 780 A.2d 494 (2001).

Slewett & Farber v. Board of Assessors, 80 A.D.2d 186, 189, 438 N.Y.S.2d 544 (1981).

Smith v. Ring, 250 So. 2d 913 (Fla. Dist. Ct. App. 1971).

Southern Burlington County NAACP v. Township of Mt. Laurel, 67 N.J. 151, 336 A.2d 713 (1975).

Springfield Marine Bank v. Property Tax Appeal Board, 44 Ill.2d 428, 256 N.E.2d 334 (1970).

Spring Hill, L.P. v. Tennessee State Board of Equalization, No. M2001-02683-COA-R3-CV (Tenn. Ct. App. 2003).

Stadium Concessions, Inc. v. City of Los Angeles, 60 Cal. App. 3d 215, 131 Cal. Rptr 442 (1976).

State v. Birmingham Southern Railway, 182 Ala. 475, 62 So. 77 (1913).

State v. Moore, 12 Cal. 56 (1859).

State v. Thayer, 69 Minn. 170, 71 N.W. 931 (1897).

Steele v. Town of Allenstown, 124 N.H. 487, 471 A.2d 1179 (1984).

Stewart Title & Trust v. Pima County, 156 Ariz. 236, 751 P.2d 552 (Ariz. Ct. App. 1987).

Stone Brook Limited Partnership v. Sisinni, 224 W.Va. 691, 688 S.E.2d 300 (2009).

Strand v. Escambia County, 992 So. 2d 150 (Fla. 2008).

Supervisor of Assessments v. Har Sinai West Corp., 95 Md. App. 631, 622 A.2d 786 (1993).

Swan Lake Moulding Company v. Department of Revenue, 257 Or. 622, 478 P.2d 393 (1970).

Tech One Associates v. Board of Property Assessment, Appeals, and Review, 617 Pa. 439, 53 A.3d 685 (2012).

Town of Sanford v. J & N Sanford Trust, 1997 ME 97, 694 A.2d 456 (1997).

Town of Sudbury v. Commissioner of Corporations & Taxation, 366 Mass. 558, 321 N.E.2d 641 (1974).

Townsend v. Town of Middlebury, 134 Vt. 438, 365 A.2d 515 (1976).

Tregor v. Board of Assessors, 377 Mass. 602, 387 N.E.2d 538 (1979).

United States v. City of Manassas, 830 F.2d 530 (4th Cir. 1987), *aff'd*, 485 U.S. 1017, 108 S. Ct. 1568, 99 L. Ed. 2d 884 (1988).

United States v. County of Fresno, 50 Cal. App. 3d 633, 123 Cal. Rptr. 548 (Cal. Ct. App. 1975), *aff'd*, 429 U.S. 452, 97 S. Ct. 699; 50 L. Ed. 2d 683 (1977).

United States v. New Mexico, 455 U.S. 720, 102 S. Ct. 1373, 71 L.Ed. 2d 580 (1982).

Village of Ridgewood v. The Bolger Foundation, 6 N.J. Tax 391 (1984), *aff'd* in part, *rev'd* in part on other grounds, 202 N.J. Super. 474, 495 A.2d 452 (1985), *rev'd*, 104 N.J. 337, 517 A.2d 135 (1986).

Walt Disney Productions v. United States, 327 F. Supp. 189 (C.D. Cal. 1971), *modified*, 480 F.2d 66 (9th Cir. 1973).

Wells National Services Corp. v. County of Santa Clara, 54 Cal. App. 3d 579, 126 Cal. Rptr. 715 (1976).

Western Reserve Christian Church Inc. v. Testa, No. 2011-Q-380 (Ohio Bd. Tax App. 2013).

Woda Ivy Glen Limited Partnership v. Fayette County Board of Revision, 121 Ohio St. 3d 175, 902 N.E.2d 984 (2009).

Yadco, Inc. v. Yankton County, 89 S.D. 651, 237 N.W.2d 665 (1975).

Statutes, Ordinances, Constitutional Provisions, and Administrative Rulings

10 Pa. Stat. § 372(b).

35 Ill. Comp. Stat. Ann. 200/10–30(a).

35 Ill. Comp. Stat. 200/15-170.

49 U.S.C.S. § 11501.

Alaska Stat. § 29.45.110(d).

Ariz. Rev. Stat. § 42-13301.

Ark. Code Ann. § 26-26-303.

Calif. Rev. & Tax Code § 988(a).

Colo. Const. Art. X, § 20 (4).

Cook County, Illinois, Code of Ordinances § 74-63 (2015).

Fla Stat. § 193.461(3)(b).

Fla. Stat. § 193.461(4)(c) (2012), repealed by H.B. 1193; Fla. Laws ch. 2013-95.

Idaho Code § 55-2109.

Ill. P.L. 93-715.

La. Atty. Gen. Op. No. 1997-336 (October 1, 1997).

La. Rev. Stat. Ann. § 9:1271.

Maryland Declaration of Rights, Art. 43.

Md. Code Ann. Tax-Property § 9-105.

Mass. Const. Art. CXII.

Mass. Gen. Laws, ch. 40, § 56.

Mass. Gen. Laws, ch. 58, §§ 4A–4C.

Mass. Gen. Laws. ch. 59, § 2A(b).
Mass. Gen. Laws, ch. 59, § 51.
Mass. Gen. Laws, ch. 184, § 31.
Mass. H.4375, Chapter 286 (2014).
Me. Const. Art. IX, § 8(2)(D).
Me. Rev. Stat. title 36, §§ 1102 (6); 1109 (3).
Neb. Rev. Stat. § 77-201.
New York City Admin. Code § 11-2101(7).
N.H. Rev. Stat. Ann. § 75:1-a.
N.J. Stat. Ann. §§ 54:4-23.5.
N.M. Stat. Ann. § 7-37-3.
N.Y. Laws of 2008, ch. 332.
N.Y. Real Prop. Tax Law § 581 (1) (a).
N.Y. Real Prop. Tax Law § 1805 (1).
Ohio Rev. Code § 5715.01 (B).
Or. Const. Art. XI, § 11.
Or. Rev. Stat. § 308.146.
R.I. Gen. Laws § 44-3-9.
S.D. Codified Laws § 10-12-42.
Tex. Tax Code § 11.1825 (x)(3).
Utah Code Ann. § 59-2-102(20)(b).
Wash. Rev. Code § 84.40.030.
Wisc. Stat. § 66.0602.

U.S. Internal Revenue Code, Treasury Regulations, and Internal Revenue Service Rulings

I.R.C. § 42(h)(6)(B)(v).
I.R.C. § 170(f)(3)(B)(iii).
Rev. Rul. 64-205, 1964-2 C.B. 62.
Treas. Reg. § 1.170A-13(c)(4).
Treas. Reg. §§ 1.170A-14(h)(3)(i)–(iii).

Index

About the Author

JOAN YOUNGMAN is a senior fellow and chair of the Department of Valuation and Taxation at the Lincoln Institute of Land Policy in Cambridge, Massachusetts. She is an attorney and author of numerous articles concerning the taxation of land and buildings. She is the author of *Legal Issues in Property Valuation and Taxation: Cases and Materials* (2006), a coauthor of *State and Local Taxation: Cases and Materials* (10th edition, 2014), and coeditor of *Erosion of the Property Tax Base* (2009), *Making the Property Tax Work—Experiences in Developing and Transitional Countries* (2008), and *The Development of Property Taxation in Economies in Transition: Case Studies from Central and Eastern Europe* (2001).

ABOUT THE
Lincoln Institute of Land Policy

The Lincoln Institute of Land Policy is an independent, nonpartisan organization whose mission is to help solve global economic, social, and environmental challenges to improve the quality of life through creative approaches to the use, taxation, and stewardship of land. As a private operating foundation whose origins date to 1946, the Lincoln Institute seeks to inform public dialogue and decisions about land policy through research, training, and effective communication. By bringing together scholars, practitioners, public officials, policy makers, journalists, and involved citizens, the Lincoln Institute integrates theory and practice and provides a forum for multidisciplinary perspectives on public policy concerning land, both in the United States and internationally. Lincoln Institute's work is organized into three thematic areas: planning and urban form, valuation and taxation, and international studies.

LINCOLN INSTITUTE
OF LAND POLICY

113 Brattle Street
Cambridge, MA 02138-3400 USA
P 1.617.661.3016   1.800.526.3873
F 1.617.661.7235   1.800.526.3944
help@lincolnist.edu
lincolninst.edu